D1483864

eyes like butterflies

eyes like butterflies

A TREASURY OF SIMILES AND METAPHORS

compiled by
Terence Hodgson

CHAMBERS

CHAMBERS

An imprint of Chambers Harrap Publishers Ltd
7 Hopetoun Crescent
Edinburgh, EH7 4AY

This edition first published by Chambers Harrap Publishers Ltd 2006
Previous edition published by Steele Roberts Publishers Ltd 2003

A CIP catalogue record for this book is available from the British Library.

ISBN-13: 978 0550 10272 0
ISBN-10: 0550 10272 8

Publishing Manager: Patrick White
Editors: Vicky Aldus, Ian Brookes
Prepress Controller: Heather Macpherson

Designed and typeset by Chambers Harrap Publishers Ltd, Edinburgh
Printed and bound by Clays Ltd, St Ives plc

Introduction

Details. The natural world plies us with any amount of them, as does the immense catalogue of the creative works of humankind. We notice details, we may be intrigued with them, they can enchant and invigorate us. We may be in thrall to a musical detail like, say, the alarming opening theme of Bach's stupendous Fugue in D Minor for organ. We are drawn to architectural detail; perhaps some weather-nibbled saint tucked away in an alcove high on a cathedral. Or we may become dreamily lost in a detail from a work of art, such as some walled city in the background of a Medieval manuscript illustration.

Literature is also a rich source of details and among these is imagery: the use of similes and metaphors. They are particularly memorable when they are original and resonant.

This book presents a treasury of such imagery, to savour and linger over – no rushing on with the plot here. These images put across in a concise, adroit manner feelings which might otherwise take pages to describe. They condense ideas into a single phrase. The more astounding the images, the more likely we are to notice and delight in them. They can become collectables. Literature in cameo, they lend themselves to be lifted off the page and enjoyed on their own account, just as we enjoy quotations, aphorisms or epitaphs. In savouring the images we may wonder about the relish the authors felt when fashioning them.

For their sources of imagery, authors do not seem circumscribed by many limits. Inspiration comes from anywhere: from history, science and popular culture through to music and art. For example, where the image is underpinned by a knowledge of art, the author might well indulge in an exercise of association. William Eastlake's
   a pink face, red on all the highlights, like a Degas peach
transports the reader to the artist's work. Similarly Desmond Hogan's

    a damaged El Greco storm sky

conjures up the dramatic backgrounds of many of El Greco's paintings, while Bernard Kops's

    a Paul Klee sea

takes the mind's eye effortlessly into cubic waves and blocks of colour.

If authors' sources of imagery are diverse, then so too is the range of feelings and impressions evoked. We encounter humour when Hugo Charteris writes

    a smile like a torch with a weak battery

and Norman Mailer writes

    she looked like a house whose lawn was landscaped and whose kitchen was on fire.

There is intrinsic delight in images such as Todd McEwen's

    a baklava of ideas

and William Faulkner's

    a procession of small clouds like an ancient geographical woodcut

while there is a wistfulness about Faulkner's

    twilight ran in like a quiet violet dog.

Conversely, such ideas as Edmund White's

    the terrible decaying Camembert of my heart

and Mark O'Donnell's

    she looked like a child with progeria

are successfully grim, whereas Penelope Shuttle may well perplex with

    you kissed me like a man crossing out a sentence

as may Janet Frame with

    a voice like hundreds and thousands.

Then there are images which demand specific prior knowledge, such as this from Anthony Burgess:

    the rain began to hiss outside, like the chorus in Bach's St John Passion demanding crucifixion.

They can be memorable, these images, even if not memorized. I have found it intriguing that by far the majority of images pertain to human features and attributes – there are abundant entries for *face*, *mouth*, *eyes*, *voice*, *hair*, *smile* and *thought*. This is not surprising when we remember that most literature is essentially about people and characterization. Also numerous, although not as extensive, are the images devised for such universals as *house*, *sea*, *sky*, *sun* and *star*.

In compiling this treasury I have limited myself to modern literature written in English. Specifically, I have drawn from novels and short stories written since the Second World War, occasionally allowing compelling images from the 1920s and 1930s. This catchment excludes plays, scripts, poetry, journalism and the like, yet even so the range has proved vast, and the inventiveness displayed by the authors, magnificent.

Terence Hodgson

Publisher's Note

The quotations in this collection have been reproduced as they appear in the editions consulted by the compiler. Occasional inconsistencies and apparent irregularities with regard to spelling, capitalization and punctuation are due to the different countries of publication and the different house styles of the original publishers.

abstraction

She ... had the abstracted and disorganised air you might expect
from somebody who was related to the Queen
MARTIN AMIS *The Information*

accent

Her mill-town accent kissed me on the ear
SIMON BREEN *Down in One*

The accent cracks eggshells from the other side of the room
JANICE GALLOWAY *The Trick Is to Keep Breathing*

[Their] accents are blunt, pompous with coal and cash
PHILIP CALLOW *The Bliss Body*

The voice had a touch of an accent, like cinnamon, cloves,
unknown spices
HELENA ECHLIN *Gone*

acne

The acne on your face ... is like an ancient map of Ireland after a
smattering of napalm
DESMOND HOGAN *Martyrs*

the green-brown shrapnel of his dried acne cysts, like lentils buried
in the skin
LORRIE MOORE *Beautiful Grade*

Adam's apple

He had a most extraordinary Adam's apple that bobbed up and down the long neck like a lost marble with limited powers
JENNIFER LASH *Blood Ties*

[his] Adam's apple gulping in his stringy old throat like a danger signal
PHILIP CALLOW *Going to the Moon*

his wonderful Adam's apple gliding up and down his throat, a tiny flesh elevator
LORRIE MOORE *Go Like This*

adolescence

adolescents like spies in a cold waiting-room
HUGO CHARTERIS *The Lifeline*

the leveling storm of adolescence
JAY MCINERNEY *Brightness Falls*

aerial

television aerials like a jumbled alphabet consisting mainly of aitches
JOHN BANVILLE *The Untouchable*

afternoon

varicose-veined afternoons
CHARLES DENNIS *The Next-to-Last Train Ride*

The empty afternoons fill the world with beach fatigue
MARTIN AMIS *Success*

The afternoon was in need of blood
PETER VANSITTART *Pastimes of a Red Summer*

[a] long, slow, tea-shoppe-lit style of English afternoon
JOHN UPDIKE *A Madman*

That afternoon had outlines fine as a perfectly drawn invoice
PETER VANSITTART *Three Six Seven*

afternoons like fingertips, like dreams of blood
JEFF NUTTALL *The Gold Hole*

the afternoon is holding its finger to its lips
    ELIZABETH BERG *Until the Real Thing Comes Along*

a delphinium blue afternoon
    EMMA TENNANT *Queen of Stones*

a long slow afternoon that stretched out and rolled over like a dog
on a rug
    T CORAGHESSAN BOYLE *Drop City*

the last ninety minutes of the afternoon dance away like spatters of
grease
    DAVID LONG *The Falling Boy*

afternoon ... went on like a long calm out-breath
    DAVID IRELAND *The Chosen*

the afternoon wore on like a tattered fabric of used and borrowed
moments
    T CORAGHESSAN BOYLE *The Tortilla Curtain*

the afternoon was getting dolled up in extravagant pinks and
violets for the evening
    NICOLA BARKER *Wide Open*

It is one of those shimmery, light-headed, pollen afternoons
    MARTIN AMIS *Success*

The afternoon passed like a slow, humid dream
    TIM GAUTREAUX *Sorry Blood*

air

the slightly misty air ... moved very slightly as if a man was pulling
cubic yards of it with a rope
    JAMES FORDEN *The Love Chase*

The air vomited hot tar, then scratched with its sharp nails
    FD REEVE *White Colours*

the air was like cold washing-up
    MARTIN AMIS *Money*

Cold air rushed up and down the stairs like a cranky child in bare
feet
    CHARLES DICKINSON *Crows*

raw sea-groined air
  JEREMY LELAND *Lirri*

the conditioned air purred like a doctored cat that never went out
  ANTHONY BURGESS *Devil of a State*

The air is cooler now, laying itself along the backs of her hands like chilly satin gloves
  MICHÈLE ROBERTS *The Visitation*

chill, cathedral air
  EMMA TENNANT *The Ballad of Sylvia and Ted*

At sunset the air hung low, striated like a weird plowed field of pigmented earth
  KATE CHRISTENSEN *In the Drink*

the night air smelled like the deepest roots of a tree
  STEPHEN MARION *Hollow Ground*

The air was gaudy with birdsong
  JOHN BANVILLE *Ghosts*

the lighted grayish rain-teased air holding a glow as of a decomposing moon
  HAROLD BRODKEY *Profane Friendship*

The air smelt of cheap ghosts – those that had died cheaply: street accidents, bludgeonings, mattress fires
  MARTIN AMIS *Yellow Dog*

The air had the dull flat inertia of an exhibit under glass
  DARIN STRAUSS *The Real McCoy*

The air felt unsure, as though it had landed in the wrong place
  HESTER KAPLAN *Kinship Theory*

The air pressed down ... like thick scorched sandpaper
  JANETTE TURNER HOSPITAL *Oyster*

the air around him ... was a rich brown as deep and virtually narcotic as the shadows prevailing at the edges of late Rembrandt self-portraits
  REYNOLDS PRICE *The Promise of Rest*

The air ... felt clotted, sluggish, hot, partisan and impassioned,
like the breathing of a vindictive judge
   CYNTHIA OZICK *The Doctor's Wife*

The air against her face had the warm kiss of fever
   WILL CHRISTOPHER BAER *Penny Dreadful*

ambulance

ambulance ... like a white sigh
   YAËL DAYAN *Death Had Two Sons*

anger

her anger sparking around her like an electric outline
   MOLLY GILES *Iron Shoes*

a hot coin of anger twirled against his rib cage
   MICHAEL GRANT JAFFE *Skateaway*

a thickish selfsatisfaction-anger that was like a secret along my
spine
   HAROLD BRODKEY *Innocence*

anger rising off her like a mirage, a molten corona
   MICHAEL CAHILL *A Nixon Man*

My anger became a white dome inside my skull
   ALYSON HAGY *Ballad and Sadness*

The ball of anger in her split open, she was all sour juice and fine
eyes spitting
   PHILIP CALLOW *The Subway to New York*

anxiety

those underground mists of personal anxiety
   JENNIFER LASH *Blood Ties*

an awful anxiety ... like a strange rot in the windowsills
   SEBASTIAN BARRY *Annie Dunne*

[He] woke into a sovereign state of anxiety
   JAY MCINERNEY *Ransom*

applause

a sustained applause ... like the steady wash of sea on shingle
T CORAGHESSAN BOYLE *The Road to Wellville*

argument

Huge, library-sized arguments
MELINDA HAYNES *Mother of Pearl*

arms

arms ... were as beautiful as the soul of St Catherine of Sienna
ALDOUS HUXLEY *Antic Hay*

Her arms ... opened like landing gear
FD REEVE *White Colours*

arms like peeled wands
ANAÏS NIN *Ice*

arms out like the ears of a mouse
SUSAN KERSLAKE *Middlewatch*

The girl's arms, bone-skinny and white ... like the stems of peonies that have been grown in darkness
MARGARET ATWOOD *Spring Song of the Frogs*

His arms are dangling at his sides like broken awnings
JANETTE TURNER HOSPITAL *Borderline*

Her forearms spoke of enemas and other terrifying eviscerations
TOBY LITT *Dreamgirls*

[He] habitually kept his arms folded across his chest like a Civil War general in a daguerreotype
TOBIAS WOLFF *Old School*

audience

audience settled down like a gaudy ship
PETER VANSITTART *Landlord*

The audience was on its feet in a molecular furore
ALISON DYE *An Awareness of March*

aunt

aunt ... like a Savings bank, but more mobile and whimsical
AL KENNEDY *The Mouseboks Family Dictionary*

autumn

autumn drove through the valley ... scraping and violining
GEORGE MOOR *Fox Gold*

Autumn, like grief, changes everything
NICOLA GRIFFITH *Stay*

back

Her bare back a lunar surface beneath his hands
JOHN UPDIKE *Bech: A Book*

his back arched like an overcooked cannelloni which had lost its stuffing
ERICA JONG *Fear of Flying*

her perfect eighteenth-century back, the age of flesh and dimples
JIM CRACE *Being Dead*

beaches

beaches spread out like damp smudged foolscap pages ravelled at the edges
CHRISTY BROWN *Wild Grow the Lilies*

beard

his impenetrably black beard, an obsidian canopy that covered the lower half of his face like a moonless night
STEPHEN AMIDON *The Primitive*

a failed beard that suggested a toddler who'd crawled under a bed with jam on his chin
CHRISTOPHER BRAM *Gossip*

[a] beard like a bad pubic graft
IAIN SINCLAIR *Radon Daughters*

a small confrontational beard
ANNE SCOTT *Calpurnia*

a little bullion of a goatee
DESMOND HOGAN *A Farewell to Prague*

beauty

Her beauty is still there, somewhat rotted, like a fading painted-wood fish
HAROLD BRODKEY *Largely an Oral History of My Mother*

birds

birds began to creak, some like rusty winches, some like door hinges and some like fishing lines unreeled at a great rate
CHRISTINA STEAD *The Man Who Loved Children*

birds that rose and fell in the sky, like supplementary breathings of the tide
JANET FRAME *The Edge of the Alphabet*

birds squeaked like blunt chalk
JILL NEVILLE *The Living Daylights*

[the] sound of birds, tiny, industrious whistles and chirps like the coming to life of some vast, miniature household
NINO RICCI *Where She Has Gone*

a rush of birds rising up ... black dots high up in the sky, shimmering pepper
ELIZABETH BERG *Range of Motion*

Tilting blackbirds burnished by the noon sun gleamed like contrivances of tinfoil
WILLIAM GAY *Provinces of Night*

nameless birds were moving patternlessly against a gunmetal sky, like random markings on a slate
WILLIAM GAY *Provinces of Night*

cockatoos ... graze in the grass like hundreds of wisps of very clean washing
MARION HALLIGAN *The Point*

the sky was black with [buzzards], descending like so many priests to a Eucharist below
COLUM MCCANN *Songdogs*

returning geese passed overhead in their great formations like the wakes of grain ships reflected on the sky
STEVEN HEIGHTON *The Shadow Boxer*

pigeons muttering like makeshift witches
JANET FRAME *Scented Gardens for the Blind*

pigeons settled like a quilt
EL WALLANT *Children at the Gate*

pigeons coming down like shattering slate
JULIE ORRINGER *Care*

pigeons take off like applause
PAULETTE JILES *Sitting in the Club Car*

sparrows sit like fists
WILLIAM H GASS *In the Heart of the Heart of the Country*

a flock of dingy city birds, starlings, rose up chattering from someone's back yard, like pepper thrown into the sky
JEAN THOMPSON *City Boy*

bitterness

A bitterness flowed from him, not from a deep, tragic wound, but rather, it rolled along his surface like winds across a desolate planet
DJ LEVIEN *Wormwood*

bland

bland as a parent who won't hear
THOMAS KENEALLY *Passenger*

blood

blood ... like artificial marbling
ROY CHRISTY *The Nightingales Are Sobbing*

blood, that warm traitor
JOHN UPDIKE *Roger's Version*

blood like a wet reflection of the light, beautiful and trivial
WILLIAM BURGESS *Second-Hand Persons*

His blood was rushing around like a woman who cleans up the house after the company has come
FLANNERY O'CONNOR *Wise Blood*

A thin line of blood ... marshalled itself along his cheekbone then widened itself downwards like a sudden advance of redcoats
  MICHAEL BALDWIN *The Gamecock*

Tiny apple seeds of blood
  SHANE CONNAUGHTON *A Border Station*

The blood spurted out like pips from a lemon
  MARGARET ATWOOD *Significant Moments in the Life of My Mother*

big red asterisks of [blood]
  ALAN GOULD *Close Ups*

an octopus of blood advanced down his brow
  TIBOR FISCHER *The Thought Gang*

your blood, dark as wet bark
  WILLIAM H GASS *Omensetter's Luck*

A traffic light of blood
  MARTIN AMIS *The Information*

blush

a fierce blush – like two clumsily upended measures of sweet cherry brandy
  NICOLA BARKER *Behindlings*

boats

sailing boats ... like a collection of small white metronomes rocking on the horizon
  JEREMY LELAND *The Jonah*

The boats were thin and curved, like ancient dried-up pods, like bits of rind
  RUPERT THOMSON *The Book of Revelation*

body

[her] body which hung from her shoulders like an ill-fitting storage bag
  EDWARD COHEN *Two Hundred and Fifty Thousand Dollars*

... body moved like channelled water
  JULIA O'FAOLAIN *First Conjugation*

her body was as rich as a side of beef
HE BATES *A Dream of Fair Women*

... body was a breathing bas-relief which might have appealed to a corkscrew on shore-leave
LAWRENCE DURRELL *Monsieur*

My body that long sleek car someone spun on curves
JAYNE ANNE PHILLIPS *Accidents*

her slight body like a wire run through drapery
PAMELA HANSFORD JOHNSON *A Summer to Decide*

[a] body ... like the shape of a fish inside a damp wrapping of tissue
JEREMY LELAND *The Jonah*

her body curved like the still of an action shot
MICHÈLE ROBERTS *A Piece of the Night*

her thin body folded into itself like a reprimand
SARAH MYLES *Transplanted*

he had felt her body beside him like an immense word on the verge of being spoken
JOHN UPDIKE *The Man Who Became a Soprano*

Her body was a trembling bag of soft fraying strings and bubbles that burst
KEITH RIDGWAY *Never Love a Gambler*

Her body is a softish, anatomical coral reef in which bits of dream flittered
HAROLD BRODKEY *The Runaway Soul*

His body felt like piled gravel
DANIEL BUCKMAN *Morning Dark*

Her body had been fashioned in the school of Egon Schiele, sharp curvings of bone, adamantine breasts, a musculature suggesting anguish and extremity
JOHN MARKS *War Torn*

Her body like moonlight
JANET FITCH *White Oleander*

Her body was a three-dimensional relief map of the beaches of
Southern California
> STEVE AYLETT *The Crime Studio*

her slight, wiry dancer's body poised tight and firm as an
exclamation point
> GEORGIA COTRELL *Shoulders*

his body looked as if it had been whittled, late at night in the light
of the moon, by an absentminded sailor who did not know when to
stop
> KATHRYN DAVIS *Labrador*

[his] drooping, joyless body, like some mollusk cast from its shell,
living on without its usual support
> CAI EMMONS *His Mother's Son*

His body is thin and Jesuitical, his skin has seen no sun
> ALISON FELL *Mer de Glace*

bones

bones ... like cutlery slack in a bag
> JULIA O'FAOLAIN *Godded and Codded*

big bungling bones that sprouted ... like scrub timber
> AL BARKER *The Joy Ride*

Her bones felt like a child had traced them out on a piece of paper
and toted them to school underneath his arm. Thin like that
> OLYMPIA VERNON *Eden*

books

books ... ironic lighthouses sweeping a confused, interior darkness
> PETER VANSITTART *Sources of Unrest*

books ... on shelves that sagged like cumbersome abdomens.
Others were in semi-collapsed piles as if the Manhattan skyline
had suffered an earthquake
> JEREMY LELAND *A River Decrees*

books, old, old books, heavy as centuries
> CYNTHIA OZICK *Levitation*

[Books] packed tall bookcases like rows of gritted teeth
> MICHAEL LOWENTHAL *The Same Embrace*

boredom

boredom creeps over her like vines
MARGARET ATWOOD *Bad News*

boredom clung to my mouth, chilly and deadening, like anaesthetic
MICHÈLE ROBERTS *Reader, I Married Him*

brain

her brain a black aperture eating shaped light
ELIZABETH KNOX *Paremata*

His brain as charred as a hamlet in the path of the Tet offensive
JAMES BARKER *Fuel Injected Dreams*

eyes blinking to the metronome of his brain
NORMAN MAILER *Barbary Shore*

branches

Branches like the necks of birds scanning the sky for food
REBECCA JOSEPHS *Early Disorder*

The branches ... swayed like immense oars dipping into a sea rolling and chilled by the far far stars
TRUMAN CAPOTE *The Grass Harp*

bravery

Bravery descended upon him like sudden rain
DONALD BARTHELME *110 West Sixty-First Street*

breasts

her breasts tilted like soft cupolas
JEREMY LELAND *A River Decrees*

great breasts tossing like shipwrecks
FREDERICK BUECHNER *Treasure Hunt*

breasts like searchlights
JOHN RECHY *City of Night*

breasts ... like two calm edible moons rising side by side
JOHN UPDIKE *The Centaur*

her breasts crouched beneath the blankets, two snug creatures
waiting for Spring
    ANDREW SINCLAIR *The Project*

breasts like fresh boiled eggs with their shells just off
    ROBERT NYE *Falstaff*

breasts ... hard and still like turtles
    COLIN CHANNER *Waiting in Vain*

her breasts as small and sharp as the last inch or two of ice-cream
cones
    VINCENT O'SULLIVAN *The Last of Freddie*

gargoyle breasts
    PATRICK WHITE *The Full Belly*

her breasts were two extinct volcanoes
    PATRICK WHITE *The Vivisector*

the fine big bosom like one of the walled imperious towns of the
Middle Ages whose origin antedates writing
    WILLIAM FAULKNER *Pylon*

[Her] bosom ... heaved like a sentimental sea
    MICHÈLE ROBERTS *The Visitation*

her breasts had drooped down to her knees as if they yearned for
the floor
    STEVE YARBROUGH *The Oxygen Man*

Her breasts are eggplants, watermelons, cacao pods. Sacks of yams.
Tamarind balls. Anthills of the savanna
    COLIN CHANNER *Satisfy My Soul*

her breasts were like people, two slouching fat white people in caps
having a conversation across the four-lane highway of her rib cage
    T CORAGHESSAN BOYLE *Drop City*

My breasts grew like young doves
    ANGELA CARTER *A Very, Very Great Lady and Her Son at Home*

Her breasts were like great stone pillars at the entrance to an estate
    JOE COOMER *Apologizing to Dogs*

Her breasts were small but droopy, like tiny bread rolls in two
translucent plastic bags
  Nicola Barker *Reversed Forecast*

her sugar-in-gunnysacks large breasts
  Harold Brodkey *The Nurse's Music*

small breasts like sachets
  Harold Brodkey *The Runaway Soul*

Her breasts are like mad faces
  Harold Brodkey *Car Buying*

huge German *Hausfrauen*, shelf-breasted like escritoires
  Thea Astley *Coda*

My breasts are like ... twin white doves coming down from Mount
Gilead
  Cynthia Ozick *The Suitcase*

her breasts were pneumatic with joy
  Mavis Cheek *Getting Back Brahms*

those breasts, magnificent things ... like pneumatic roundels of
chocolate blancmange
  Mavis Cheek *Janice Gentle Gets Sexy*

Breasts like appalled witnesses
  Glen Duncan *Love Remains*

breath

... breath made a sound like two pancakes cooking
  Janet Frame *The Edge of the Alphabet*

breath like a salt mine
  Christina Stead *The Man Who Loved Children*

breath coming like puffs of Morse code all in vapor
  Lucas Webb *Stribbling*

breath like a dead moggy on a hot day
  Alan Bleasdale *Scully*

breath like a laser-beam
  Martin Amis *Dead Babies*

His breath smelt, it was a kind of wet, sharp pantry smell, like
some sour thing left too long in a warm cooking place
  JENNIFER LASH *Blood Ties*

[a] breath ... like a brush passing over a leather strap
  JOHN WRAY *The Right Hand of Sleep*

his breath was bad, like the gasps from cellars beneath buildings
  HARLAN GREENE *What the Dead Remember*

breath like a sewage beach shovelled into a spin-dryer
  IAIN SINCLAIR *Radon Daughters*

Her breath smells like a bad accident
  MARGARET ATWOOD *Cat's Eye*

each drawn-in breath rattled like a truckful of gravel being poured
through a giant tin culvert
  MATT COHEN *Elizabeth and After*

her breath has the sound of a dry leaf on a marble floor
  HAROLD BRODKEY *The Runaway Soul*

her intent little animal breath, a faint damp wind across the desert
of my face
  BETH NUGENT *Live Girls*

Their breaths steamed like little private pockets of thought, or
desire
  JOYCE CAROL OATES *Death Mother*

I feel my breath stuck in my chest like an eel I've swallowed whole
  CAROL SHIELDS *Unless*

His breath was minty, like a little blow torch
  MAVIS CHEEK *Pause Between Acts*

she let out an angry breath like ... sibilant chimneys
  PETER CONRAD *Underworld*

breeze

a breeze like a quick kiss from a ghost
  BENEDICT KELLY *Proxopera*

When the breeze struck our cheeks, it was like the sloppily
affectionate lick of a dog you secretly hate
  TOBY LITT *Deadkidsongs*

A cat-curl of breeze
SONYA HARTNETT *Surrender*

bruise

the bruise ... tucked away like a secret letter
CHARLOTTE BACON *Lost Geography*

a bruise blossoms on his jaw, like a purple flower unfolding under dirty snow
BETH NUGENT *Live Girls*

building

a building shooting upward like a railway track set for the moon
ANAÏS NIN *Winter of Artifice*

buildings ... like mumbling mental patients turned out on the street
JOHN UPDIKE *Roger's Version*

buildings glistening with night stood dark grey and worn smooth like stone pillars by centuries of leaning darkness and rain
JANET FRAME *The Adaptable Man*

darkened buildings ... like vast blinded nuns
PETER VANSITTART *A Little Madness*

That graceful old building was beginning to look like the temporary headquarters of an invading army during some particularly nasty war
CALVIN TRILLIN *Tepper Isn't Going Out*

tall buildings, pink and ethereal in a haze, like cromlechs of painted plasticine
EDNA O'BRIEN *House of Splendid Isolation*

apartment buildings as always faced the sea: weary sentries, ossified guards to a kingdom of air
EMILY CARTER *Glory and the Angels*

The factory buildings rise like tired mourners
ERIC SHADE *Kaahumanu*

The apartment building ... was like something out of *Metropolis* – the walls glistened and the tenants were pale
STEVE AYLETT *The Crime Studio*

calves

Her calves were like slivers of almond
  DAVID LONG *Lightning*

car

[The] great car stood like a bruise against the passage of eternity
  MICHAEL ARLEN *The Green Hat*

shiny cars ... like a border of enormous artificial flowers
  ELSPETH HUXLEY *A Man from Nowhere*

a car went by, like a heavy blanket being dragged along the street
  ALAN SILLITOE *The Chiker*

cars go by in the street like boats and soft bubbles
  JP DONLEAVY *A Fairy Tale of New York*

cars like special sleek slugs
  RICHARD HUGHES *The Fox in the Attic*

the car urbane as a metal butler
  LAWRENCE DURRELL *The Black Book*

expensive cars ... moving like ointments
  LAWRENCE DURRELL *Tunc*

cars ... queued ... like liqueur chocolates with intentions
  HUGO CHARTERIS *Marching with April*

cars ... trudged down the streets ... as though they were large gray animals being led home on a long rope
  DAVID RHODES *The Easter House*

A car coming up behind sounded like a slow claustrophobic pursuit
JEREMY LELAND *A River Decrees*

The car was a suitcase of childhood memories
MICHAEL HORNBURG *Downers Grove*

The car roared like angered wildlife
RICK MOODY *Garden State*

Outside the windows a low car full of black youths swung past,
stately, like a hippopotamus, its stereo pounding bass
ALISON FELL *Mer de Glace*

cat

[A] cat picked its way through the street as if looking out for model
sinners on a model Day of Judgement
RUSSELL HOBAN *Turtle Diary*

cats like pipe cleaners
PENELOPE GILLIATT *Mortal Matters*

neighbourhood cats curled along the drive like punctuation marks
TERRY WOLVERTON *Bailey's Beads*

[She] watched the cat breathing, its small body like a heart in a
grey purse
KEITH RIDGWAY *The Long Falling*

cats curled their tails like alien clefs
CYNTHIA OZICK *Heir to the Glimmering World*

cathedral

The cathedral was like a great pomegranate fruit: alluring on the
outside but stony and sterile within
NINA FITZPATRICK *Daimons*

St Paul's across the Thames – a fat bishop boxed in and stranded
flat on his back
EDWARD DOCX *The Calligrapher*

centuries

the blind weight of centuries, the full avoirdupois
JOAN CHASE *The Evening Wolves*

chair

a chair as artistic as a theorem
WO MITCHELL *Who Has Seen the Wind?*

chairs ... like a lot of stiff-legged old creatures waiting to jump through a hoop
AL BARKER *The Joy Ride*

chairs where ladies from fiction sit
JUNE ARNOLD *Baby Houston*

chandelier

a chandelier like a bush of ice hung upside down
JONATHAN BUCKLEY *Invisible*

charm

Her charm ... like a sunbeam entering a tinsel factory
EUGENE WALTER *The Untidy Pilgrim*

the flame of her charm adjusted like a blowtorch
IAIN SINCLAIR *Radon Daughters*

cheek

[She] presents her cheek like a passport
MICHAEL ARDITTI *Easter*

cheeks like mixed petunias
JULIA O'FAOLAIN *That Bastard Berto*

cheeks ... smooth like good writing paper, cream-laid
ADRIAN MITCHELL *Wartime*

Her cheek on my shoulder was like a wafer in a field of snow
PATRICK KAVANAGH *Tarry Flynn*

His rough, scarred cheeks suggested the cheeks of an old statue corroded by its own tears
CHRISTOPHER BRAM *The Notorious Dr August*

the soft barricades of his cheeks
MARGARET ATWOOD *Life Before Man*

cheekbones

When she laughed, her cheeks rose with the strange, graceful bulk of glaciers
STEVE ALMOND *Run Away, My Pale Love*

His cheeks ballooned as if to contain a mouthful of prancing vomit
MARTIN AMIS *The Rachel Papers*

Her cheeks the red of the Virgin Mary's cheeks on roadsides in Ireland
DESMOND HOGAN *A Farewell to Prague*

Pin-cushion cheeks
THYLIAS MOSS *Tale of a Sky-Blue Dress*

his cheeks pouching as if he is rolling a thick thought around in them
CAI EMMONS *His Mother's Son*

cheekbones

his skyscraper cheekbones
MICHAEL HORNBURG *Downers Grove*

her cheekbones flying off to either side in a crucifix
LORRIE MOORE *Who Will Run the Frog Hospital?*

Age has abseiled her cheekbones
COLUM MCCANN *Sisters*

high cheekbones like an arctic explorer's
JOHN CROWLEY *The Translator*

cheekbones from which the chin had taken a suicide dive
IAIN SINCLAIR *Radon Daughters*

his cheekbones protrude like the tops of cliffs
GLEN HIRSHBERG *The Snowman's Children*

child

[children] ... brass-fisted tow-headed devil's anchors
ALAN SILLITOE *Isaac Starbuck*

London children looked like ... crisps ... This one looked like cheese-and-onion. This one looked like beef-and-mustard. This one looked like salt-and-vinegar
MARTIN AMIS *The Information*

children were like healing scar tissue over a wound. They were like white stepping stones over a river
JENNIFER DAWSON *Judasland*

the years of her childhood lay across her mind like the weight of a pile of sleepers
JEREMY LELAND *A River Decrees*

Her children tumbled like balls on the street, like balls escaping gloves and bats
WILLIAM H GASS *Mrs Mean*

chimney

[a] stone chimney standing like a stunned person above the small ruins of the house
JON CLEARY *The Sundowners*

long chimneys like the fingers of drowning men clutching upwards at the sunstraws of the morning
PAMELA HANSFORD JOHNSON *Too Dear for My Possessing*

chin

[He] shot his chin forward like a piece of machinery
MERVYN PEAKE *Titus Groan*

her powerful chin ... like a handle for her head
CHRIS OFFUTT *The Good Brother*

Her chin became Mount Rushmore
T CORAGHESSAN BOYLE *A Friend of the Earth*

... chin quivered like the reed of a musical instrument
RICHARD HUGHES *The Fox in the Attic*

the rudiments of a chin, like a child's hand poking through a sheet
EDMUND WHITE *A Boy's Own Story*

Her chin dribbled away like a melting vanilla cone
KEN KESEY *Sailor Song*

his chin ... a scrum of melted beef lard in a furious blue-white, an unguent waterfall
NICOLA BARKER *Behindlings*

His chin was like something you might see in a cavern – underground, spot-lit – in a *gorge*
NICOLA BARKER *Behindlings*

the sharpness of [her] chin like a drop of water upside down
JANET FITCH *White Oleander*

She stood defiantly, hands on hips, chin up like a furious daisy
MAVIS CHEEK *Getting Back Brahms*

a raw, protuberant chin, deeply cleft and mercilessly shaved, like a tiny pair of smarting buttocks
JOHN BANVILLE *Mefisto*

church

a church stood out against the darkness in a forbidding Gothic trance
PETER VANSITTART *A Little Madness*

ruddy Victorian churches loom like freighters in the sea of bastard architecture
JOHN UPDIKE *The Witches of Eastwick*

cigarette

the red nub of his cigarette in bloodscript scrawl against the night
LEON ROOKE *A Good Baby*

city

the city was a dark cloth on which the pubs glowed like flashy gems
DUDLEY BARKER *The Ladder*

[the] city ... lumped like a lot of glacial boulders refusing to split in the cold
ROY CHRISTY *No Time Like the Past*

[The] city lay curled up below like an animal infested with electric lights
ANGELA CARTER *Several Perceptions*

this city is like a handkerchief put together from bits of dirt
DESMOND HOGAN *The Leaves on Grey*

The city was asleep on its right side and shaking with violent nightmares
ANAÏS NIN *Ragtime*

a city like an edgy encampment of several tribes
ELIZABETH KNOX *Glamour and the Sea*

The city unfurled slowly, highrises separating like the ribs of a fan
ELIZABETH KNOX *Treasure*

this uncorseted city, dusk-veiled, whose entrails lay open to the sky
SUNETRA GUPTA *Memories of Rain*

cities like clusters of Drambuie bottles
JOHN LEONARD *Crybaby of the Western World*

slum-grey cities
DESMOND STEWART *The Pyramid Inch*

the city was a woman, a lusty, bawdy creature who strutted and swung her hips and kicked her voluminous skirts, and promised shuddering adventures
LOUIS ZARA *Dark Rider*

on into the wet chambered heart of the city
KEITH RIDGWAY *The Parts*

The city looked foreign, a maze of Möbius streets
BRET ANTHONY JOHNSTON *Waterwalkers*

we stared out at the city that hummed and glittered like a computer chip deep in some unknowable machine, holding its secret like a poker hand
JANET FITCH *White Oleander*

The city is comfortable here, relaxed, as unconsciously nestled in this point of land as the last bone in my finger
JOE COOMER *Beachcombing for a Shipwrecked God*

Now as spring quickened around me, the city came alive, like a garden indeed, flushed and rustling, impatient and panting, with vague shrills and swoopings on all sides in the lambent, watercolour air
JOHN BANVILLE *Mefisto*

The city was smiling with a heartbreaking indifference, a *cocotte* refreshed by the darkness
LAWRENCE DURRELL *Justine*

The city settled wistfully into night, drew darkness about it like codeine
THOMAS GLYNN *Watching the Body Burn*

Then the city itself, London, as taut and meticulous as a cobweb
MARTIN AMIS *London Fields*

voluptuous, oppressive, corrupt, self-regarding London marinating in the syrup of her own decay like *baba au rhum*, while the property speculators burrow away at her guts with the vile diligence of gonococci
ANGELA CARTER *Reflections*

London was a huge map of misery soaking in September sun, like a mockery of paradise
PHILIP CALLOW *The Bliss Body*

all of Manhattan lying before me like an antipasto tray
RALPH LOMBREGLIA *Inn Essence*

Manhattan shone before him like the biggest illuminated target on earth
DENIS HAMILL *Sins of Two Fathers*

New York ... the sour stink of ten million people, all streaming by at a thousand frames per second
NICOLA GRIFFITH *Stay*

New York piling up like so many stacks of nickels and pennies in the light
WILLIAM LYCHACK *The Wasp Eater*

clock

The clock made a noise as if it was clearing its throat
ROBERT NYE *Faust*

cloud

cloud like a drenched swab
MERVYN PEAKE *Titus Groan*

clouds ragged like different brands of lipstick
DESMOND HOGAN *Teddyboys*

[Clouds] drifted homeward bound, like the sad profiles of a retreating menagerie
ISIDORE OKPEWHO *The Victims*

a stately ice-pudding of a cloud
PATRICK WHITE *A Fringe of Leaves*

clouds hung in the sky like bits of a baroque apocalypse
WILLIAM SANSOM *A Gift of Tongues*

the mysterious archaeology of the clouds
EMMA TENNANT *Wild Nights*

the cloud bars of an early sunset; linen soaked in blood
LAWRENCE DURRELL *Mountolive*

[clouds:] the heavens scattered with sheep-shearings
PAUL SMITH *Come Trailing Blood*

the clouds like down asking to be danced upon
EDNA O'BRIEN *Night*

corpse-thin clouds
CYNTHIA OZICK *Trust*

sulphurous boulders of cloud
GEOFF PIKE *Henry Golightly*

pillow-fighting clouds
MICHÈLE ROBERTS *A Piece of the Night*

warm cottony clouds, downy behind the knees and in the spine
HELEN WYKHAM *Cavan*

a procession of small clouds ... like an ancient geographical woodcut
WILLIAM FAULKNER *Mosquitoes*

a cloud, like an obsolete god
PETER VANSITTART *A Little Madness*

pale clouds slipped back ... like returns of consciousness
PETER VANSITTART *A Little Madness*

A cloud like trousers draped over a rock
  WILSON HARRIS *Ascent to Omai*

pearl-blue clouds like big empty hospital rooms
  FRED CHAPPELL *I Am One of You Forever*

The clouds ring the neck of the light with grey knuckles
  ANDREW SINCLAIR *The Hallelujah Bum*

[a cloud] like a wing ripped from the body of an eagle ... moved
northwards through the awakening air quilled with blood
  MERVYN PEAKE *Titus Groan*

the clouds like a field of gray tumuli, the remnants of a mound-
building people
  VERLYN KLINKENBORG *The Last Fine Time*

light musical clouds
  LAWRENCE DURRELL *Livia*

clouds sidled past each other like uneasy giants
  JG BALLARD *Vermilion Sands*

clouds like lung tissue were packed around the moon,
soundproofing the heavens
  PAUL RADLEY *My Blue-Checker Corker and Me*

clouds like a great hunt of wolfhounds
  HUGO CHARTERIS *The Indian Summer of Gabriel Murray*

clouds with their rough, unsympathetic faces
  A MANETTE ANSAY *River Angel*

a closing valve of cloud
  ELIZABETH KNOX *Treasure*

Scraps of cloud passed over me, half ticklish
  ALLAN GURGANUS *Plays Well with Others*

sudden sardine clouds in the newborn afternoon
  SUNETRA GUPTA *The Glassblower's Breath*

arm-in-arm clouds
  DAVID IRELAND *The Chosen*

storm clouds marble the horizon, grey sliding over black like a low roof of corrugated iron
  SARAH MYLES *Transplanted*

purple clouds ... hung over us like terraces as though we dwelt in Babylon
  JOAN CHASE *During the Reign of the Queen of Persia*

the clouds ... moved off like zeppelins in the last light of day
  BRAD KESSLER *Lick Creek*

The cloud was ... tilted, like a mattress being carried upstairs
  ELIZABETH KNOX *Black Oxen*

hydrocephalic clouds
  MARTIN AMIS *Time's Arrow*

Chagall-like clouds rolled in ... as if they were flying, screaming people
  JOYCE WEATHERFORD *Heart of the Beast*

toiling oceans of basaltic cloud
  FRED CHAPPELL *Look Back All the Green Valley*

The trace of blown cloud in the brilliant sky, like ice cream smudged over chrome
  MARGARET ATWOOD *The Blind Assassin*

clusters of small clouds are grouped around the horizon like the white blank faces of peeping girls
  ANNA KAVAN *Mouse Shoes*

huge clouds that ruddered the sky
  PETER GOLDSWORTHY *Maestro*

The clouds were heavy and late, expected elsewhere
  IAIN SINCLAIR *Radon Daughters*

streaky mackerel clouds are spreading in over the sky, paint on a wet page
  MARGARET ATWOOD *Surfacing*

the clouds which ... gathered in the late afternoon along the coastline like cattle coming in to drink
  JOHN BERGER *Lilac and Flag*

Superb clouds, menacing and charged with iron, squadroned in from the sea: continents of cloud, shaping and parting, overlaying the last brave peepholes of blue
  IAIN SINCLAIR *Downriver*

massive clouds, black-bellied and with lightning in their guts, swung ponderously across the skyscape. A medieval gouache
  THEA ASTLEY *It's Raining in Mango*

clouds hung low and black as bowels
  STEPHEN MARION *Hollow Ground*

clouds zebra'd with lightning
  WILLIAM H GASS *The Tunnel*

Torn clouds are in slow gait to the south, like a straggle of gray and white house dogs hobbling to their beds
  RON HANSEN *Mariette in Ecstasy*

A bundled, lead-coloured cloud burning like magnesium all along its edge
  JOHN BANVILLE *Ghosts*

clouds were sailing on like kingdoms
  MARTHA BERGLAND *A Farm under a Lake*

a mudflat of clouds
  TIM GAUTREAUX *The Clearing*

mountain-sized brackish clouds move like barracks or fat wooden ships
  HAROLD BRODKEY *S.L.*

clouds drifted like layers of licorice
  JACK CADY *The Off Season*

the shattered lamp of clouds
  HAROLD BRODKEY *The Runaway Soul*

Dun clouds rest their bellies on a layer of wind
  CHARLES FERNYHOUGH *The Auctioneer*

a bright blue sky, crossed rapidly by little-lamb clouds
  CHARLES FERNYHOUGH *The Auctioneer*

a few white clouds ... like defeated daisies
  DESMOND HOGAN *Miles*

a low ceiling of storm clouds coiled like entrails
STEVEN HEIGHTON *The Shadow Boxer*

The clouds were flat-bottomed and they gathered in formation like freshly built ships, absurdly shaped, massive, sailing in a gray sky, shot through with mock structural rods of sunlight
SAM NORTH *Chapel Street*

the few clouds were like handfuls of mud
DANIEL BUCKMAN *Morning Dark*

opaque, dully white, layers of stained cumulus clouds like ill-fitting flagstones
JOYCE CAROL OATES *The Hand-Puppet*

clouds sat above the mountains like strange horses
COLUM McCANN *Songdogs*

the rags of sea-dragging cloud
THEA ASTLEY *Coda*

rain-clouds progressing like noble wreckage across the jumbled rooftops of the city
JOHN BANVILLE *Athena*

a thin banner of cloud … like a shred from a passing spirit's robe
JAY McINERNEY *Ransom*

clouds had collected in disorderly heaps: wool waiting to be sorted, graded, baled
KATE JENNINGS *Snake*

the sky pale with fleet, untrussed clouds, a bunker of them, now darkening, low bellied, like the lone cow, milk-swollen, heavy with its own curdle
JULIANNA BAGGOTT *The Madam*

The clouds formed to the west like rimrock mountains
DANIEL BUCKMAN *The Names of Rivers*

small white clouds like old men's faces scudding across the sky
PETER CAREY *Oscar and Lucinda*

clouds hurtle by like islands cut loose from below
ALEXANDER CHEE *Edinburgh*

Clouds scalloped the sky in crazy wisps like uncombed hair
MICHAEL LOWENTHAL *The Same Embrace*

clouds ... moving across the sky like grey-suited dictators
JEAN MCNEIL *Private View*

There would be clouds and mist ready to burst in on their day like spoiling boys
JIM CRACE *Being Dead*

A grey-hulled taskforce of destroyer clouds was moving in from the west
EDWARD DOCX *The Calligrapher*

[Clouds] crossed the sky, stark white where the sun bleached them, like the ghosts of icebergs, hauling their own shadows
DELIA FALCONER *The Service of Clouds*

storm clouds, hurtling by at vampire-movie speed
JEAN MCNEIL *Hunting Down Home*

late-afternoon sunlight coloring the western clouds like layers of a parfait
MARK O'DONNELL *Let Nothing You Dismay*

the outlines of cloud, giant octaves of ochre
LAWRENCE DURRELL *Justine*

cold

the cold rode his shoulders like a hitchhiker
T CORAGHESSAN BOYLE *Drop City*

as cold as a plate-glass negative at night
DELIA FALCONER *The Service of Clouds*

complexion

[her] complexion merely a cardiovascular or alcoholic pink
JOHN FULLER *Tell It Me Again*

a complexion like a baking potato
MICHAEL GRIFFITH *Bibliophilia*

the impeccable cream cotton tablecloth of her soft complexion
NICOLA BARKER *Behindlings*

consciousness

her consciousness swirling back into her body like food coloring
invading a jar of water
CINTRA WILSON *Colors Insulting to Nature*

consonants

consonants clicked like a belt
ANTHONY BURGESS *The Worm and the Ring*

consonants like leading in a window of stained glass
JOHN UPDIKE *The Poorhouse Fair*

a long name of all consonants like a bad Scrabble hand
EDMUND WHITE *His Biographer*

the consonants were flints that decorated the unchanging desert of
his speech
THEA ASTLEY *The Well Dressed Explorer*

the soft knobs of consonants
ANGELA CARTER *Shadow Dance*

conversation

conversation as useless as wet newspaper
JAMES FORDEN *The Love Chase*

conversation lurched like iron trams through the afternoon
PATRICK WHITE *The Vivisector*

spermy, lying conversation
STEFAN KANFER *The Eighth Sin*

Little popcorn bursts of conversation
CHARLES HALDEMAN *The Sun's Attendant*

conversations ... hung like wedges of cold pudding, unexplained
and out of context
GRACE INGOLDBY *Across the Water*

weak conversations that pass over the flat water like tired sparrows
DENNIS BOCK *Olympia*

conversation broke into monochrome phrases like the glaze on a
plate
THEA ASTLEY *The Multiple Effects of Rainshadow*

the conversation began creaking like strained pond ice at the first weight of any serious view
TIM FARRINGTON *Blues for Hannah*

Their conversations had a sprung, argumentative quality, like regurgitated panel discussions
JONATHAN LETHEM *The Fortress of Solitude*

Conversation flowed stiffly, like papier mâché
PHILIP HENSHER *Kitchen Venom*

much of what passes for conversation is the simplest filler; like the down in a huge quilt, it shifts and settles and warms
ROSELLEN BROWN *Tender Mercies*

their conversation has begun to seem like a tired minuet, something so old and obvious it's not worth doing anymore
CAI EMMONS *His Mother's Son*

cough

a cough like … dry paper flapping against a cactus
AIMEE BENDER *An Invisible Sign of My Own*

She coughed me a transient rainbow of germs
MARTIN AMIS *The Rachel Papers*

a succession of cold-engined coughs
CHARLES FERNYHOUGH *The Auctioneer*

countryside

It was the sort of namby-pamby countryside you could imagine Virginia Woolf walking through in her long skirts
SUSAN SWAN *The Wives of Bath*

cow

Cows like tiny ceramic cows from a knickknack shelf grazed placidly in the weight of the sun
WILLIAM GAY *Provinces of Night*

Beyond the velvety lawn and ha-ha grazed golden cattle, sweet-eyed, glistening-mouthed, as pastorally perfect as any De Cuyp
MAVIS CHEEK *Getting Back Brahms*

curl

black curls like the silhouette of a grassfire
ALAN GOULD *Close Ups*

[an] unruly head of curls like the sun coming up behind her head
ROSELLEN BROWN *Civil Wars*

curse

curse like a mob wiretap
DENIS HAMILL *Sins of Two Fathers*

darkness

storms of darkness ... like tides summoned by a moon
HENRY GREEN *Party Going*

the dark, a live monster, leaned on the roof and tried the glass doors
DAVID IRELAND *The Glass Canoe*

darkness ran over her like ink over a fly
AL BARKER *The Narrow Boat*

dark as a plush-lined pistol-case
BRIGID BROPHY *In Transit*

darkness hanging like a Japanese print of an extinct volcano
LAWRENCE DURRELL *Nunquam*

a vulva-shaped volume of gleaming city-garden darkness
ELIZABETH KNOX *Treasure*

the flocculent, moth-laden darkness
JOHN BANVILLE *Ghosts*

dawn

... squirt of dawn
CLIVE BARRY *Crumb Borne*

the arched back of the dawn had humped the sheet of the night away
ANDREW SINCLAIR *The Project*

The dawn looks like a beautifully-tuned piano made entirely of sea-shells
　PETER REDGROVE *In the Country of the Skin*

the festering gray maw of the dawn
　T CORAGHESSAN BOYLE *Riven Rock*

the nacreous hush of a winter dawn
　MICHEL FABER *Under the Skin*

the few experimental chirps and bronchitic engines of our city's dawn
　AL KENNEDY *So I Am Glad*

She watched the dawn leak between the buildings and into the streets and the sky, a capillary action of amber
　JANETTE TURNER HOSPITAL *Borderline*

Dawn came, so pink, so pastel, so silly
　HAROLD BRODKEY *Innocence*

dawn … seeping higher and higher, until it cast itself across the sky, a vertical violet light, like a risen watchtower
　CYNTHIA OZICK *Heir to the Glimmering World*

the gnat-swarms of dawnlight
　NICHOLSON BAKER *A Box of Matches*

the first cobalt scabs of [dawn]
　GLEN DUNCAN *Weathercock*

day

Day came in like Joshua, with ramshorn blasts of sun
　GERALDINE McCAUGHREAN *The Maypole*

day, like a lift out of control
　JANET FRAME *Scented Gardens for the Blind*

day was burning up like some old dry-grassed ruin with sick white convolvulus flowers clinging to its broken windows and crumbling brick walls
　JANET FRAME *Intensive Care*

ticking dry bones of the day
　JOHN BANVILLE *Birchwood*

day ... like a baby dumped on a doorstep, gorgeous but unwanted
  REYNOLDS PRICE *The Happiness of Others*

the day, a nightmare of many parcels, beckoned with a child's cruel eyes and a grubby nail-bitten finger
  ANTHONY BURGESS *The Worm and the Ring*

days were as pointless as childhood afternoons
  CYNTHIA OZICK *Trust*

day was beautiful and dead, a coloured photograph
  PJ KAVANAGH *A Happy Man*

a cold-blooded, rent-demanding, hanged-drawn-and-quarter day
  WILLIAM SANSOM *The Almighty Test*

The day arched like a blinding headache
  JOHN UPDIKE *The Coup*

days passed as if they dragged a ball and chain
  DAVID IRELAND *The Glass Canoe*

days like letters written in pencil
  ELLEASE SOUTHERLAND *Let the Lion Eat Straw*

Our radiant days together had become barium tracers within me
  JOHN UPDIKE *A Month of Sundays*

days strolled by like polite children in the parks
  DESMOND HOGAN *The Ikon Maker*

It was an eighteenth-century day, windswept and bright, the distances all small and sharply defined, as if painted on porcelain
  JOHN BANVILLE *The Newton Letter*

the day insisted on going crooked, like a cross-threaded screw
  WALLACE STEGNER *Crossing to Safety*

Every day was a lithograph of the one before
  T CORAGHESSAN BOYLE *Riven Rock*

each remaining day ... like another wine in a series of increasingly rare vintages, each complecting, elaborating, the one that came before
  NEIL GORDON *The Gun Runner's Daughter*

By June the days were long slabs of sun
  CHRIS OFFUTT *The Good Brother*

The days braided together in a rope of noise and cooled cinder
  MICHAEL GRANT JAFFE *Skateaway*

a clear, gold, late-summer day that almost had a hum to it, a chord
in a minor key
  MARTHA BERGLAND *Idle Curiosity*

The day was a long pallid worm arching up out of darkness and
back again
  JOHN UPDIKE *Toward the End of Time*

With its tramp-dread and street-sadness, the day has special terrors
  MARTIN AMIS *Success*

The whole day felt distant, like someone else's dream
  GLEN HIRSHBERG *Dancing Men*

It was the kind of day they polish steel for
  ROBERT FORD *The Student Conductor*

Her days are baroque, they curl into each other like acanthus
leaves, she lives somewhere between now and then
  JANETTE TURNER HOSPITAL *Borderline*

death

my father's sad minor-key death
  MATT COHEN *The Bookseller*

death might come, like delicious sleep, with the rich fragrances of
rotting flowers
  SUNETRA GUPTA *Memories of Rain*

death has already entered, it is like a black star, a soft black star
being hauled up the stairs on its iron shanks
  EDNA O'BRIEN *House of Splendid Isolation*

death stretches away like a valley crossed with lazy streams
  WILLIAM H GASS *The Tunnel*

death was an ill-lit corridor with all its greater rooms beyond
  JIM CRACE *Being Dead*

desire

Death, a high velvet tide, smothered him
DELIA FALCONER *The Service of Clouds*

death's elaborate, unfunny door
BRUCE WAGNER *I'm Losing You*

desire

the sly hinge of my adult desires
DELIA FALCONER *The Service of Clouds*

A drowned coal seam of desire
ALAN WALL *China*

the nimble rabbits of his desire
RUSSELL HOBAN *Angelica's Grotto*

Desire lies on her tongue like morning breath
COLUM MCCANN *This Side of Brightness*

despair

despair ... washes over them like gray ink
MARGARET ATWOOD *Alien Territory*

dimple

deep dimples like parentheses that hold up his cheeks
KRISTIN WATERFIELD DUISBERG *The Good Patient*

disbelief

I sprouted Corinthian columns of disbelief
TIBOR FISCHER *The Thought Gang*

distraught

the vaguely distraught air of a kitten that had seen visions
RONALD FIRBANK *Concerning the Eccentricities of Cardinal Pirelli*

dog

The dog wriggled through the basement like a large black muscle
RALPH LOMBREGLIA *One-Woman Blues Revival*

doors

huge front doors had the magnificent discouragement of a butler's facade
JON CLEARY *The High Commissioner*

doors that clicked shut like a mind made up
STEFAN KANFER *The Eighth Sin*

doubt

the dreadful torque of his doubt
SALMAN RUSHDIE *Fury*

a sickle of doubt
DJUNA BARNES *Nightwood*

doubts would stand by her bed like giants with upraised clubs
LAURENS VAN DER POST *The Face Beside the Fire*

doubt stirred like a centipede
PAMELA HANSFORD JOHNSON *The Unspeakable Skipton*

like a pickled plum inside a rice ball, lurked a tiny malignant ball of doubt
DEBORAH BOEHM *Hungry Ghosts in Love*

A trichinosis of self-doubt undermined the shank and brisket of my soul
RICK DEMARINIS *Life Between Meals*

doubt made a trapdoor in her stomach
JANICE GALLOWAY *Clara*

a flea's leap of doubt
JULIA O'FAOLAIN *Man in the Cellar*

dread

Dread, like a scrap of stale bread was stuck in her throat
REGGIE NADELSON *Somebody Else*

Dread kindles in my chest
JULIE ORRINGER *When She Is Old and I Am Famous*

Dread disperses and hangs on the air like a thick roux
CAI EMMONS *His Mother's Son*

dream

Some quivering butterfly dream soaked in sunlight in a doorway
PETER CAREY *Bliss*

dreams like light imprisoned in bright mineral caves
ANNA KAVAN *Asylum Piece*

the tight-fisted cabin of her dreams
SUSAN DODD *Mamaw*

Night after night, the same dreams, fault lines along which my
sleep repeatedly cracked and broke
ANN HARLEMAN *Imagined Colors*

Her dreams were a mockery of sleep, another shade of haunting
ALYSON HAGY *Kettle of Hawks*

A long, slow, blue-skied, green-grassed, yellow-hued, daisy-kissed,
wheat-smelling, poppy-bleeding, bee-buzzing, stonechat-smacking
pastureland of dreaming
NICOLA BARKER *Behindlings*

Her dreams are as beautiful and mysterious as a hand-painted
tarot pack – the Visconti set in the Pierpont Morgan Library, for
example
JANETTE TURNER HOSPITAL *Borderline*

dusk

dusk was like a hand of caution on the shoulder
DIANA FARR *Choosing*

the dusk raked like a black searchlight across the hills
MARTIN AMIS *Dead Babies*

Dusk was settling over the highway like a mood
LORRIE MOORE *Joy*

dust

dust still suspended in the air like a confession
HESTER KAPLAN *Kinship Theory*

ears

ears were small and rigid, like dried apricots
    FD REEVE *White Colours*

her ears fragile mollusks
    KELLY DWYER *Self-Portrait with Ghosts*

her pretty ears stood out pointed from her head, like gnomes at prayer
    LAWRENCE DURRELL *Livia*

big brown ears like tea-dunked ginger-biscuits
    MARTIN AMIS *The Rachel Papers*

old women whose aged ears hang off their heads like tree fungus
    AMY BLOOM *Rowing to Eden*

the great guitars of [his] ears
    MARTIN AMIS *Time's Arrow*

elbow

His elbow looked like a gray, unlit light bulb
    CLYDE EDGERTON *In Memory of Junior*

elegance

there's a severe and unadorned elegance about her – like a Quaker meetinghouse
    MARGARET ATWOOD *Alias Grace*

emotion

emotion ... still present in her voice like a shadow on sunlit water
  LAURENS VAN DER POST *The Face Beside the Fire*

emotion boiled down to a highly charged sediment
  GILLIAN TINDALL *The Youngest*

armed only with braille emotions
  PENELOPE SHUTTLE *Wailing Monkey Embracing a Tree*

the emotion in his voice as dazzling as a suddenly and rarely drawn sword
  ELIZABETH KNOX *After Z-Hour*

emotions ... were as ornate as girls' breasts
  HAROLD BRODKEY *Profane Friendship*

I was constantly up to the waist in a lukewarm sump of thin, over-scented emotions
  AL KENNEDY *So I Am Glad*

His emotions washed easily across his face like water in a tipped dish
  ROSELLEN BROWN *Civil Wars*

evening

evening ... cracking like a mirror in the flames
  LAURENS VAN DER POST *The Face Beside the Fire*

the evening was dead, like a cinema ticket held forgotten as the film glides past
  PETER VANSITTART *Quintet*

evening like a nun shod with silence
  WILLIAM FAULKNER *New Orleans*

evening like a girl slipping along the wall to meet her lover
  WILLIAM FAULKNER *New Orleans*

evening came sad as horns among the trees
  WILLIAM FAULKNER *Mosquitoes*

[the] end of the evening looming darkly ahead like rusty buffers at the end of a shining railway line
  ROBIN MAUGHAM *The Wrong People*

the broad fiery arson of evening
CHRISTY BROWN *A Shadow on Summer*

the evening falling outside so starkly she could nearly hear it, a faint exhalation, like a sigh of defeat
NEIL GORDON *The Gun Runner's Daughter*

an evening so cold it seemed milled from lead
CHARLOTTE BACON *Lost Geography*

It's evening, one of those grey watercolour washes, like liquid dusk, the city comes up with in fall
MARGARET ATWOOD *Cat's Eye*

the blurred sepia of early evening
MICHAEL GRANT JAFFE *Skateaway*

That evening was a slow, broad falling of fire. Dusty heat rose, lazy, from the ground while the burning of the sea and sky commenced with peach and egg yellow and ended with sparking iron, bright mercury and blood that cooled to a thickening, ashy dusk
AL KENNEDY *Everything You Need*

expression

He had the expression of someone who wishes the rain would stop
WILL CHRISTOPHER BAER *Kiss Me, Judas*

an expression of laboratorial interest on her face
GREG HRBEK *The Hindenburg Crashes Nightly*

[a] fixed expression you might have seen on a piece of rock
VS PRITCHETT *Blind Love*

an expression like a wrecked Volkswagen
PENELOPE GILLIATT *Mortal Matters*

Her sponge-cake expression
ELLIOTT BAKER *Klynt's Law*

an expression like Elizabeth Barrett Browning's spaniel
PENELOPE GILLIATT *One by One*

that wistful expression, almost as though she were visited by a spirit
JOAN CHASE *The Evening Wolves*

She looked up at him with an expression as if he'd asked her the color of her dead husband's eyes
  BRAD WATSON *The Heaven of Mercury*

that tolerant, capable-urban-man-approaching-silly-rural-woman expression
  NICOLA GRIFFITH *Stay*

his face ... was screwed into the I'm-going-to-get-you expression of a convict who's already started digging a tunnel with a nail file
  LIONEL SHRIVER *We Need to Talk about Kevin*

[his] expression fruit-on-a-bough-ish
  HAROLD BRODKEY *Lila and S.L.*

the tolerant expression of somebody watching a small animal attempt something inexplicable
  JIM SHEPARD *Nosferatu*

Expressions moved across his face slowly, elegantly, like the passing shadows of clouds over mountains
  RENÉE MANFREDI *Above the Thunder*

the expressions of repentant murderers who have called their victims up in a séance
  ANDREW SEAN GREER *The Confessions of Max Tivoli*

He always wore the surprised expression of a frog run over in the road
  PHILIP CALLOW *Some Love*

[He] bore the facial expression of one being approached by a pterodactyl
  MAVIS CHEEK *Getting Back Brahms*

Her face wore the superior, peevish expression of aged servants who have chosen to stay up longer than they are expected to
  PATRICK WHITE *The Vivisector*

[His] expression was filled with a numinous and unthinking glow, common to all self-styled nineteenth-century explorers
  KATHRYN DAVIS *Labrador*

[She had] a sweet shipwrecked expression at the eyes
  LEIF ENGER *Peace Like a River*

eyeballs

[His] eyeballs moved under his lids like nether creatures
  TIM GAUTREAUX *The Clearing*

His eyeballs was [sic] black olives floating in hot sauce
  TIM GAUTREAUX *Deputy Sid's Gift*

eyebrows

eyebrows as pronounced and swift in their curve as two angry strokes of unsharpened charcoal
  JOHN UPDIKE *A Month of Sundays*

thick converging eyebrows that lean on each other like the sides of a fur tent
  CHARLES HALDEMAN *The Sun's Attendant*

[His] eyebrows were twin Norman arches
  GRAHAM JOYCE *Dreamside*

[Her eyebrows] were faint and wispy, like an aerial shot of grain
  LORRIE MOORE *Who Will Run the Frog Hospital?*

her eyebrows shooting together like twin complaints over her nose
  ELIZABETH JORDAN MOORE *Cold Times*

wiry eyebrows that twisted off his forehead like spray
  DAVID PROFUMO *Sea Music*

Quizzical eyebrows (curls of unlit gunpowder)
  IAIN SINCLAIR *Landor's Tower*

Heavy eyebrows like the tracing of muddy thumbs on clean Irish linen
  IAIN SINCLAIR *Landor's Tower*

[Her] eyebrows snailed in effort
  SARAH STONICH *These Granite Islands*

The black eyebrows were wobbling like rocking-horse manes
  CYNTHIA OZICK *The Messiah of Stockholm*

[eye]brows like cutlass slashes
  IAIN SINCLAIR *Downriver*

raising one of her perfectly defined eyebrows, which looks like a
crow in flight in the far distance of a painting by Van Gogh
    JAY MCINERNEY *Model Behaviour*

his dark eyebrows rising like the shadows of twin hawks on the
sheer cliff of his forehead
    JAY MCINERNEY *Brightness Falls*

tufted eyebrows that arched as though he were in a continual state
of intellectual surprise
    RICHARD BAUSCH *Violence*

[Her] eyebrows came together like a small thunderhead
    TIM GAUTREAUX *Died and Gone to Vegas*

an eyebrow, thin and dark as a line drawn with water
    BERNARD COOPER *A Year of Rhymes*

his eyebrows two thatches of unkempt wire
    CHRISTOPHER COOK *Robbers*

The strong dashes of her eyebrows were knitted together like
caterpillars in a collision
    SAM NORTH *Chapel Street*

His eyebrows … looked like two accents that had been stuck on his
brow
    TIBOR FISCHER *Voyage to the End of the Room*

her eyebrows knitting together like offended caterpillars
    JANETTE TURNER HOSPITAL *Borderline*

His eyebrows were now higher than a drag queen's in a
planetarium
    TOBY LITT *Map-Making among the Middle-Classes*

my eyebrows were now expressing the kind of enraptured greeting
towards each other that Italian and French engineers make when
their tunnelings meet perfectly in the middle of a mountain
    MAVIS CHEEK *Getting Back Brahms*

his eyebrows frail as Oriental brushstrokes
    ROSELLEN BROWN *Before and After*

[His] eyebrows collapsed into an adorable curving V, like a child's crayon rendition of a bird, all wings
  MICHAEL LOWENTHAL *The Same Embrace*

his bristly brows, courtesy of Holbein or Cranach the Elder
  BRUCE WAGNER *The Chrysanthemum Palace*

eyelashes

her [eye]lashes moved dustily like moths, in sudden antennal jerks
  PHILIP CALLOW *Clipped Wings*

her blinking eyelashes freighted with mascara
  MARTHA WITT *Broken As Things Are*

eyelids

eyelids ... fluttering like a medium
  JAMES PURDY *Malcolm*

eyelids slipping down like two mauve shells
  ANITA DESAI *Fire on the Mountain*

her cast-down eyelids gleamed like the backs of teaspoons
  HELEN SIMPSON *Send One Up for Me*

The thin paper of his eyelid
  AIMEE BENDER *An Invisible Sign of My Own*

her eyelids flashed like small change at the bottom of a wishing well
  TRUDY LEWIS *Private Correspondences*

[Her] eyelids seemed carved by the hands of a saint-maker
  TINA DE ROSA *Paper Fish*

eyes

their eyes levelled on each other's and were like cold windows behind which each one had just pulled shut venetian blinds
  SUMNER LOCKE ELLIOTT *The Man Who Got Away*

his rheostat eyes turning up to 300 watts
  TOM WOLFE *The Electric Kool-Aid Acid Test*

eyes like marbles of gristle
  MERVYN PEAKE *Titus Groan*

... eyes had faded to the innocent blue of baby ribbon
ANGELA CARTER *Fireworks*

eyes wander like tangled searchlights
JAMES ALDRIDGE *Mockery in Arms*

eyes like one of the mourners around the dead Christ in an El Greco painting
CHRISTOPHER ISHERWOOD *The World in the Evening*

eyes ... like those of a dying man who looks everywhere for healing
JAMES BALDWIN *Giovanni's Room*

brandy-ball eyes
AL BARKER *The Joy-Ride*

wild egg-yolk eyes
KEN KESEY *Sometimes a Great Notion*

eyes ... perfect, murky globes that would have made suitable novelties for a czar
GILBERT ROGIN *Earnest Observers*

Her eyes look like snot
TONI MORRISON *The Bluest Eye*

blue eyes as fresh and wild as a full pardon
EDMUND WHITE *Nocturnes for the King of Naples*

cash-register eyes
PHILIP CALLOW *Flesh of Morning*

She had eyes like Tierra del Fuego butterflies
DESMOND HOGAN *A Curious Street*

eyes like moths that had escaped out of apple trees
PAUL SMITH *Come Trailing Blood*

rheumy boiled-onion eyes
EVA HANAGAN *In Thrall*

His eyes were facts
SUSAN KERSLAKE *Middlewatch*

... raised his eyes to heaven like a Guido Reni martyr
PETER ABRAHAMS *The Fury of Rachel Monette*

The eyes of a Belsen stoker
 HUGO CHARTERIS *Marching with April*

eyes like intelligent bonfires
 ROBERT NYE *Falstaff*

her largo eyes
 PENELOPE SHUTTLE *Wailing Monkey Embracing a Tree*

eyes like mud with fog caught in it
 RICHARD STERN *Packages*

eyes ... playing like twin radios broadcasting a romantic concerto
 ANTHONY BURGESS *The Right to an Answer*

small jetty eyes
 AL BARKER *Novelette*

eyes like trespassers
 PETER VANSITTART *Landlord*

eyes stiff, like italics
 PETER VANSITTART *Landlord*

eyes like pages in last winter's magazine left in the waiting room of
a dentist
 ANNE ROIPHE *Up the Sandbox*

Her eyes were twin black furnaces demanding constant loads of
dark grief to keep them fueled
 SARAH BIRD *Alamo House*

eyes as forlorn as the last two olives in a relish jar
 EDWARD STEWART *Rock Rude*

driving his eyes at me like two hounds in a strange yard
 WILLIAM FAULKNER *As I Lay Dying*

Her eyes were snails in mustard
 DESMOND HOGAN *A New Shirt*

the hand-up-your-skirt eyes
 ALISON FELL *The Bad Box*

her High Street eyes
 MARTIN AMIS *Money*

eyes like violets under glass
T CORAGHESSAN BOYLE *World's End*

narrow anthracite eyes
JEREMY LELAND *A River Decrees*

dense brown eyes like the eyes of men in Goya portraits
BARBARA BENSON *The Underlings*

frayed eyes gazing like a misprint
PETER VANSITTART *Landlord*

the-Cossack-came-by eyes
AMY BLOOM *The Gates Are Closing*

the blank eyes of a giver of bad news
COLIN CHANNER *Waiting in Vain*

He looked into her eyes and they were floodplains of madness
T CORAGHESSAN BOYLE *Riven Rock*

her eyes looked like destroyed rifle targets
KEN KESEY *Sailor Song*

empty-eyed, like an old uncle baby-sitting
KEN KESEY *Sailor Song*

eyes ... like the desolating gaiety of a fundless paediatric hospital
MARTIN AMIS *London Fields*

eyes ... like a criminal's cream Rolls-Royce, parked at dusk between
a tube station and a flower stall
MARTIN AMIS *London Fields*

eyes that shone like melting bitumen
DAVID IRELAND *The Chosen*

her eyes candid and innocent as an STD receptionist
DAVID IRELAND *The Chosen*

eyes like depopulation
DAVID IRELAND *The Chosen*

her eyes wore that squinting, world-weary expression one finds on
girls who were still dressing Barbies when they started having sex
GABRIEL EVERETT *A Story of Scorpions*

flashing white eyes moons of madness desperately trying to avoid eclipse
 SHANE CONNAUGHTON *The Run of the Country*

eyes leaking like egg-white into the cheeks
 JOHN FULLER *Tell It Me Again*

her ... eye had turned brown, like a blossom dying, like madness leaving its mark
 CONNIE MAY FOWLER *River of Hidden Dreams*

Her dark eyes ... burn without light: icon eyes
 ANN HARLEMAN *The Cost of Anything*

the blue of her eyes, like tiny gifts
 NINO RICCI *Where She Has Gone*

Her left eye looked like the letter e if you typed it on the hotel typewriter and then went back and typed another e on top of it
 RUPERT THOMSON *The Insult*

I could feel the eyes of men on her like postage stamps that were already licked and looking for an envelope
 RUPERT THOMSON *The Insult*

her eyes like two sourceless holes
 SARAH MYLES *Transplanted*

her brown eyes gold-shot at times like the ripe skins of pears simmering, spiced dark with cinnamon and cloves
 JOAN CHASE *During the Reign of the Queen of Persia*

his eyes gray from clouds that had passed over his heart
 JOAN CHASE *During the Reign of the Queen of Persia*

eyes the color of glacial melt
 T CORAGHESSAN BOYLE *Termination Dust*

eyes ... like casual acquaintances, like neighbours on their way to a P.T.A. meeting
 T CORAGHESSAN BOYLE *She Wasn't Soft*

eyes clear as Christ
 SHANE CONNAUGHTON *A Border Station*

She had the violet eyes of fate
 JOYCE WEATHERFORD *Heart of the Beast*

her eyes would flick open, stare into mine, blue, like still-wet-from-
the-dye denim
  NICOLA GRIFFITH *Stay*

his eyes ... shone in deep sockets like splashes of solder
  IAIN SINCLAIR *Landor's Tower*

their eyes already gone whoring
  BARRY HANNAH *Yonder Stands Your Orphan*

his eyes pressing me like hot breaths
  MERLE DROWN *The Suburbs of Heaven*

eyes, like two bright breves on an otherwise unaccented page
  JOHN UPDIKE *Cruise*

his eyes behind his glasses are like plums cut in half
  JOHN BERGER *To the Wedding*

eyes shifting like a naughty blonde hamster
  SIMON BREEN *Down in One*

his eyes grateful and shy, like magnets brushed with gold
  EDNA O'BRIEN *House of Splendid Isolation*

his glasses making his eyes look extinct, like capped wells
  EDMUND WHITE *His Biographer*

her glassine Tiffany eyes like two jewels set in shadow
  NEIL GORDON *The Gun Runner's Daughter*

loud-mouthed eyes
  MELINDA HAYNES *Mother of Pearl*

your eyes shining like digital wristwatches
  MARGARET ATWOOD *Men at Sea*

The eyes ... are Monday at the fishmongers, glazed and dull
  GRACE INGOLDBY *Bring Out Your Dead*

dark blue eyes that looked as though they had come from some
deep part of the sea
  JENNY HOBBS *The Sweet-Smelling Jasmine*

those prying boiled-sweet eyes
  JENNY HOBBS *The Sweet-Smelling Jasmine*

Chocolate-drop eyes
  MOLLY GILES *Iron Shoes*

eyes, abysmal, inimical, like the sea seen through holes in an icefield
  ELIZABETH KNOX *The Vintner's Luck*

Her eyes were dark, tending toward strap-leather brown, and there were times they'd hold the light like plugs of smoldering hickory
  ALYSON HAGY *Hardware River*

His eyes were like mixed metal
  ALYSON HAGY *Kettle of Hawks*

Wide-set eyes that read you like an autocue
  IAIN SINCLAIR *Radon Daughters*

his eyes with their flat hot surfaces, a glint like nailheads. Copperheads. Pennies on the eyes
  MARGARET ATWOOD *Life Before Man*

her eyes, like two pieces of gravel, cold and unreflecting
  MARGARET ATWOOD *Life Before Man*

His eyes were deep, and the brown in them was the brown of winter forests and the walk home
  KEITH RIDGWAY *The Parts*

dark eyes, fierce with sorrow, staring up out of deep pits like drowning rodents
  STEVEN MILLHAUSER *The King in the Tree*

blank puddle eyes
  THEA ASTLEY *It's Raining in Mango*

the shiny metallic tackheads of his eyes
  T CORAGHESSAN BOYLE *Drop City*

His eyes were bloodshot and full of stoically endured pain which only tsunamic revenge and the grovelling apologies of world leaders could hope to cure
  MICHEL FABER *Under the Skin*

his narrow, police eyes
  MICHAEL PYE *The Pieces from Berlin*

eyes like sequins sewn on a shroud
WILLIAM H GASS *The Tunnel*

eyes like the holes of pebbles in the moment after striking water
WILLIAM H GASS *Cartesian Sonata*

her eyes like seeds fallen on the vast facial terrain
SONYA HARTNETT *Of a Boy*

His little eyes gleamed with the brilliance of proof coins
ALAN WALL *The School of Night*

her eyes had the cool, unsparing beauty of two cathode-blue security monitors
NICK FOWLER *A Thing (or Two) about Curtis and Camilla*

eyes like wasps trapped in bottles
JOE COOMER *Apologizing to Dogs*

[His] eyes were watery, wandering; tadpoles in the jelly of his face
NICOLA BARKER *Small Holdings*

eyes like peanut brittle
NICOLA BARKER *Wide Open*

her eyes [were] unbearably smug and confident, like nuns or traffic wardens
NICOLA BARKER *Reversed Forecast*

[His] eyes are fathom-deep with patience
LOUIS BAYARD *Endangered Species*

She had those big liquid reproving eyes. Like chocolates
DEBORAH BERGMAN *River of Glass*

his eyes the gray of old bullets
TIM GAUTREAUX *The Clearing*

his eyes in the mirror like something dirty
JAMES BRADLEY *The Deep Field*

there were gold lights in his light brown eyes, like foil was behind them
MARTHA BERGLAND *Idle Curiosity*

[His] eyes shone sparkly, like the tiny saucers of a child's tea set
JACK CADY *The Off Season*

his eyes were flickering over her like lightning over grass
ANGELA GREEN *The Colour of Water*

Her eyes are not fully lit; they are stirring like half-lit theatres
HAROLD BRODKEY *The Bullies*

the thin man's eyes are ... like carpenters' levels with green liquid in them
HAROLD BRODKEY *Car Buying*

her eyes like pieces of deluding, maybe poisoned candy
HAROLD BRODKEY *The Runaway Soul*

beautiful large hazy blue eyes like an undecided summer sky
MATT COHEN *Elizabeth and After*

her eyes like malevolent currants in rising dough
AL KENNEDY *Everything You Need*

her eyes were a pure liquefaction of lapping thought
AL KENNEDY *Breaking Sugar*

His eyes glowed like sun-splendid lizards
DARIN STRAUSS *The Real McCoy*

blue eyes full of humour; their constant gaze made them seem like the riding lights of an anchored yacht
LAWRENCE DURRELL *Quinx*

the eyes of a mouse being stepped on
ERIC SHADE *Eyesores*

his eyes ... the color of damp tobacco, sunk wrong like bent nails pounded in from frustration
ERIC SHADE *Blood*

Their eyes are like fireflies, hot and erased of memory
CHRISTINA GARCIA *Dreaming in Cuban*

eyes mean as blotting-paper
JANICE GALLOWAY *Foreign Parts*

Hard cop's eyes, like shards of agate splintered off by the blow of a hammer
WILLIAM GAY *Provinces of Night*

anchovy-paste eyes
NICOLA BARKER *Behindlings*

She had disconcertingly pale blue eyes. Eyes the colour of the
exact spot where the winter sky brushed the sea
NICOLA BARKER *Behindlings*

irreversibly agnostic eyes
ANNE SCOTT *Calpurnia*

Those telegrammatic liquid-black eyes like the eyes of a Madonna
in an ikon
DESMOND HOGAN *A Farewell to Prague*

They were spooky enough, those eyes, like the changing show at a
planetarium
TRUDY LEWIS *Private Correspondences*

his eyes were little black cavities in the moon
BETH NUGENT *At the End of My Life*

eyes like a road accident
IAIN SINCLAIR *Dining on Stones*

her eyes, which used to puppy-leap about the room, had been
leashed and trained by the necessity of the streets
ANDREW SEAN GREER *The Confessions of Max Tivoli*

she looked at me with those light-catching girandole eyes
ANDREW SEAN GREER *The Confessions of Max Tivoli*

her eyes, in moonlight, seem like precious things brought round
the Horn
ANDREW SEAN GREER *The Confessions of Max Tivoli*

His mother's eyes baggy and sad as her ironing pile
MARY KAY ZURAVLEFF *The Frequency of Souls*

eyes small and mean as blood blisters
GRANT BUDAY *A Sack of Teeth*

Her eyes are as grey as the storm scud of the sea
ALISTAIR MACLEOD *The Lost Salt Gift of Blood*

His eyes were twisted lifer-mean
DANIEL BUCKMAN *Morning Dark*

eyes like a strangling
  PETE DEXTER *Train*

his inkwell eyes
  JOYCE CAROL OATES *Old Budapest*

her eyes tapered like two slender fish
  JULIE ORRINGER *The Smoothest Way Is Full of Stones*

her eyes were … figure-of-eighting over my features
  PHILIP HENSHER *The Fit*

his eyes fixed on hers, like a courtier leaving a monarch
  PHILIP HENSHER *The Fit*

her Torquemada eye
  THEA ASTLEY *The Well Dressed Explorer*

his eyes like apples just bitten into and discoloured
  COLUM MCCANN *Songdogs*

her grey eyes fixed on emptiness, like an animal pausing on a
forest track to drop its mark
  JOHN BANVILLE *Athena*

her blue eyes were as clear as a high note on a violin
  JANET FITCH *White Oleander*

his eyes on me like whips, like cold pans of water first thing in the
morning
  T CORAGHESSAN BOYLE *The Inner Circle*

There was something animated in his eyes, like pond life
  LORRIE MOORE *Community Life*

his eyes were blue and scornful as mints
  LORRIE MOORE *Agnes of Iowa*

her uncapturable minnow eyes
  HAROLD BRODKEY *The Abundant Dreamer*

her … enormous seaside-gray eyes
  HAROLD BRODKEY *Bookkeeping*

His eyes were lockets of distraction
  LORRIE MOORE *Vissi D'Arte*

Her eyes were bright as icepicks
REYNOLDS PRICE *Kate Vaiden*

his eyes, light gray – so light the whole eyeball seemed one color,
like ancient white statues (we had some in the library)
REYNOLDS PRICE *Kate Vaiden*

[He had] the eyes of some sky god hacked out of granite five
thousand years back but fulminant still
REYNOLDS PRICE *The Promise of Rest*

his eyes were as dim and marginal as the lights of a car left on all
night and well into the next day
MARTIN AMIS *The Information*

eyes like steel ingots trembling on the smelter rim
STEVE AYLETT *Atom*

[His] eyes were flat with malevolence. It was like being watched by
something you just put in the garbage
STEVE AYLETT *Atom*

the dullness of the child's eyes deepened and deepened, like a
voluptuous ember
CYNTHIA OZICK *The Doctor's Wife*

bomb-shelter eyes
CHARLES BAXTER *The Feast of Love*

He had stare-at-the-jury eyes
CHARLES BAXTER *The Feast of Love*

her … eyes burst open – whoosh! like blue umbrellas
ANGELA CARTER *Nights at the Circus*

Her eyes … were the gray-blue of a choppy ocean shot in 1950s
film stock
CINTRA WILSON *Colors Insulting to Nature*

His eyes dark like the color the Atlantic takes, when there's no land
in sight
ALEXANDER CHEE *Edinburgh*

[her] blue eyes like the sky reflected in a sword
ALEXANDER CHEE *Edinburgh*

clear blue eyes that were as sunlit pools by a fiord
  MAVIS CHEEK *Mrs Fytton's Country Life*

The eyes accused him, like index fingers at an identification parade
  PETER CONRAD *Underworld*

[her] eyes into which her smile had not quite reached
  MAVIS CHEEK *Janice Gentle Gets Sexy*

her eyes opaque as a winter sea
  ITA DALY *Dangerous Fictions*

[She's] got the bluest eyes I've ever seen, a kind of mist you fall into
  LUKE DAVIES *Candy*

Her eyes … were blue but devoid of brightness, like drowned lights
  STEVIE DAVIES *The Element of Water*

She has nice eyes. They're green, a living green the color of a stained-glass pasture on the sundown side of church
  CLINT MCCOWN *The Weatherman*

their eyes are swift shots of light in their dust-gray faces
  TINA DE ROSA *Paper Fish*

his eyes blazing like a forest fire, like a burning tenement
  BILL DRUMMOND & MARK MANNING *Bad Wisdom*

His eyes were the color of the sky in the morning when it was foggy out
  KELLY DWYER *Self-Portrait with Ghosts*

her green eyes light up like splashed beach glass
  HELENA ECHLIN *Gone*

their mother's eyes … reverting to their still gray, faraway dullness, like stones beyond reach of the polishing sea
  CAI EMMONS *His Mother's Son*

His eyes were windows through which I glimpsed an awful country
  LEIF ENGER *Peace Like a River*

the whites of his eyes showed tiny, livid capillaries, long since detonated
  GLEN DUNCAN *Love Remains*

angry iron-ore eyes
  THOMAS GLYNN *Watching the Body Burn*

eyes bright and darting like small birds looking to alight
  MARION HALLIGAN *The Point*

[his] eyes, warm and dark and sexy as the inside of a London cab
in wartime
  ANGELA CARTER *Wise Children*

His eyes were so sunken into his head it was like looking into a
cave for the distant silty shine of a pool or patch of water in its
depths
  MARION HALLIGAN *Wishbone*

[His] eyes are deep and brown and serious, like two very carefully
blown-out holes in his head
  COLUM MCCANN *This Side of Brightness*

[her] unvariegated brown eyes, the pale color of instant bouillon
that had been lengthened for more than one serving
  MARIA FLOOK *Lux*

his eyes gave you the sense of a bright blue flame atop a pale wax
candle
  LAURA KALPAKIAN *Caveat*

face

... face ... like ... a peasant on bended knee waiting for the bayonet
  JONATHAN STREET *Rebarbative*

... face fallen in like a demolished building
  BJ CHUTE *The Story of a Small Life*

... face had slipped back to the bones
  CAROLYN SLAUGHTER *Columba*

... face like the planet Saturn girdled with huge rings of concentric
fat
  EDWARD STEWART *Rock Rude*

... face like a good-natured bun
  ANNE MULCOCK *Landscape with Figures*

faces pass like derelict paper bags
  ELIZABETH SMART *The Assumption of the Rogues*

... face like a tragic magnolia
  WILLIAM FAULKNER *Absalom, Absalom!*

... eroded sandcastle of his face
  ANGELA CARTER *Several Perceptions*

... face, slippery with indecision
  PETER VANSITTART *Landlord*

... face was like the leather of thin gloves tight on the hands of a
tall and silent woman in a good store
  FREDERICK BUSCH *I Wanted a Year Without Fall*

... face like a Landseer lion
JOYCE CARY *The Horse's Mouth*

... face ... hangs curling like a postage stamp in a glass of water
JEREMY LELAND *Lirri*

... face was a doomed waffle
CHARLES DYER *Staircase*

... face like ... an effigy in a cold church
JOHN GOODING *People of Providence Street*

... unshaven wastepaper basket of a face
KEN KESEY *Sometimes a Great Notion*

a man with a clean-shaven, intelligent face, like he thinks he's
going to be entertained by a string quartet
KEN KESEY *Sometimes a Great Notion*

... face was pock-marked like a wall against which men had stood to
take the bullets of a firing squad
PENELOPE GILLIATT *The Cutting Edge*

his arc-lamp face
BRIGID BROPHY *In Transit*

her long cupboard of a face
PATRICK WHITE *The Vivisector*

a pink face, red on all the highlights, like a Degas peach
WILLIAM EASTLAKE *The Bamboo Bed*

His face looked as if it had a shout closed up in it
FLANNERY O'CONNOR *Wise Blood*

... face like an empty playground waiting for children
LAWRENCE DURRELL *Livia*

a face like a ripped-up flower
VALERIE KERSHAW *The Snow Man*

a meatpie face without the crust
ANN QUIN *Three*

her face at halfmast
CHARLES HALDEMAN *The Sun's Attendant*

her face reminded him of a grotesque, shiny, astringent orchid in a bale of straw
    CLIVE MURPHY *Summer Overtures*

... face beamed like a gold-toothed pudding
    GEOFF PIKE *Henry Golightly*

... face was as tight and mean as broccoli
    TONI MORRISON *Tar Baby*

His face was creased like old mine tailings gullied by rain
    PAUL HOGAN *The Thin Mountain Air*

her face, a cross between a Pieta and rare steak
    HUGO CHARTERIS *Marching with April*

a face like an ill-briefed astronaut who has just landed, quite out of schedule, on the wrong side of the moon
    BARBARA BENSON *The Underlings*

The face of an infant surprised by senility
    LEONARD MICHAELS *The Men's Club*

Her face was a tragic mask, that of a woman who has sent all her sons to a war and waits hourly for the death telegram
    ANGELA CARTER *The Magic Toyshop*

A face like an interested hedgehog
    DESMOND HOGAN *The Last Time*

his expensive face
    SHIRLEY HAZZARD *The Transit of Venus*

the face of a smiling valuable mink
    WOLF MANKOWITZ *Raspberry Reich*

her face was a sad afternoon landscape
    CHRISTY BROWN *A Shadow on Summer*

a George-Washington-crossing-the-Delaware face
    T CORAGHESSAN BOYLE *Green Hell*

His face was scrap-metal
    PENELOPE SHUTTLE *Rainsplitter in the Zodiac Garden*

he has the face of a pig gelder
    PENELOPE SHUTTLE *Wailing Monkey Embracing a Tree*

her face a memento mori
T CORAGHESSAN BOYLE *Water Music*

a face reminiscent of a pale 'cello
PATRICK WHITE *The Aunt's Story*

the kind of face you saw in grainy photographs of whaling
captains' wives
JAMES ATLAS *The Great Pretender*

faces as thin as credit cards
MARTIN AMIS *Money*

... face looked like an aerial photograph of a dirt farm
TIM SANDLIN *Western Swing*

a softness in her face, like the folded-under paws of a cat beside a
saucer empty of milk
JESSE HILL FORD *A Strange Sky*

a long, disciplined face like a horse on parade
WALLACE STEGNER *Crossing to Safety*

... face had the pale and polished look of the nuns who pass you in
the city streets
JENNIFER JOHNSTON *The Old Jest*

Her face was in profile, one-eyed and prim, like the Jack of
Diamonds
JOHN UPDIKE *Couples*

a colouring-book face with just one feature filled in
ELIZABETH KNOX *Glamour and the Sea*

his fat face was worryingly colourless, like an internal organ left too
long on its tray
MARTIN AMIS *Heavy Water*

A tall, fierce woman, a face out of a daguerreotype
DAVID LONG *The Falling Boy*

his face like a little gun turret, with its two red panic buttons
MARTIN AMIS *Night Train*

His face ... looking like a pizza: heavy on the pepperoni
MARTIN AMIS *The Information*

her face battered with grief till it looked like a piece of luggage dragged from port to port
T Coraghessan Boyle *Riven Rock*

her wide baleful face like a picked-over field
T Coraghessan Boyle *Riven Rock*

Her face was like the third act of a tragedy
T Coraghessan Boyle *Riven Rock*

His face looked like a limp dream
Ken Kesey *Sailor Song*

His whole face looked like history
Michael Hornburg *Downers Grove*

He had a long thin face, like that pattern of stains on the Turin Shroud
David Ireland *The Chosen*

his long, smooth face, like a teenaged Easter Island statue
Mark O'Donnell *Getting Over Homer*

her slightly heavy face, like a Pre-Raphaelite muse who'd eaten too many slices of jam toast
Gabriel Everett *A Story of Scorpions*

his lunch-meat face
Mark O'Donnell *Let Nothing You Dismay*

His lived-in face has such deep ruts and ridges that she imagines the glory a blind woman might have climbing it with her fingers
Bart Schneider *Blue Bossa*

his face went solemn as any costly horse
Reynolds Price *Roxanna Slade*

a face that didn't seem designed to hold an expression long
Calvin Trillin *Tepper Isn't Going Out*

Her face is silting up, like a pond; layers are accumulating
Margaret Atwood *The Robber Bride*

faces like piles of scrap metal and string
Margaret Atwood *The Robber Bride*

his face blank as the earl of hell
PAULETTE JILES *Enemy Women*

His face was creased like a haemorrhoid cushion left too long in the bath
IAIN SINCLAIR *Landor's Tower*

a bottom-line face
MARGARET ATWOOD *Hairball*

a big shining planetoid of a face
T CORAGHESSAN BOYLE *Killing Babies*

his face looked long and hard as a milestone
SHANE CONNAUGHTON *A Border Station*

My face a sculpture by Oldenburg, monumental, impenetrable
T CORAGHESSAN BOYLE *A Friend of the Earth*

the sweet full-moon of her face
T CORAGHESSAN BOYLE *A Friend of the Earth*

a face like a sweating cheese
MICHAEL ARDITTI *Pagan's Father*

Her face was full but pale, like a plate of oysters covered with gauze
JACQUELINE ROSE *Albertine*

faces like the dulled blades of knives
JEAN THOMPSON *All Shall Love Me and Despair*

the face of someone urinating in the country club pool
SUZANNE FINNAMORE *Otherwise Engaged*

her face assuming that spurious but rigid tolerance of a cabinet minister confronted by genuine grievance
THEA ASTLEY *Coda*

a face like dirty dough
CHRISTOPHER BRAM *The Notorious Dr August*

The man's face was sour, the gift of early handsomeness pressed from it like grappa from the dregs
T CORAGHESSAN BOYLE *Respect*

his face a quivering chiaroscuro on which was painted misery
enough for a hundred lifetimes
  ROLAND MERULLO *In Revere, In Those Days*

a battered and misshapen face, prototype for some Rushmore of
the bankrupt and broken hearted
  ROLAND MERULLO *In Revere, In Those Days*

a delicate oval art-deco face
  RUSSELL HOBAN *Angelica's Grotto*

hers was a sweet face ... a Forties face, the loyal sweetheart in black-
and-white war films, working as a riveter in an aircraft factory while
her fiancé fought overseas
  RUSSELL HOBAN *Angelica's Grotto*

His big scraped face ... a worn old landscape lost to any habitation
  CYNTHIA OZICK *The Messiah of Stockholm*

His face that he pulled around and pushed at, him behind it
somewhere, a skeleton with a smell, an earthy breath of bad
thoughts
  KEITH RIDGWAY *Never Love a Gambler*

His face hung before me like an etching or a print, a surface to
study, not touch
  ALYSON HAGY *Ballad and Sadness*

that mother's face looming like a moon, a moon seen close, cold
and ravaged
  MARGARET ATWOOD *Life Before Man*

the pale ball of his face hanging there in the night like a broken
streetlight
  T CORAGHESSAN BOYLE *Drop City*

his face like a censorious turnip
  HELEN SIMPSON *Four Bare Legs in a Bed*

a pale expressionless face like a reflection in a china plate
  J ROBERT LENNON *On the Night Plain*

The rotten handwriting of time scribbled up and down her face
  JEFFERY RENARD ALLEN *Rails under My Back*

[He] has a scrambling face that always looks like it's just about to deny an accusation
NICK FOWLER *A Thing (or Two) about Curtis and Camilla*

his thin face chiselled and clean like a chip of marble
NICOLA BARKER *Wide Open*

his face is like a cursor, a dead blink
STEVE ALMOND *Geek Player, Love Slayer*

She has the face of a Modigliani, exotically crooked, long and pale, cow-eyed
STEVE ALMOND *The Pass*

Her face looked like a rusty shovel
STEVE ALMOND *Pornography*

His face wrinkled like a leather glove cast in deep thought
IRA SHER *Gentlemen of Space*

His cavernous face like one of Caravaggio's soldiers or saints
JAMES BRADLEY *The Deep Field*

His father's face is a stupid, silly county-fair balloon
GREG BOTTOMS *Levi's Tongue*

[He] thought of her face as a flat, lipsticked radar screen
HAROLD BRODKEY *Bookkeeping*

a face like the Bible
HAROLD BRODKEY *The Abundant Dreamer*

His face ... was ... oddly leonine: something top-of-the-food-chain in the contented wreath of the mouth
MARTIN AMIS *Yellow Dog*

Her face is a somewhat contemptuous wound
HAROLD BRODKEY *The Bullies*

faces like hoofprints of stagnant water
IAIN SINCLAIR *Radon Daughters*

His face a chalk moon among posters, wimpish clouds and a city of rain
IAIN SINCLAIR *Radon Daughters*

His face looked as absent as a drifting cloud
  MARGARET SKINNER *Molly Flanagan and the Holy Ghost*

Her face had gone as sharp as a bramble in the fork of a tree
  DARIN STRAUSS *The Real McCoy*

a face like an unpaved street
  DARIN STRAUSS *The Real McCoy*

her face has an odd neutral beauty, like an idealized court portrait
of someone plain
  MARTIN AMIS *Success*

Her face like the face of a girl being mussed in the backseat of a
family Chevrolet was built all of shadows, a ruin of little slabs
  JOHN UPDIKE *Toward the End of Time*

a woman with a face like grinning wood
  ROBERT DREWE *The Drowner*

his face gave him away, was potato-peel bleak
  CANDIDA CREWE *The Last to Know*

[her] face ... dark and corrugated as an old walnut kicked out of
the leaves in the woods
  WILLIAM GAY *Provinces of Night*

Her face, drunk, was an aurora borealis of bitterness
  DESMOND HOGAN *Lebanon Lodge*

Her face looked like a Georges de la Tour face, a beautiful face
cracking into pieces
  DESMOND HOGAN *A Farewell to Prague*

He had the smooth sulky face of a Renaissance courtier
  NINA FITZPATRICK *Daimons*

a beautiful ruined face like a smeared Matisse
  JOYCE CAROL OATES *Faithless*

Her face made him think of cats sleeping among white flowers
  DANIEL BUCKMAN *Morning Dark*

her face of absolute astonishment like the inside of a mollusk
whose shell has been prized off
  JOYCE CAROL OATES *Man Crazy*

my face as determined as Napoleon's returning from Moscow
    PHILIP HENSHER *The Fit*

She had a face like a disappointed haddock
    DAVID BOWKER *The Death You Deserve*

a face like a stiffened work glove
    NANI POWER *Crawling at Night*

Her thin face, clever as an eagle's
    THEA ASTLEY *The Slow Natives*

[His] face ... formed an unwitting, paint-by-numbers version of St. Sebastian
    RICHARD POWERS *Prisoner's Dilemma*

a face like a poppyseed roll
    COLUM MCCANN *Songdogs*

a wrinkled face that was not unlike an old vegetable patch
    COLUM MCCANN *Songdogs*

She had a face that looked like it had been fashioned from some brown bank of soil
    COLUM MCCANN *Songdogs*

He wished ... his face wasn't an assembly of bruised potatoes
    TIBOR FISCHER *We Ate the Chef*

Her face was inches from mine, floating there in the dark of the car like a husked shell on a midnight sea
    T CORAGHESSAN BOYLE *The Inner Circle*

Imagine the landscape of that face: no crayon could engender it; soft wax is wrong; thin wire in trifling snips might do the trick
    WILLIAM H GASS *In the Heart of the Heart of the Country*

his face was the colour of a baked bean with the sauce washed off
    JANICE GALLOWAY *The Trick Is to Keep Breathing*

His face was plaintive and suntanned, the notes and varnish of a violin
    LORRIE MOORE *Community Life*

a face like a used bandsaw still spinning
    REYNOLDS PRICE *Kate Vaiden*

a face you'd follow through narrow straits
  REYNOLDS PRICE *The Promise of Rest*

her face … was the ground plan of pain
  REYNOLDS PRICE *The Promise of Rest*

His face opened like a pit in a nimbus cloud
  STEVE AYLETT *Atom*

a face you'd want to vote for, or see on a postage stamp
  AL KENNEDY *Paradise*

Time, like the wind in some dry land, had carried away whatever
was extra in [her] face
  TOM ENGELHARDT *The Last Days of Publishing*

boys from the Indiana steel towns with faces like ore barges rusting
in filthy rivers
  DANIEL BUCKMAN *The Names of Rivers*

her face disciplined into a steel-helmet smile
  CHARLES BAXTER *A Relative Stranger*

[He] has the face of one who will believe the beautiful promise of
the Statue of Liberty
  ANGELA CARTER *Nights at the Circus*

Her face … flushed like the glowing rocks around a campfire
  MICHAEL LOWENTHAL *The Same Embrace*

the old man's [face] was so scrawled and scribbled on, cross-
hatched and coloured-in, revised a dozen times and then written
on diagonally once the horizontal lines were full, that it could no
longer be read
  PETER CONRAD *Underworld*

our aunt's face glittered, a small, sucking, chewing planet hauled
down to sparkle before us
  MARTHA WITT *Broken As Things Are*

[His face] was as candid as the moon
  JIM CRACE *The Gift of Stones*

the breaking cloud of his face
  KATHRYN DAVIS *Labrador*

You … brought your face down, closer and closer, so that it was enormous, like the moon when it rolls across the horizon, when it has stopped being the moon and is imperious, rolling up and unrolling whole oceans
  KATHRYN DAVIS *Labrador*

The cream-at-the-top-of-the-milkpail face of someone who will never work for anything
  TONI MORRISON *Jazz*

An eroded black-bedrock wasteland of a face
  RICHARD FLANAGAN *Death of a River Guide*

each waiter's face was as blank and gormless as a new-laid egg
  DELIA FALCONER *The Service of Clouds*

Suddenly [her] face chilled with concern, her snowy pallor scaling down to permafrost
  ALAN WALL *China*

his face a terrified marshmallow
  LORRIE MOORE *To Fill*

His face was dark red as if full of old angry blood
  MARION HALLIGAN *Wishbone*

[Her] face was like a Tornado Alley weather vane – the tremble before the wild-ass spin
  BRUCE WAGNER *The Chrysanthemum Palace*

[Her] face became a flowery field overtaken by dark clouds
  BRUCE WAGNER *I'll Let You Go*

a close-to-forty face anguished with the despair of a nineteen-year-old who has just discovered all things are not possible
  LAURA KALPAKIAN *Habits*

Faces are rooms, and [she] thought of her own as clean, rich, but carelessly arrayed
  ANDREW SEAN GREER *The Path of the Minor Planets*

her fascinated smart face … gleaming like a paste tiara
  ANDREW SEAN GREER *The Path of the Minor Planets*

facts

facts punched into the ground like fence posts
IAIN SINCLAIR *Landor's Tower*

The facts would quickly slide away from him like smooth laughing
girls on ice in pompoms, away from a learning fat top-heavy boy
skater
PHILIP HENSHER *Kitchen Venom*

faint

faint as a landing moth
CRAIG CLEVENGER *The Contortionist's Handbook*

fame

your newborn fame, like a cloud of cheap racehorses around you
SUNETRA GUPTA *A Sin of Colour*

family

A family is like one of those little mortarless arch bridges they used
to build
MERLE DROWN *The Suburbs of Heaven*

the family returned ... for the funeral like separate drops of
condensing water pooling in the bowl of a cold spoon
JOE COOMER *One Vacant Chair*

fear

tiny moist raisins of fear
DK MANO *The Death and Life of Harry Goth*

fear that lay like ice-cold steel rods along her blood
JANET FRAME *The Adaptable Man*

fear, a monstrous sore planted by a rabbit exterminator
DAVID IRELAND *The Unknown Industrial Prisoner*

fear lay like a pair of crossed paws on his chest
TONI MORRISON *Song of Solomon*

fear gathered like wolves
DIANNE BENEDICT *The Stone Angel*

the deep-freeze of fear
    LINDA GRAY SEXTON *Points of Light*

fear surfaced on his skin like a sharp, hot scent
    RUPERT THOMSON *The Book of Revelation*

A gray fear began to gather behind his eyes like iron filings
    BRAD WATSON *The Heaven of Mercury*

He was folded up in a human origami of fear
    MICHAEL LOWENTHAL *Avoidance*

the cold little balloon of fear
    RICHARD BAUSCH *Violence*

Fear shadowed her like somebody lonesome
    MARGARET SKINNER *Molly Flanagan and the Holy Ghost*

a bitter paste of fear coats his tongue
    STEVEN HEIGHTON *The Shadow Boxer*

Fear gatecrashed unhelpfully
    TIBOR FISCHER *We Ate the Chef*

fear plain as billboards
    JANET FITCH *White Oleander*

A small void opened within his belly: fear
    JAY MCINERNEY *Ransom*

Fear mapped me to the bed
    DEREK BEAVEN *Newton's Niece*

features

her every feature like so many tucks and pleats in a piece of pastry
    NICOLA BARKER *Reversed Forecast*

his features rounded like those of a statue left for centuries out in
the rain
    TIM GAUTREAUX *The Clearing*

[his] features barely pinched out on the surface like the decorations
of a cookie
    WILLIAM H GASS *Omensetter's Luck*

feel

I feel like an oversize Lolita without anyone to seduce
MICHAEL HORNBURG *Downers Grove*

I feel like the second movement of the Marcello Oboe Concerto in C Minor
SHEILA BALLANTYNE *Untitled – Ink on Paper*

I felt like the man who discovered the *Marie Celeste*
SUSAN WEBSTER *Small Tales of a Town*

he felt like a well-to-do land-owner who had just bought himself a mountain
JG BALLARD *High-Rise*

I felt ... like a piece of butter melting into warm toast
MICHAEL HORNBURG *Downers Grove*

he felt like a man might feel whose mother was scrubbing floors while he was sailing in the Mediterranean
GEOFF BROWN *My Struggle*

he felt like the captain of a small tug looking, up through the mist, at the Statue of Liberty
HUGO CHARTERIS *The Lifeline*

He felt like a potato in the soil dreaming of the vodka that was to be made of it
PENELOPE GILLIATT *Known for Her Frankness*

She felt like a stray particle moving outside the laws of physics
JEAN THOMPSON *Paper Covers Rock*

She felt like a piano in a country where everyone had their hands cut off
ANGELA CARTER *Black Venus*

He felt like a comet approaching a green planet
GRAHAM BILLING *The Primal Therapy of Tom Purslane*

[He] felt like something in a ten-gallon bag behind a nuclear power plant
MARTIN AMIS *The Information*

[He] felt like a man in a paperweight snowstorm
GRAHAM JOYCE *Dreamside*

He felt like Gauguin wielding a Polaroid camera
JOHN FULLER *Tell It Me Again*

I felt like a syphilis patient who blushes with pleasure on catching a glimpse of the local viscount leaving the clinic by the side door
ANNE ROIPHE *Loving Kindness*

He felt numb, inconsequential, like a cardboard space; brown, pointless, scooped out and dull; unutterably dull
JENNIFER LASH *Blood Ties*

She felt like the dot on a domino
MICHAEL ARDITTI *Easter*

[She felt] ancient, like a volcano that never erupted
ELENA LAPPIN *Inhaling New York*

she [felt like] an escapee from a bestiary
JEAN THOMPSON *The Little Heart*

He felt like a minnow stuck on the end of a fishhook
RICK MOODY *Garden State*

He felt like a fierce old king besieged by rebellious underlings, like Laocoön in the grip of the serpents
T CORAGHESSAN BOYLE *The Road to Wellville*

altogether he feels like a mildewed mattress
MARGARET ATWOOD *Life Before Man*

He felt ... like something in parentheses, an afterthought, an aside
KEITH RIDGWAY *The Parts*

[She felt] like a letter in an envelope waiting to be read
MICHÈLE ROBERTS *The Visitation*

I feel like an arctic explorer at the moment his supply ship disappears over the horizon
GLEN HIRSHBERG *The Snowman's Children*

I felt like a theatre-goer trapped in the middle of a long second act who hears, outside, a fire engine howling past in the direction of his own house
JOHN BANVILLE *The Untouchable*

He felt moist and serene, like a crocodile
MICHAEL GRIFFITH *Bibliophilia*

I felt like a bad third of a corrupt fraction
  SIMON BREEN *Down in One*

he felt like a fly struggling in sap
  TIM GAUTREAUX *People on the Empty Road*

she feels like an energetic pencil-tip doing a detailed connect-the-dots
  SOPHIE POWELL *The Mushroom Man*

He feels like a high-powered sports coupe stalled, out of gas, on a rush-hour freeway
  STEVEN HEIGHTON *The Shadow Boxer*

He felt like a balloon let loose before being knotted
  MARY KAY ZURAVLEFF *The Frequency of Souls*

she felt like a child bridesmaid who has sneaked early into a wedding breakfast and, unobserved, taken a bite from the immaculate cake
  PHILIP HENSHER *The Fit*

[She] feels like a runner who hasn't heard the starting gun
  KATE JENNINGS *The Magazine for Pool Families*

I felt like the last Mrs Bluebeard
  JOHN BANVILLE *Athena*

I felt like an undeveloped photograph that he was printing, my image rising to the surface under his gaze
  JANET FITCH *White Oleander*

[He] felt like a Fifth Avenue store window dusted with snow on Christmas eve
  ALLISON BURNETT *Christopher*

I felt like a grapefruit tumbling from the Eiffel Tower
  TIBOR FISCHER *The Thought Gang*

I felt like an empty tiger
  JANICE GALLOWAY *The Trick Is to Keep Breathing*

[He was] feeling like a ship's captain who has come to a port where the native customs seem dangerously out of the ordinary
  DAVID LONG *Life As We Know It*

I feel as blue and hushed as the horizon
DAVID LONG *Other People's Stories*

I felt like a mammal with a hard winter at hand
DAVID LONG *Other People's Stories*

[She] feels like a paper mouse in the talons of the Almighty
JANETTE TURNER HOSPITAL *Charades*

I felt like a wind sock on a windless day
NICHOLSON BAKER *A Box of Matches*

[She] felt like a giantess, broken in half
JENNIFER STEVENSON *Trash Sex Magic*

[He felt] like a sack of something bought in a garden centre
MAVIS CHEEK *Three Men on a Plane*

She felt herself studded with false pretenses, like a clovy apple
ROSELLEN BROWN *Civil Wars*

He felt like a spy who'd bluffed his way into the palace
JEAN THOMPSON *City Boy*

he felt suddenly like a glove with the hand inside it slipping away
RUSSELL HOBAN *Kleinzeit*

I felt like a small valise that had been used for baggage-handler soccer all the way from Reykjavik to Delhi, including connecting flights
TOBY LITT *Finding Myself*

feet

her slender feet, pale and as thickly veined as two expensive slices of blue cheese
MARTHA WITT *Broken As Things Are*

figure

his figure emaciated like a sketch rubbed out and refined one too many a time
SUNETRA GUPTA *A Sin of Colour*

fingernails

fingernails like a grave digger's
T CORAGHESSAN BOYLE *East Is East*

short [finger]nails like little dabs of glue
MAURICE GEE *Loving Ways*

her short, white nails thin as ten tight crescent moons; bright as albumen
NICOLA BARKER *Behindlings*

fingers

long staccato fingers with the snap and spring of mousetraps
EDWARD STEWART *Rock Rude*

fingers like trained setters
ANTHONY BURGESS *The Worm and the Ring*

gelignite fingers
PENELOPE SHUTTLE *Wailing Monkey Embracing a Tree*

fingers ... like five pale, unsteady snakes
CONNIE MAY FOWLER *Before Women Had Wings*

moth-soft fingers
JOHN GREGORY BROWN *The Wrecked, Blessed Body of Shelton Lafleur*

His fingers were drawn together like a feeding sea anemone
JOYCE WEATHERFORD *Heart of the Beast*

Small blunt fingers, like those round-edged scissors they give to schoolchildren
JEAN THOMPSON *Antarctica*

His fingers were heating up like the staves of a fence on fire
CYNTHIA OZICK *The Messiah of Stockholm*

fingers built like commandments
OLYMPIA VERNON *Eden*

His own fingers were useless: Cumberland sausages burst in the pan
IAIN SINCLAIR *Radon Daughters*

his fingers were shaking – like hummingbird wings about to lift
COLUM McCANN *Songdogs*

Her poor fingers were stiff as chapel hat-pegs
ANGELA CARTER *Nights at the Circus*

fist

His fists clenched like a pair of grins
BRUCE ROBINSON *The Peculiar Memories of Thomas Penman*

[He] had fists as big as market-stall cauliflowers
BILL DRUMMOND & MARK MANNING *Bad Wisdom*

flesh

flesh clung to his bones like grave wax
CHRISTINA STEAD *The Man Who Loved Children*

litmus flesh
BERYL BAINBRIDGE *Harriet Said*

She shifted the hills of her spent flesh
JOHN RECHY *City of Night*

the slumbering brickwork of her flesh
WILSON HARRIS *The Waiting Room*

The flesh was time-thinned, shrunken from back-country summers
THEA ASTLEY *The Multiple Effects of Rainshadow*

His flesh is so condensed, so dense. Fine-grained, charred. She'd
seen ashtrays carved out of wood like that
MARGARET ATWOOD *The Blind Assassin*

The flesh was spread unevenly over the bones, like cold butter on
bread
JEAN THOMPSON *Who Do You Love*

fog

the dirty milk-jug of increasing fog
JANET FRAME *Scented Gardens for the Blind*

fogs ... clung like grey stoppers at every window
JULIA O'FAOLAIN *Melancholy Baby*

fog ... nuzzles at my window like some friendly blind animal
JOHN BANVILLE *Nightspawn*

fog came in wisps ... like the hair of maiden aunts
TONI MORRISON *Tar Baby*

fog sits forward like a big boy on the horizon's broad shoulders
BART SCHNEIDER *Blue Bossa*

fog like the wallpaper of a dream
T CORAGHESSAN BOYLE *A Friend of the Earth*

fog like gray hair in a comb
WILLIAM H GASS *Emma Enters a Sentence of Elizabeth Bishop's*

The fog still gliding in and out – like a suspicious moorhen
treading water with its prodigious pale toes on a busy river
NICOLA BARKER *Behindlings*

a Stephen King-caliber fog
MARIA FLOOK *Lux*

forehead

... forehead was like the smoothly plastered front of an empty
house, deserted save by the ghost of a bird-like tenant which
hopped about in the dust and preened its feathers in front of
tarnished windows
MERVYN PEAKE *Gormenghast*

her forehead a little scrubbing-board running moisture
PATRICK WHITE *The Vivisector*

a polished forehead of a smooth Brancusi elegance
PHILIP ROTH *The Dying Animal*

his tall white forehead [like] a ravenous bald eagle (Falconiformes
Accipitridae, Audubon, plate 107)
JAY MCINERNEY *Brightness Falls*

a forehead ruled like a music staff with creases
ROSELLEN BROWN *Before and After*

She had the broad sweet forehead of an untested saint
ROSELLEN BROWN *Before and After*

Her forehead's high and spotty and as delicate as a Fabergé egg
GLEN DUNCAN *Love Remains*

freckles

fair skin marked with big pale freckles, like water sprinkled on the surface of sifted flour
ELIZABETH KNOX *Paremata*

a few freckles dotted ... like tiny lost islands from summer
MATT COHEN *The Bookseller*

a brown sugar spill of freckles
JENNY HOBBS *The Sweet-Smelling Jasmine*

freckles ... spattered across his skin like a Pollock painting, like the stars at night, like Morse code
SARAH WILLIS *Some Things That Stay*

the freckles standing out on her root-white skin like bug bites
MARGARET ATWOOD *Cat's Eye*

the faint smattering of freckles suggestive of a Celt in the woodpile
JAY MCINERNEY *Brightness Falls*

freckles like asperities on the skin of a new potato
MARTIN AMIS *Straight Fiction*

all those freckles dancing in her face like the Fourth of July
MARTHA WITT *Broken As Things Are*

frost

a biting lacquer of frost
ALAN SILLITOE *The Death of William Posters*

hedgehogs of frost
JERZY PETERKIEWICZ *Green Flows the Bile*

a debacle of frost
PENELOPE SHUTTLE *Rainsplitter in the Zodiac Garden*

frost ... a colourless Lego of ice crystals
ELIZABETH KNOX *Treasure*

frost coated the pavements like mismatched skin grafts
JOEL LANE *The Blue Mask*

furniture

Heavy ornate furniture like ancient kings and queens, hostile at having their kingdom invaded
ANN QUIN *Three*

fragile furniture that seemed to be tiptoeing
JOHN UPDIKE *The Stare*

old furniture squatted like bears in the airless rooms
ANNIE GREEN *Bright River Trilogy*

fury

a purple churn of insatiable fury
LIONEL SHRIVER *We Need to Talk about Kevin*

future

the future I carried in myself like an empty amphitheatre
GLEN DUNCAN *Weathercock*

garden

The garden … looks like a set for a film about Passchendale
JANICE GALLOWAY *The Trick Is to Keep Breathing*

gargoyle

gargoyles … peering down at him, some with hollow eyes and
strawberry noses, like alcoholics down the ages
CANDIDA CREWE *The Last to Know*

gaze

a gaze like the clear fuel thrown ahead of a flamethrower's burst of
fire
ELIZABETH KNOX *Black Oxen*

that toilet-plunger gaze
JAY MCINERNEY *Brightness Falls*

his gaze when it fell on me was like a scrape
EMILY CARTER *Glory and the Angels*

the moist treasure, in its shining lashed vessels, of her gaze
JOHN UPDIKE *Toward the End of Time*

his pale blue gaze coolly Nordic, set for distances
JOYCE CAROL OATES *Son of the Morning*

glance

a glance like a lasso
CARSON MCCULLERS *The Heart Is a Lonely Hunter*

[His] glance was like the flick of a scorpion's tail
    KATE CHRISTENSEN *Jeremy Thrane*

an oblique glance like the upturned cover of a bedspread, the edge of a petticoat
    ANAÏS NIN *Children of the Albatross*

She glanced at it like the Empress Theodora
    JOHN BERGER *Photocopies*

hummingbird f-stop glances
    CRAIG CLEVENGER *The Contortionist's Handbook*

their glances had met and held ... like the probing, seeking beams of two lonely mountain freight trains which round a bend at midnight
    ALISTAIR MACLEOD *The Golden Gift of Grey*

gloom

oniony gloom
    JOHN BANVILLE *Birchwood*

gloom could be felt like grit between the teeth
    GWYN THOMAS *Good Night Julius*

the green winebottle gloom
    JEREMY LELAND *A River Decrees*

gossip

gossip clinging stickily to the current victim
    JOAN ALEXANDER *Bitter Wind*

living on gossip like people on rafts live on plankton
    JOHN POLLOCK *They Wouldn't Stop Talking*

spreading gossip from house to house like a line of smoke from a sinner's pipe
    OLYMPIA VERNON *Eden*

grass

The dull grass was like a coarse hospital blanket too hastily pulled over a corpse that refuses to shut its eyes
    IAIN SINCLAIR *Downriver*

the heavenly odour of grass new-cut. A Purcell smell, so delicate it
is, so laced, so graced with the immanence of nostalgia
TOBY LITT *Deadkidsongs*

the cool grass curled round her feet like loving tongues as she
wandered downhill
ANGELA CARTER *Heroes and Villains*

graves

graves like polished front rooms
JANET FRAME *Daughter Buffalo*

graves like flocks of sheep grazing on the hillside
CONRAD RICHTER *The Waters of Kronos*

graves ... like nameless and forsaken Iron Age monuments
PAULETTE JILES *Enemy Women*

grief

the sirocco of her grief
JOHN UPDIKE *Augustine's Concubine*

grief was a blooming flower in the mouth. It was a gardenia: white,
redolent, untouchable
KELLY DWYER *Self-Portrait with Ghosts*

My grief is a great cathedral and the hand nestling in the neck is a
small bird perched on the corbel of one of its arches
MARION HALLIGAN *The Fog Garden*

Grief grows fat and richly fleshed, and sits in her chest like a big
suety pudding
MARION HALLIGAN *The Fog Garden*

my own grief murmured and tugged at me, came like chanting just
over a hill
DAVID LONG *Eggarine*

her cadenzas of grief
PHILIP HENSHER *The Fit*

Grief is like another country. [She] traveled there for months
LESLEY GLAISTER *Sheer Blue Bliss*

She felt grief closing in at the back of her throat as though she had swallowed sand
SUSIE BOYT *Only Human*

a grief so hard I could actually hear it inside, scraping at the lining of my stomach, an audible ache, dredging with hooks as rivers are dredged when someone's been missing too long
LEIF ENGER *Peace Like a River*

grin

a welded grin
KEN KESEY *One Flew over the Cuckoo's Nest*

a grin like a cut melon
JENNIFER DAWSON *Fowler's Snare*

a deckle-edged grin
LAWRENCE DURRELL *The Black Book*

that 'oh shit' grin of a man caught in the rain without a coat or umbrella the moment he learned he was required to perform a special duty at the highest level
LLOYD JONES *Biografi*

a grin like what was left of a baked Virginia ham
KEN KESEY *Sailor Song*

grinned like a released bunch of pigeons taking off
SEAN HIGNETT *A Cut Loaf*

a grin like a headlight
CHARLES HALDEMAN *The Sun's Attendant*

grinning like a piano
AL BARKER *The Gooseboy*

grinning ... like a walnut about to split open
T CORAGHESSAN BOYLE *World's End*

grinning like a man inviting us to come and view the huge gold nugget he has just lifted from some Californian stream, changing forever the course of American history
ALLAN GURGANUS *Plays Well with Others*

a prison-burning sort of grin
HELEN ZAHAVI *Dirty Weekend*

her foxy look: an eyes-narrowed grin
JENNY HOBBS *The Sweet-Smelling Jasmine*

her big, open confessional grin
PHILIP ROTH *The Dying Animal*

He grinned so broadly it was like an incision slicing his head in two
MICHEL FABER *Under the Skin*

a grin placed on his face like bacon on a plate
WILLIAM H GASS *The Tunnel*

a huge hambone grin
MICHAEL LOWENTHAL *Avoidance*

he grinned sleepy-eyed like somebody in a movie with secrets he couldn't tell
JOYCE CAROL OATES *You Must Remember This*

he gave his sunrise-over-the-Grand-Canyon grin
REYNOLDS PRICE *The Tongues of Angels*

[His] grin is a large plastic comb of teeth
LORRIE MOORE *Anagrams*

He grins like his mouth is full of locusts
WILL CHRISTOPHER BAER *Hell's Half Acre*

He grinned like Gorgonzola
BILL DRUMMOND & MARK MANNING *Bad Wisdom*

[a] grin like a moonlit knife
GLEN DUNCAN *Weathercock*

guilt

guilt like some wounded animal, trembling in my chest
GREG HRBEK *The Hindenburg Crashes Nightly*

guilt tracks her like a security camera
MICHAEL ARDITTI *Easter*

guilt descends, billowing softly like a huge grey parachute, riderless, the harness empty
MARGARET ATWOOD *The Robber Bride*

guilt glittered on them like tinfoil
MARGARET ATWOOD *Surfacing*

His guilt bounced three inches
  THEA ASTLEY *The Slow Natives*

the yappity-yap terrier of guilt
  BEVERLY LOWRY *The Track of Real Desires*

hair

hair like a night waterfall
ALAN DIPPER *The Golden Virgin*

grey hair like snow that remains by the roadside long after the thaw
JEREMY LELAND *The Tower*

high-tensile hair
DE CHARLEWOOD *An Afternoon of Time*

hair ... stiff like a field of wire whisks
ANNE ROIPHE *Torch Song*

hair careful as a hat
PETER VANSITTART *Quintet*

corrugated plates of senatorial white hair
CJ NEWMAN *We Always Take Care of Our Own*

hair like the plumage in a deserted crow's nest
JAMES PURDY *I Am Elijah Thrush*

hair ... streamed like a Communist banner
GEORGE MOOR *Fox Gold*

black hair wild and as crossed as blackberries
DESMOND HOGAN *Embassy*

rain forest of ... hair
JAMES BALDWIN *Just Above My Head*

hair curls in charming question marks
    JENNIFER JOHNSTON *The Old Jest*

her hair was so thin it looked like ham gravy trickling over her skull
    FLANNERY O'CONNOR *Wise Blood*

His hair was that special mad yellow, like an omelette
    MARTIN AMIS *Money*

hair intricate as Velasquez's rendering of lace
    EDMUND WHITE *A Boy's Own Story*

hair ... like the insides of a Salvation Army mattress
    GEOFF PIKE *Golightly Adrift*

hair like sporadic cotton manna
    DESMOND HOGAN *A New Shirt*

his hair that unkempt American TV margarine colour
    DESMOND HOGAN *A New Shirt*

red hair like a peat fire above a potato-famine face
    CHARLES BAXTER *First Light*

hair was tied in tight plaits about her head as though to bind in any accidental kind thoughts
    CAROLYN SLAUGHTER *Columba*

the fantastic shoeshine of her hair
    MARTIN AMIS *State of England*

hair which looks like an aquatint of moonlight on surf
    VERLYN KLINKENBORG *The Last Fine Time*

her hair the color of a Fabergé egg
    RICHARD POWERS *Plowing the Dark*

black hair like a curtain of crushed flies and spiders
    EMMA TENNANT *The Ballad of Sylvia and Ted*

the menagerie of her hair
    T CORAGHESSAN BOYLE *Achates McNeil*

a Medusa-shake of dirty hair
    IAIN SINCLAIR *Landor's Tower*

hair that looked as if it had been the major reason for Brylcreem's success
  STEVE YARBROUGH *The Oxygen Man*

a tight brown bun in her hair like an onion God drew forth from her mind
  BRAD WATSON *The Heaven of Mercury*

her snarled Ophelia hair
  MARGARET ATWOOD *Bad News*

lank chip-pan hair
  IAIN SINCLAIR *Radon Daughters*

hair combed back like a rinsed paintbrush
  MICHEL FABER *Under the Skin*

His curly hair erupted out of his cap like humidity-activated popcorn
  GLEN HIRSHBERG *The Snowman's Children*

his hair like cotton in an aspirin bottle
  TIM GAUTREAUX *The Clearing*

her blonde hair like the flare on a gas-well
  JAMES BUCHAN *The Golden Plough*

flat red smalltown hair
  MARTIN AMIS *Success*

her hair a shocked sea anemone
  JANICE GALLOWAY *Foreign Parts*

hair red at the tips with white roots like a sheep on fire
  JANICE GALLOWAY *Foreign Parts*

His hair is spun sugar, candy-floss and demerara
  CHARLES FERNYHOUGH *The Auctioneer*

a small republic of hair
  CHARLES FERNYHOUGH *The Auctioneer*

A steeple of hair leaned out of his left ear
  TIBOR FISCHER *I Like Being Killed*

hair wild like a *New Yorker* cartoon of a shrink
  JONATHAN LETHEM *The Fortress of Solitude*

His hair was poking out in all directions like rude tongues
LESLEY GLAISTER *Now You See Me*

Her long straight hair like a downpour
DAVID IRELAND *A Woman of the Future*

His hair had a frailty about it, beautiful, soft, and without a future
HESTER KAPLAN *Kinship Theory*

His hair shone like monofilament line
DAVID LONG *Eggarine*

her hair … like sunspots, like pollen unclipping in the wind
ROBERT OLMSTEAD *America by Land*

a nosegay of nostril hair
IAIN SINCLAIR *Dining on Stones*

his hair that lies black in short sine waves
THYLIAS MOSS *Tale of a Sky-Blue Dress*

My hair turned white-gray in color, similar to 000-gauge steel wool
DJ LEVIEN *Swagbelly*

[his] remaining chest hairs curled, like acolytes of grey
COLUM MCCANN *Songdogs*

her hair had been Medusa'd into all sorts of strange curls that probably had names
TIBOR FISCHER *We Ate the Chef*

Her hair is straight, an arras
HAROLD BRODKEY *The Abundant Dreamer*

His frosted hair was an ice pack for an angry boil of a head
STEVE AYLETT *Atom*

The man's hair … suggests he has been quite recently burned at the stake
AL KENNEDY *Paradise*

His hair resembled damp ripe hay that had undergone reckless chemical enrichment
MARTIN AMIS *The Information*

Her hair stuck out in a demented Struwwelpeter mop
ANGELA CARTER *Shadow Dance*

His father's hair was black, signed with silver fire
PETER CAREY *Oscar and Lucinda*

His hair was a masterpiece, black and smooth as shellac, as if a
gramophone record had been moulded to his skull
JOHN BANVILLE *Mefisto*

Her hair falls down her back like a lot of wilderness resisting
agriculture
PAULETTE JILES *Sitting in the Club Car*

the clear nearly forbidding purity of her hair pulled back from
her forehead, like an impossibly even shoreline seen from a great
distance
ROSELLEN BROWN *Civil Wars*

Her hair was now as lifeless as the leaf tuft on a pulled beetroot
JIM CRACE *Arcadia*

[her] cirrus-light hair
WILL EAVES *The Oversight*

her hair spiraling in a hive of curls gave her a wild appearance,
like a sun-bleached haystack delirium on a van Gogh postcard
MARIA FLOOK *Lux*

hand

... hand, white as rice paper inscribed with a calligraphy of blue
veins
DANIEL STERN *The Suicide Academy*

her hand extended like a minor saint
FORBES BRAMBLE *Stone*

hands drifted to rest like white doves drowned on peat water
HENRY GREEN *Party Going*

hands lying before him like trained dogs
LEONORA CARRINGTON *The Stone Door*

wringing my hands like a lady in a novel
VICTORIA BRANDEN *Mrs Job*

blotting-paper hands
URSULA HOLDEN *Endless Race*

Her hands were the shape of unbroken gothic stone
    PATRICK WHITE *The Living and the Dead*

His hands like pale gloves filled with wet sand
    ROBERT NYE *The Voyage of the Destiny*

... hands looked like separate living animals facing one another
    ARTHUR MILLER *The Prophecy*

hands ... lay like little furless pets
    JOHN LEONARD *Crybaby of the Western World*

hands ... like the crabbed, spiky drawings of Edward Ardizzone
    JOHN METCALF *Private Parts; A Memoir*

she folded her hands like a large church bulletin
    JONATHAN WESLEY BELL *The Prairie Dancers*

hands dangled out like big price tags
    FRED CHAPPELL *I Am One of You Forever*

her strong roughened she-never-had-a-maid hands
    MICHAEL FELD *The Short Cut Life of Bacchus Pocock*

... hand had the dry cool scratch of clean writing-paper or pressed
flowers
    PATRICK WHITE *The Solid Mandala*

Her hands ... kept touching each other nervously as though to
make sure they were still there, like an old blind couple
    EVA FIGES *Nelly's Version*

His large white hands lay motionless in his lap, like a pair of
clumsy implements fallen from his grasp
    JOHN BANVILLE *Mefisto*

... limp hand like a slab of putty
    MERVYN PEAKE *Titus Groan*

His hands must have been left over from early Irish farmers
    AMY BLOOM *The Story*

Her hands are like wild kittens she doesn't know how to hold
    KELLY DWYER *Self-Portrait with Ghosts*

Her hands moved rapidly, like shorebirds
    RICHARD POWERS *Plowing the Dark*

Her hands dry-pointed the air in front of her
RICHARD POWERS *Plowing the Dark*

her hands fixed like delicate fan clasps upon her jutting hips
JOAN CHASE *During the Reign of the Queen of Persia*

an old man with ... bony, Cocteau-like hands
EDMUND WHITE *Palace Days*

his bony Pilgrim-father hands
MAURICE GEE *Sole Survivor*

his hands ... on the table like a couple of side plates
BRUCE ROBINSON *The Peculiar Memories of Thomas Penman*

Her hands were pallid pale, a length of moonlight doubled, one
on the other, resting
KEITH RIDGWAY *The Long Falling*

like swifts writing their souls in the air, her hands fluttered
KEVIN McILVOY *Hyssop*

hands as big as paperback mysteries
MICHAEL LOWENTHAL *Avoidance*

her hands like insufficient shields against what Life can do to a life
ALBERT GOLDBARTH *Pieces of Payne*

He had large fleshy arms and hands ... hands for hurling Bavarian
villagers out of your path
LOUIS BAYARD *Fool's Errand*

his strong, atta-boy hand
MICHAEL CAHILL *A Nixon Man*

Her hand fluttered a little like a dove that wants desperately to
perch on a forbidden tree
JANETTE TURNER HOSPITAL *The Tiger in the Tiger Pit*

his hands like crepuscular rays appearing from behind a cloud,
promising an establishment of light
THYLIAS MOSS *Tale of a Sky-Blue Dress*

Her hands were gathered humbly in her lap – an apron full of
chopped fingers
LAWRENCE DURRELL *Justine*

His hand lies over the sheet like a slim fish
  THOMAS GLYNN *Watching the Body Burn*

handsome

handsome ... like a marble figure at the far side of a lawn
  JOHN BANVILLE *The Book of Evidence*

he's almost handsome like a healthy hog would be handsome up
on his hind legs and his eyes shining
  JOYCE CAROL OATES *Man Crazy*

handwriting

small neat handwriting that looks as if it's been done by fastidious
mice
  MARGARET ATWOOD *The Robber Bride*

the lines of blue pentel handwriting accumulated like something
ductile at the end of a factory production line
  ALAN GOULD *Close Ups*

The writing was tiny, neat, and compressed, like something to be
smuggled out of prison
  RUSSELL HOBAN *Kleinzeit*

hangover

My hangover, like a drunken Glaswegian in the opposite seat at the
beginning of a long train ride, sweating and swearing and wanting
to be friends
  EDWARD DOCX *The Calligrapher*

happiness

a wash of happiness ... like an oil-slick
  ANNE MULCOCK *Landscape with Figures*

as happy as a couple of dead pigs in the sunshine
  KIT REED *Armed Camps*

a shadow of happiness, blowing like a tumbleweed across those
high cheekbones and defiant black eyes
  CONNIE MAY FOWLER *Before Women Had Wings*

memory-cluttered happiness
  JOHN WRAY *The Right Hand of Sleep*

a strange and fragile happiness, an eerie rainbow-colored bubble that hovered around her heart
  Molly Giles *Iron Shoes*

[His] happiness was vertiginous, steep-sided like a cliff
  Harold Brodkey *The Abundant Dreamer*

hate

a liquid trail of hate
  Toni Morrison *Sula*

hatred is clear, metallic, one-handed, unwavering; unlike love
  Margaret Atwood *Cat's Eye*

She hands me her hatred done up like a fruitcake soaked six months in sherry
  William H Gass *The Tunnel*

She felt hate boiling like gas through the veins, up and through the skin like branding
  Janice Galloway *Need for Restraint*

hate welling up in his eyes like dark ice
  Daniel Buckman *Morning Dark*

he

Young, handsome, wholesome, [he] was like a milkshake moving creamily through its straw
  William H Gass *The Tunnel*

he was like an old sandwich with curling edges, left on a plate at a pointless leaving party which nobody wished to attend
  Nicola Barker *Wide Open*

[He] was a self-contained vessel of sorrow that needed to be broken open
  Tim Gautreaux *The Clearing*

He was darkly open, an entire eye
  Harold Brodkey *Profane Friendship*

He was plain, brown and clean; like peat or coya bark, or fine, rich, fertilizer
  Nicola Barker *Behindlings*

[He was a] sepia felthatted old man like a curling Walker Evans photograph, brittle and fragile as memory
  WILLIAM GAY *Provinces of Night*

he was effete, oily, like the film that warmed cognac leaves on the sides of a crystal snifter
  STEVEN HEIGHTON *The Shadow Boxer*

[He] was an arabesque of remarks
  DESMOND HOGAN *The Airedale*

He was like one of those Battle of Britain pilots dug out of a Kentish hop field
  IAIN SINCLAIR *Dining on Stones*

Everything about him is long and unhealthy-looking, bloodless and pale, like some rootbound plant kept in a basement so long it's turned white as it stretches blindly across the floor in search of light
  BETH NUGENT *Live Girls*

he was as airy and light on his feet as a Chagall lover
  JOYCE CAROL OATES *The Man Whom Women Adored*

[He] is unpuncturable jelly
  WILLIAM H GASS *Mrs Mean*

He is the type to have hobbies: sad ones that he'll want to talk about
  AL KENNEDY *Paradise*

He was like a handsome house that has been let, furnished
  ANGELA CARTER *Nights at the Circus*

He was like a small, torn remnant that couldn't be used
  ELIZABETH COX *The Ragged Way People Fall out of Love*

He was, she supposed, vaguely Heathcliffian – the eyes, at least, might have pleased a Brontë
  JENNIFER GOSTIN *Peregrine's Rest*

His head thrown back, his features varnished by the light [he was] a quattrocento figure: beautiful, dominant and yet impotent
  ITA DALY *Dangerous Fictions*

[He] hunkers on his bar stool like a liquor-soaked question mark
    LISA REARDON *The Mercy Killers*

He was like a small, hot, talkative planet
    LEIF ENGER *Peace Like a River*

He is like a piano of perfect tone but with no sustaining pedal
    LAWRENCE DURRELL *Constance*

head

head like a gobbet of raw meat
    JOHN BANVILLE *Doctor Copernicus*

head like an empty American cinema, full of ghostly distorted
voices and the terrible sickly smell of stale popcorn
    JULIAN MITCHELL *A Circle of Friends*

head tilted happily back, like a sparrow egg perched on a duck egg
    SYLVIA PLATH *The Bell Jar*

[He] tipped his head slightly, like a radar dish
    JOHN UPDIKE *Bech: A Book*

his head felt like a nest of cotton-wool in which a few phrases lay
supine
    ISABEL COLEGATE *Agatha*

heads bold as sweetbreads
    DYLAN THOMAS *Adventure in the Skin Trade*

a head like that of a suckling pig lying glazed on a doyley
    PENELOPE GILLIATT *One by One*

head close-cut, like a helmet
    PETER VANSITTART *Quintet*

the bony silence of his steep head
    PETER VANSITTART *The Friends of God*

His great big head … like a yellow salt lick somebody carved his
face in
    CLYDE EDGERTON *In Memory of Junior*

[a] phrenologist's wet dream of a head
    GLEN DUNCAN *Weathercock*

headache

My headache came down like a sentence
JOAN CHASE *The Evening Wolves*

my headache lifts off like a velvet hat and leaves without me
AL KENNEDY *Paradise*

her headache was knitting needles buried to the hilt up each
nostril
CINTRA WILSON *Colors Insulting to Nature*

headlands

headlands loomed out of sleep like an extra dream or nightmare
JANET FRAME *The Edge of the Alphabet*

A torn-paper outline of advancing headland
IAIN SINCLAIR *Downriver*

headlights

huge probing headlights like monstrous feelers
WILLIAM VINCENT BURGESS *Second-Hand Persons*

headlights flowed over the white posts like a perfect liquid eraser
LEONARD COHEN *Beautiful Losers*

our headlights boring across the gorge as in a cheap film
JOHN HAWKES *Travesty*

the headlights ... made a painting of the rain
COLUM MCCANN *Everything in This Country Must*

headlights like holes poked through into a purer world
ELIZABETH KNOX *Black Oxen*

headlights ... were matches struck in haunted rooms
IAIN SINCLAIR *Radon Daughters*

The stab of his headlights was like a poke at a sleeping beehive
ALYSON HAGY *Keeneland*

The headlights stuttered over dark, wet-shingled summer cottages
DAVID LONG *Eggarine*

heart

... heart crashed in and out like an oxygen bag
ALAN SILLITOE *The Rope Trick*

Her heart fell parachuteless
JEREMY LELAND *A River Decrees*

his heart began to grip him like a little ape clutching the bars of its cage
FLANNERY O'CONNOR *Wise Blood*

the delicate tappets of a heart
LAWRENCE DURRELL *The Black Book*

the dressing-up box of the heart
ANGELA CARTER *Flesh and the Mirror*

the terrible decaying Camembert of my heart
EDMUND WHITE *A Boy's Own Story*

His heart pounded, taut strings of crimson
PAGE EDWARDS JNR *Touring*

a heart like a bear market
ANDREW SINCLAIR *Beau Bumbo*

his heart knocking in his ribs like something trying to hatch
JAYNE ANNE PHILLIPS *The Patron*

Her heart was crashing its two halves together like a boxer's fists
PAULETTE JILES *Enemy Women*

her heart like a bird fluttering the mites out of its feathers
BRAD WATSON *The Heaven of Mercury*

Her heart knocked like a gnarled fist against the hollow door of her chest
TERRY WOLVERTON *Bailey's Beads*

her heart [was] a kind of crusty anchor whose weight she'd never quite gauged
CHARLOTTE BACON *Lost Geography*

the old woman's heart beating like a gong at the top of a mighty staircase in some palace
JOHN BERGER *Lilac and Flag*

The blackness in my heart, that fetid ditch of sorrow and suspicion
ALAN WALL *The School of Night*

My heart was a sour heavy stone
DEBORAH BOEHM *The Samurai Goodbye*

his heart clumping in his ears like an increasingly weary man climbing wooden stairs
AL KENNEDY *Everything You Need*

the heart; a place where love rose, and a place where killing sat, and dwelt
PHILIP HENSHER *Kitchen Venom*

My heart did a fast crawl out and onto the hilly dirt road of aloneness and escape
LORRIE MOORE *Anagrams*

Their hearts are swept as clean as Shaker houses
HELENA ECHLIN *Gone*

heat

heat like blades working from a cracked sky
PETER VANSITTART *Landlord*

dense heat hung like an immense bell jar that threatened in tiny ticking sounds to crack
EL WALLANT *Children at the Gate*

the heat was like a hand on the face all day and night
JOSEPHINE W JOHNSON *Now in November*

the heat tightened on the city like a drumskin
PENELOPE GILLIATT *One by One*

The heat like a hypnotist
ANAÏS NIN *Collages*

The morning heat bulged and swore, trapped in the confines of the forest, a bully pinned furious to the ground
SONYA HARTNETT *Surrender*

The heat, like a remorseless unwanted guest
LAURA KALPAKIAN *A Time Change*

helpless

helpless as sunflowers leaning on a fence
TONI MORRISON *Sula*

Their helplessness is like ... soft unraveled blue cloth
JANETTE TURNER HOSPITAL *Oyster*

hill

hill ... arched like a promise against the sky
STUART JACKMAN *The Burning Men*

hills that lay like a crowd of studded, leather-covered backs
DOMINIC COOPER *Sunrise*

hills ... rearing up ... like stone horses
EMMA TENNANT *Wild Nights*

the shaven hills like penitents bowed around us
LAWRENCE DURRELL *Tunc*

hills ... like coils of paint out of a tube
ANITA DESAI *Fire on the Mountain*

the curve of the hills ... melt into quiet debate
THEA ASTLEY *A Descant for Gossips*

black foothills lay like whales in the mist
ANNE RIDER *A Light Affliction*

hills like black steam trains
MAURICE GEE *Sole Survivor*

hills and valleys that hunched out beyond her like the weird
undulations of brains or crumpled papers
AL KENNEDY *Everything You Need*

hills steep as attic steps
JOYCE CAROL OATES *Because It Is Bitter, and Because It Is My Heart*

[The hill] printed its indigo triangle to the south
THEA ASTLEY *Girl with a Monkey*

the line [of hills] was a calligraphed sentence
REYNOLDS PRICE *The Tongues of Angels*

Hills bent like pensive brows
LAWRENCE DURRELL *Constance*

history

history lunged at me with its brittle tin bayonet
WILLIAM HERRICK *Strayhorn*

history, like the tyrannical motor in the powerhouse, had started up again
MICHAEL HARDING *Priest*

history rumbled like thunder in the distance and worked up from underneath, like tree roots splitting the concrete
HARLAN GREENE *What the Dead Remember*

honest

honest as erections
WILLIAM H GASS *The Tunnel*

hope

hope like a wavering marsh-light
MERVYN PEAKE *Titus Alone*

hope like a pale sun
MERVYN PEAKE *Titus Alone*

the unmistakable electricity of hope
BRET ANTHONY JOHNSTON *Corpus Christi*

the old surge of hope was there in my veins like a secret shake, an excitement
PHILIP CALLOW *Clipped Wings*

hope quits her like a limp sail
STEVIE DAVIES *Kith and Kin*

horizon

single stretched black hair of the horizon
PATRICK WHITE *The Eye of the Storm*

The western horizon was a thin, strangling, copper wire
PATRICK WHITE *The Solid Mandala*

the empty horizon with its blue and endless forgetting
SARAH MYLES *Transplanted*

the horizon, written over with small farms like confessions on an unending scroll
EMMA TENNANT *The Ballad of Sylvia and Ted*

the night-softened horizon ... like a miles-long floor show
ELIZABETH BERG *Range of Motion*

hours

The hours ... creep like slugs in a headwind
RICHARD POWERS *Plowing the Dark*

The hours folded down about him like three sides of a card-house
RODNEY HALL *A Place among People*

hours like tall ebony women with gongs between their legs, tolling continuously so that I could not count them
ANAÏS NIN *House of Incest*

The narrowed hours of winter light were a form of patience themselves, a stoic reply to no question
JONATHAN LETHEM *The Fortress of Solitude*

house

house ... like a two-storey bird with split-shake feathers, sitting fierce in its tangled nest
KEN KESEY *Sometimes a Great Notion*

[The] house ached with boredom
JOHN BANVILLE *Birchwood*

houses were thin like books leaning out of iron book-stacks
JENNIFER DAWSON *The Cold Country*

[The] house ... stood ... with a sort of matriarchal dignity, the verandah coming round in front of it like two arms folded over a self-satisfied bosom
JON CLEARY *The Sundowners*

houses ... seemed to lean back like disapproving dowagers
JON CLEARY *The Country of Marriage*

tall rows of houses were like cliffs with fires of barbarians burning in the mouths of caves
ANGELA CARTER *Several Perceptions*

blind houses muttered hush-hush
NICK JOAQUIN *May Day Eve*

houses that ran like awkward antipodean Utrillos up and down hills
DONALD HUTLEY *The Swan*

the new house looks like a harmless grey animal that would eat out of your hand
ANNA KAVAN *A Changed Situation*

soft gray houses leaning like tired ladies
TONI MORRISON *The Bluest Eye*

the house like a chunk of the night cut away with a serrated knife and blackened in India ink
T CORAGHESSAN BOYLE *Riven Rock*

the house looming like an enormous idea
LINSEY ABRAMS *Double Vision*

the house ... shimmered in the moonlight like a jukebox alive in a meadow
ELLEN GILCHRIST *Revenge*

the bank-holiday-morning-coma-stilled row of houses
PAUL SMITH *Esther's Altar*

The house, empty, seemed an immense, vulnerable shell, a *Titanic* throttled down to delay its rendezvous with the iceberg
JOHN UPDIKE *White on White*

exquisite houses laid out like a child's beautiful overgrown toys
WILSON HARRIS *Black Marsden*

a house like something the earth coughed up
SUSAN DODD *Mamaw*

houses looked ... like a photographic negative of teeth in a lower jaw, where light pours out of a black-lipped mouth
ELIZABETH KNOX *Treasure*

houses ... looked like the remote bundled figures of parents lining
a field
ELIZABETH KNOX *Treasure*

The house was a paper puzzle, one thousand folds, secreting
letters, pressed flowers, bloodstains
ELIZABETH KNOX *Treasure*

The house ... was listening, stiffly still, its back turned
ELIZABETH KNOX *After Z-Hour*

the terrace of little houses looked at him in a way he didn't like
RUSSELL HOBAN *Angelica's Grotto*

houses along the bay look like bit players out of *Gone With the Wind*
KIT REED *@expectations*

Raspberry haemorrhages of council houses
DESMOND HOGAN *A Farewell to Prague*

newly paved subdivisions where the houses sat like single scoops of
sherbet
DAVID LONG *Other People's Stories*

[The house] looked like something out of an American genre
painting, the kind of second-rate canvas hidden in the back of
most museums near the elevators
CHARLES BAXTER *Saul and Patsy Are Pregnant*

modest wooden houses, white and grayed white, like something
laundry soap could never soak clean again
ROSELLEN BROWN *Civil Wars*

The houses seemed to be shriveling for the season as cold took
the softness off leaves and flowers and left the meagerness of the
architecture to show like poor slight loosely strung bones, chicken
or child
ROSELLEN BROWN *Civil Wars*

Stunted little houses looked down ... from the cliffs, where they
perched precariously, like cicada shells
JENNIFER GOSTIN *Peregrine's Rest*

Their house feels as fragile as a sitcom set
HELENA ECHLIN *Gone*

Along uptown streets, Victorian mansions congregate like
parishioners sitting through an eternal sermon of rain and mist
  JACK CADY *The Off Season*

hunger

a wide surgical hunger
  TONI MORRISON *Tar Baby*

the knot of hunger pulsing inside her like a child
  A MANETTE ANSAY *Vinegar Hill*

husband

a husband like a hammer in her bed
  MICHAEL ARDITTI *Easter*

her well-fed smirk of a husband
  TIM GAUTREAUX *Good for the Soul*

idea

[The] idea tossed in his head for a moment like a sad note
EL WALLANT *Children at the Gate*

drowned ideas loom like discarded vegetables
JANET FRAME *The Edge of the Alphabet*

ideas bouncing about her head like electrons
HE BATES *A Party for the Girls*

the idea going on in my mind like a light bulb in a comic strip
WALLACE STEGNER *Crossing to Safety*

a baklava of ideas
TODD MCEWEN *Fisher's Hornpipe*

ideas ... stack like planes above an airport
GRACE INGOLDBY *Bring Out Your Dead*

One idea remained like an exclamation mark in the sweet-tasting pink wax of their heads
CYNTHIA OZICK *The Messiah of Stockholm*

The idea entered his head like a fox bellying under a fence
STEVE AYLETT *Jawbreaker*

Slowly, like Turkish coffee seeping through a sugar cube, an idea began to emerge
DEBORAH BOEHM *The Undead of Uguisudani*

the idea ... had just flown into her head like a pretty-coloured bird
MATT COHEN *Nadine*

The idea ... swam through him like a saucy ghost, fingering his hopes and tendons as it went
AL KENNEDY *Far Gone*

The idea was like a telephone ringing too far away to answer in time
HESTER KAPLAN *Kinship Theory*

Ideas sprang out of his head like showy nasturtiums
NINA FITZPATRICK *Daimons*

the pandect, the last say, the round-up, the $E=mc^2$ of ideas
TIBOR FISCHER *The Thought Gang*

imagination

[the] stethoscope of her imagination
RICHARD CHOPPING *The Fly*

the dark haylofts of her heated imagination
JESSIE KESSON *Where the Apple Ripens*

[His] imagination was flopping like a wet moth on elastic
AL KENNEDY *Everything You Need*

inconspicuous

[He is as] inconspicuous as an ant lifting an eyelash
STEVE AYLETT *Atom*

injustice

Injustice steeped in her eyes like tea in two cups, darkening them
ROSELLEN BROWN *Civil Wars*

insects

beetles with shuttered backs
JANET FRAME *The Edge of the Alphabet*

[a] beetle, minute and heraldic
MERVYN PEAKE *Titus Alone*

beetles black as phones
BRUCE ROBINSON *The Peculiar Memories of Thomas Penman*

butterflies ... huddled together ... like a lump of dark earth
PJ KAVANAGH *A Happy Man*

The abrupt butterflies darted in the jungle fog as though bringing capricious telegrams announcing the birth of millions more
WILLIAM EASTLAKE *The Bamboo Bed*

the contralto drone of the cicadas – a thousand brainless voices blended, like an inhuman radio signal from space
JOHN UPDIKE *Toward the End of Time*

In the garden, a cicada winds itself up
MARION HALLIGAN *The Fog Garden*

intensity

the curious fixed intensity of the eyes of saints painted on wood
PATRICK WHITE *The Vivisector*

irritation

the irritation … grew in her like an iris rhizome, bulbous and knotted, to be divided and planted somewhere else, time and again
KATE JENNINGS *Snake*

island

Offshore the islands prowled like whales
THEA ASTLEY *Vanishing Points*

distant islands strewn like musical notes
SARAH STONICH *These Granite Islands*

A little island lay below … frozen, like a wild duck trapped in frost-glittering sedge
LAWRENCE DURRELL *Monsieur*

isolation

the isolation of a gargoyle
LAWRENCE DURRELL *The Black Book*

jaw

... jaw ... savage as an upraised club
JON CLEARY *The Sundowners*

... jaw ... hung open like the mouth of a sepulchre
MERVYN PEAKE *Gormenghast*

[He] had a pair of jaws like church pews
PAULETTE JILES *Enemy Women*

[He] stuck out his jaw like the tray of a cash register
STEVE AYLETT *Atom*

jealousy

jealousy, profound jealousy, raged as an amphetamine
BINNIE KIRSHENBAUM *A Disturbance in One Place*

jealous ... as a Beardsleyan queen
JOHN BANVILLE *The Book of Evidence*

joy

joy is as short and straight as the blade of a pocketknife
TONI MORRISON *The Bluest Eye*

joy that rises like the fume from the *boeuf en daube*
MARION HALLIGAN *The Fog Garden*

keys

> keys ... rattled accusations from his large pockets
> STEPHEN AMIDON *Splitting the Atom*

kiss

> ... kiss was like a divining-rod which twists suddenly and trembles
> in a desert where no one believed in the existence of water
> JANET FRAME *The Edge of the Alphabet*

> kisses ... tadpole-tongued in summer parks
> JANET FRAME *The Edge of the Alphabet*

> ... kiss deeply, like knife-blades
> JANET FRAME *The Adaptable Man*

> your kisses along my arms were like tracer bullets
> ANGELA CARTER *Elegy for a Freelance*

> Her kisses were loose, somehow unspecific, as if her mouth
> couldn't choose where to stay
> LEONARD COHEN *Beautiful Losers*

> raw-liver kisses
> MARTIN AMIS *Success*

> You kissed me like a man crossing out a sentence
> PENELOPE SHUTTLE *Rainsplitter in the Zodiac Garden*

> he kissed her goodbye on the lips with a sweet little smack that
> rang through the house like one of Chopin's trills
> MOLLY GILES *Iron Shoes*

You kissed like you'd slept with a barnload of farm boys
  CHARLOTTE BACON *Lost Geography*

The kiss felt ... like something you might do to take your mind off
something else
  STEPHEN MARION *Hollow Ground*

he kissed silver into the back of my neck
  AIMEE BENDER *An Invisible Sign of My Own*

Her short kiss is a burning moth on the top of my head
  HAROLD BRODKEY *The Nurse's Music*

the slightly moist feminine tact of their kisses
  HAROLD BRODKEY *The Runaway Soul*

[She] plants rhythmic, tiny, baby-syllable kisses – like stitches in
good sewing in a schoolroom
  HAROLD BRODKEY *The Bullies*

Their kisses grew more arrowy
  MARTIN AMIS *Dead Babies*

these little kisses, like grapes, did not come singly
  JILL NEVILLE *The Love Germ*

soft probing kisses like questions
  JOYCE CAROL OATES *Because It Is Bitter, and Because It Is My Heart*

this kiss was so easy like slotting a diamond stylus into the grooves
of an old LP
  RICK MOODY *The Grid*

Her kiss was huge. It sank into his body through his mouth and
shone like moonlight on shapes inside him
  JENNIFER STEVENSON *Trash Sex Magic*

She took kisses like so many coats of paint
  LAWRENCE DURRELL *Justine*

a very long kiss, her tongue at the end of it, like a P.S. at the
end of a letter containing some further, some impossibly heady
endearment
  ANTHONY GIARDINA *Recent History*

A kiss like an interval between points in mathematics, like a cigarette-end burning in the dark
LAWRENCE DURRELL *Monsieur*

knees

knees like helpless elbows
ALAN SILLITOE *The Storyteller*

Her knees pucker above the boot tops like wizened old ladies' faces
ROSELLEN BROWN *Tender Mercies*

knowledge

knowledge ... arrived like little pieces of heartburn
JANETTE TURNER HOSPITAL *The Last Magician*

[He] carries his knowledge like a heavy gift, one he can't wait to open
NANI POWER *Crawling at Night*

knuckles

his knuckles like lines of neat mountains on the curve of the steering wheel
BARBARA ESSTMAN *Night Ride Home*

his knuckles light as shoelace knots
CHRISTOPHER BRAM *The Notorious Dr August*

the archipelagic row of knuckles
HAROLD BRODKEY *The Runaway Soul*

They were thick fingers with knuckles like small tumors
JANETTE TURNER HOSPITAL *Borderline*

lake

the oceanic lake surrounded them with its depthless epidemic of water
> JEREMY LELAND *A River Decrees*

lakes ... like a giant's ink spill
> GRACE INGOLDBY *Across the Water*

the vast grey lake, spreading like an anaesthetic
> ANITA BROOKNER *Hotel du Lac*

the still trance of the lake
> STEVIE DAVIES *The Element of Water*

a narrow lake like a blade of black iron
> GLEN DUNCAN *Love Remains*

landscape

the landscape unfurls around me like an old fan that has lost all its painted silk and left only the bare, yellowed sticks of antique ivory
> ANGELA CARTER *The Passion of New Eve*

the foreign landscapes ... beautiful and wearying, as fractionally incomplete as a repeating decimal
> MICHAEL BLAKEMORE *Next Season*

landscapes that swelled grandly by like escaping oceans
> BRIAN W ALDISS *Randy's Syndrome*

the clenched landscape
> MARGARET ATWOOD *Polarities*

A landscape scribbled with the signatures of men and epochs
LAWRENCE DURRELL *Justine*

language

pale one-storey language
JONATHAN STREET *Rebarbative*

he was speaking Spanish, a hot crazed drumroll of a language
T CORAGHESSAN BOYLE *The Tortilla Curtain*

language thick as pipe smoke
MAUREEN DUFFY *Wounds*

a liquidy language, cranky, flat, sticky as strong tea
SHANE CONNAUGHTON *A Border Station*

her language ... was full of cuts and wounds and fractures and dark night
MAURICE GEE *Sole Survivor*

a language like the ploughing of fields
JANET FITCH *White Oleander*

laughter

[a] laugh ... like the sound of something chipping nicks out of glass
JOHN BANVILLE *Birchwood*

laughing like crockery
MERVYN PEAKE *Titus Alone*

laughs were waving like flags
PETER VANSITTART *Quintet*

[a] laugh like the creasing of tin foil
CYNTHIA OZICK *Trust*

[The] rattle of laughter sounded like the trolleying off of corpses after rapid identification
TOM STACEY *The Brothers M*

laughter like the throb of a heart made of jelly
TONI MORRISON *The Bluest Eye*

a laugh like a whipped egg
ROBIN CHAPMAN *The Duchess's Dray*

[a] laugh like a rifle coughing
    HUGO CHARTERIS *The Indian Summer of Gabriel Murray*

He had a powerful luxurious laugh, like a ripe fruit being peeled,
slowly: a long, tropical, smoky rind
    CAROL MUSKE-DUKES *Saving St. Germ*

one of those single-syllable, apologize-for-existing laughs
    RICHARD POWERS *Plowing the Dark*

laughing like mudflaps
    LEON ROOKE *The Birth Control King of the Upper Volta*

laughing like a coven of drains
    DAVID IRELAND *The Chosen*

High, thin spirals of laughter
    RUPERT THOMSON *The Insult*

laughter ... like the clinking of chandeliers in a white and gold
room where soldiers have flung open the doors
    ROBERT NYE *Mary Murder*

laughed like a man who had at last dismissed his fool
    WILSON HARRIS *Palace of the Peacock*

I laughed like a dad who'd just backed over his deformed little girl
with a brand-new car
    JAMES BAKER *Fuel Injected Dreams*

laughter like the throttling of birds
    T CORAGHESSAN BOYLE *Water Music*

the theatrical laughs of boys destined for popularity, vice-
presidencies and weekend houses in the country
    A MANETTE ANSAY *Midnight Champagne*

laughing like water over stones
    MELANIE RAE THON *First, Body*

their laughter was [like] the crackling of thorns under a pot
    HUGH LEONARD *A Wild People*

His laughter sizzles like fat
    MICHAEL ARDITTI *Easter*

a carillon of laughter
ANGELA CARTER *Wise Children*

a laugh as blunt as a butter knife
JENNY HOBBS *The Sweet-Smelling Jasmine*

[a] little calliope toot of a laugh
T CORAGHESSAN BOYLE *The Road to Wellville*

his laugh, thick as gravy
MARGARET ATWOOD *Life Before Man*

She laughed, a sound like a well-oiled door swinging wide, quiet but inviting
CHARLOTTE BACON *Lost Geography*

She laughed a guttural laugh, a Nazi laugh
MICHÈLE ROBERTS *Daughters of the House*

Cold laughter, like ice shaking together
EMMA TENNANT *Queen of Stones*

her laughter, even that, seemed to come from a shallow cave of bones
KEVIN MCILVOY *Hyssop*

someone was laughing, a blunt sound like two books banged together
IRA SHER *Gentlemen of Space*

the laughter on her face as light and delicate as lint on a child's clothes
OLYMPIA VERNON *Eden*

their laughter following them like tame birds
HAROLD BRODKEY *The Shooting Range*

this makes her laugh very politely in a far-off grown-up hoarse woman-who-has-a-job-and-who-chain-smokes fashion
HAROLD BRODKEY *The Runaway Soul*

her bankrupt's laugh
TALITHA STEVENSON *An Empty Room*

Laughter, like a visitor from much deeper down, rises out of the old woman's throat
JANETTE TURNER HOSPITAL *The Last Magician*

The girl's laughter was like the abrupt agitation of bells
TONI MORRISON *Love*

laughter ... sounding like someone had dropped a bag of small bells
NANI POWER *Crawling at Night*

[Her] laugh ... chilled him: a cold breeze on a moonlit lake
MARGARET ATWOOD *Oryx and Crake*

they laugh like frightened crystal
WILLIAM H GASS *Mrs Mean*

their laughter was like music boxes being opened
JANETTE TURNER HOSPITAL *Charades*

[He] laughed like a medieval tax collector after calling on the local innkeeper
DJ LEVIEN *Wormwood*

his laughter acted on her like warm water
CAI EMMONS *His Mother's Son*

his laugh an echoing clarion noise that opened up the sky and pushed back the night
LAURIE LYNN DRUMMOND *Cleaning Your Gun*

lawn

The lawn is a stand-off
MARGARET ATWOOD *Loulou, or the Domestic Life of the Language*

The lawn with its heavy trees was Corot's material, perhaps Constable's
WARD JUST *Ambition and Love*

leaves

trees held out their leaves like playing-cards
JENNIFER DAWSON *Judasland*

leaves like thin fingers of cloud
JEFFERY RENARD ALLEN *Rails under My Back*

magnolia leaves, thick like wallets
MARTHA BERGLAND *Idle Curiosity*

leaves stood motionless, gummed to the quiet sky
  PAMELA HANSFORD JOHNSON *Catherine Carter*

leaves rustling like the thin pages of a hundred well-hidden Bibles caught in the wind
  ALAN SILLITOE *Key to the Door*

The whispering of the leaves is like the handwriting of a very ancient woman
  PENELOPE SHUTTLE *Rainsplitter in the Zodiac Garden*

The noise of tambourining leaves
  HAROLD BRODKEY *The Runaway Soul*

The leaves fluttered above us, a million muted wind chimes
  LAURIE LYNN DRUMMOND *Where I Come From*

black, patent-leather leaves
  PATRICK WHITE *The Night the Prowler*

leaves hung like the wilting hands of Lazarus
  SEAN VIRGO *Vagabonds*

Outside, the leaves ... were doing a dazzling fade, the gold, paper money of pirates
  LORRIE MOORE *Anagrams*

Leaves like little bits of peel in unset marmalade
  JANICE GALLOWAY *The Trick Is to Keep Breathing*

leaves lay precisely etched on the wet pavement, flat as if they'd fallen from diaries
  LEONARD COHEN *The Favorite Game*

leaves crackled like pale brown moustaches beneath my feet
  DELIA FALCONER *The Service of Clouds*

Dry leaves blow across the courtyard like speech in a low fanatic voice
  PENELOPE SHUTTLE *Rainsplitter in the Zodiac Garden*

leg

[a] leg like a column of pale cheese
  JANET FRAME *Intensive Care*

legs stiff as crutches
WILLIAM SANSOM *The Ulcerated Milkman*

slim legs melting, leaning into music
PETER VANSITTART *Landlord*

Belsen legs
BERYL BAINBRIDGE *The Bottle Factory Outing*

portcullis legs
SUMNER LOCKE ELLIOTT *The Man Who Got Away*

long, gleaming legs like lascivious scissors
ANGELA CARTER *The Passion of New Eve*

legs ... like those of a schoolgirl late for an appointment
EMYR HUMPHREYS *Jones*

her little pencil legs scribbling this way and that
CYNTHIA OZICK *The Shawl*

legs stretched like held notes in Mozart
HAROLD BRODKEY *Hofstedt and Jean – and Others*

her legs widespread like a weird book
HAROLD BRODKEY *The Runaway Soul*

his legs weren't crossed so much as draped over each other like wet seaweed
CRAIG CLEVENGER *The Contortionist's Handbook*

letters

letters are bracelets of the dead
JANET FRAME *The Edge of the Alphabet*

letters that bloomed like firelight on loved faces
WALLACE STEGNER *Angle of Repose*

flicking the letters off her tongue like beads across an abacus
ANNE REDMON *Emily Stone*

lie

lies were like rain repeatedly overcoming the steady work of the windshield wipers
STEVE AYLETT *Dummyland*

life

life lay round a bend in the road, like a new and frightening land
JON CLEARY *The Sundowners*

life like some private cinema performance in a rich man's house
ANTHONY BURGESS *The Worm and the Ring*

life was as deforming as an ill-fitting shoe
JANET HOBHOUSE *Nellie Without Hugo*

the first fifteen years of her life were like a special magazine offer
SERENA HILSINGER *Still Life*

So much of life hangs about like this – quiet as enamel though capable of clatter
WILLIAM H GASS *The Tunnel*

the cold, bright storage space of my waking life
EMILY CARTER *The Bride*

little flicks of life mouthed by
AL KENNEDY *Everything You Need*

life ... like an overbearingly scented rubber ice pick, a chocolate pacemaker, or an open tub of chicken giblets cast out to a man besieged by tetchy sharks
AL KENNEDY *The Mouseboks Family Dictionary*

my mother's life still stretched ahead of her like a motorway sunlit after rain
CHARLES FERNYHOUGH *The Auctioneer*

his life felt like a shabby waste, as if a paper screen had been pulled back to reveal a vast landscape of pain and regret
JAY MCINERNEY *Ransom*

His life seemed to be untacking itself, lying loose about him like a blouse
LORRIE MOORE *Places to Look for Your Mind*

You live your life like a waiter in a windtunnel
STEVE AYLETT *The Crime Studio*

His life seemed to be taking place in slow motion, like the arc of a ball thrown high for an easy catch
JEAN THOMPSON *City Boy*

light

Overhead, the first watery yellow light trickled through the clouds like iodine tracing a vein
GLEN HIRSHBERG *Shipwreck Beach*

the pure light of morning played hide-and-seek with the hills and tall maples
MATT COHEN *Elizabeth and After*

the light of a northern spring morning the colour of shined-on lead falling from a mansard window
JOHN BANVILLE *Shroud*

blinding light like a dragon in plate-mail
CHRISTINA STEAD *Seven Poor Men of Sydney*

a hurtling diapason of light
ANGELA GREEN *The Colour of Water*

clean, aristocratic, leaf-filtered light
JANET FRAME *A State of Siege*

The light was strange and pure ... a mystic butter spread on the earth's bread
HAROLD BRODKEY *The Shooting Range*

It was ... the kind of light that seems to look over your shoulder, like sunlight in a church
ELIZABETH KNOX *Daylight*

Tall windows with blinds admitting flying buttresses of dusty light
STEVIE DAVIES *The Element of Water*

The light felt like two dirty thumbs in my eyes
LEIF ENGER *Peace Like a River*

The light that entered the room was thin, like a threadbare gown
ROBERT BOSWELL *Century's Son*

a dangerous, come-hither chink of light
ROSELLEN BROWN *Half a Heart*

The light ... fell upon the floor like a bored sigh
WILLIAM H GASS *Bed and Breakfast*

the caramelised light of a below decks corridor
ELIZABETH KNOX *Glamour and the Sea*

February's is an alphabetical light, pale with dark shadows like
lines and blotches on a page
HAROLD BRODKEY *Profane Friendship*

dimmed winter light that was like airy tissue paper
HAROLD BRODKEY *Profane Friendship*

The afternoon light lay like a scrap of nylon on the torn-up fields
ELIZABETH COX *The Ragged Way People Fall out of Love*

The light began to change, thinning from rich afternoon mead to
a more sophisticated predusk Chablis
NICOLA GRIFFITH *Stay*

the light dwindling like a dream of waking
JANETTE TURNER HOSPITAL *The Ivory Swing*

The light itself had dwindled to the joyless sepia of an old
photograph
SHIRLEY HAZZARD *The Bay of Noon*

the rusty nape of evening light
IAIN SINCLAIR *Radon Daughters*

It was dusk. Lights hatched out like angry zits
NICOLA BARKER *Wide Open*

lights were going on in the mansions and neat cottages, opening
up rooms like an advent calendar
SALLY EMERSON *Second Sight*

light drains out of the house to be sopped up by the swagged
drapery of darkness
MAUREEN DUFFY *Love Child*

the city lights glow like an overturned Christmas tree
WILL CHRISTOPHER BAER *Kiss Me, Judas*

city lights shimmered across the river like sequined women of the
night
DONALD HUTLEY *The Swan*

lightbulb

[a] lightbulb like a drop of bright yellow fat
JOHN BANVILLE *Birchwood*

a single lightbulb hung from the dusty cord like an executed horsethief
ROBERT ROPER *Royo County*

[A] lightbulb hung like a diseased and undefinable sex
JAMES BALDWIN *Giovanni's Room*

lightning

lightning snapped at the world like a whip
JOHN RECHY *City of Night*

lightning kept taking her photograph
JOHN UPDIKE *The Witches of Eastwick*

lightning punished the earth
JOYCE WEATHERFORD *Heart of the Beast*

arthritic feelers of lightning
MARTIN AMIS *Yellow Dog*

the summer lightning slits the sky's throat
ANDREW SEAN GREER *The Confessions of Max Tivoli*

zigzag lightnings, like a sudden showing of teeth
CYNTHIA OZICK *Heir to the Glimmering World*

Lightning shot across the sky, like serotonin through a madman's brain
BILL DRUMMOND & MARK MANNING *Bad Wisdom*

lips

lips big and bunched like the neck of a sponge bag
JENNIFER DAWSON *The Cold Country*

lips tight as the zipper on a fat man's pants
ROBERT ROPER *Royo County*

... lips flickered with words like semaphore
DAVID THOMSON *Hungry as Hunters*

lips thin as a prude's
MERVYN PEAKE *Gormenghast*

... lips floundered like two minnows in a giant aquarium
GILES GORDON *Enemies*

brutally self-indulgent lips
JAMES BALDWIN *Just Above My Head*

cold God-praying lips
GERRY JONES *The Sin Eater*

his lips stretched back from his teeth like a skier on a tight turn
JOHN UPDIKE *A Month of Sundays*

His lips were flattened like squashed motorcar tyres dyed in a
solution of children's blood
FRANCES JESSUP *The Fifth Child's Conception in the Runaway Wife*

little blue prawn lips
LAWRENCE DURRELL *Tunc*

His lips ... are a death valley in the desert of his meteor-pocked
face
PATRICK O'CONNOR *Into the Strong City*

heavy lips like numb, dangerous fruit
JOHN UPDIKE *The Coup*

the marvelous fuchsia of her lips
ELLEN GILCHRIST *1944*

her lips a mere splash from a scarlet pen
MILES GIBSON *The Sandman*

lips trembling like beds of earth about to burst with seed
COLIN CHANNER *Waiting in Vain*

the fullness of his lower lip is a ledge for the weak English sun
SUNETRA GUPTA *The Glassblower's Breath*

His thin lips felt like an empty glass placed over my mouth
JOYCE WEATHERFORD *Heart of the Beast*

Her lips were small and brilliant, like the knot-end of a balloon
IAIN SINCLAIR *Landor's Tower*

lips like sofas
  IAIN SINCLAIR *Radon Daughters*

Her lips are thin and a cruel red, like holly berries
  EMMA TENNANT *Queen of Stones*

[Her] lips draw themselves up in a Grosz
  WILLIAM H GASS *The Tunnel*

his blunt, bee-stung lips those of Gauguin's Tahitians
  ANGELA CARTER *A Souvenir of Japan*

his lips moved over my skin like a string quartet
  AIMEE BENDER *An Invisible Sign of My Own*

his lips are sweet as orange slices on a plate on a porch in the summer with weeping willow trees and larks
  AIMEE BENDER *An Invisible Sign of My Own*

beanbag-and-pistol lips
  HAROLD BRODKEY *The Runaway Soul*

his upper lip philosophically seamed
  MARTIN AMIS *The Coincidence of the Arts*

[Her] lips had the stretch-across ambition of a railroad line gone too far
  DARIN STRAUSS *The Real McCoy*

lips uncials of sweet compliance
  LAWRENCE DURRELL *Quinx*

lips downturned like a bad luck horseshoe
  CANDIDA CREWE *The Last to Know*

Her dark lips looked like a wine stain in snow
  RICK DEMARINIS *Weeds*

Her lips curved like a sad little bell
  ERIC SHADE *Kaahumanu*

She had teensy lips narrow as pine needles
  LEON ROOKE *A Good Baby*

[His] thick lips ... vibrated, like two fat, pink molluscs performing a shifty rhumba
  NICOLA BARKER *Behindlings*

lips compressed, like a maiden aunt fetching up a shilling for sweets
JOHN BANVILLE *The Book of Evidence*

Her lips have the unmistakable pursing of someone with much knowledge and little chance of making money
TIBOR FISCHER *The Collector Collector*

Her fine lips turned into long commas of disapproval
JANET FITCH *White Oleander*

her magenta lips a wolf's stained smile
JANET FITCH *White Oleander*

Her skin was pale, her lips gotcha red
TIBOR FISCHER *Bookcruncher*

His lips were smooth and thick and hung open like a change purse
LORRIE MOORE *Starving Again*

the dry chap of her lips against his, still there, like a ten-second ghost
LORRIE MOORE *Anagrams*

My [lips] twitched uncomfortably, like clumsy, mating creatures that had landed on my face
MYLÈNE DRESSLER *The Deadwood Beetle*

soft-focus lips like bruised cherries
BILL DRUMMOND & MARK MANNING *Bad Wisdom*

[her] great salmon-sushi lips
BRUCE WAGNER *I'll Let You Go*

lipstick

the terrible gash of lipstick like heart disease
ANNA KAVAN *All Saints*

[She] stabbed lipstick around her mouth in the swift weary stroke of a teacher circling her millionth misspelled *Connecticut*
NICK FOWLER *A Thing (or Two) about Curtis and Camilla*

lipsticks like the little red sex of a thousand lapdogs lusting for love
LAWRENCE DURRELL *Sebastian*

her search-and-destroy lipstick
TIBOR FISCHER *We Ate the Chef*

listen

He listened the way a Russian icon listens: absolutely
AL KENNEDY *Rockaway and the Draw*

loneliness

I feel rather lonely ... like a little boat that no longer goes out to sea
DIANA FARR *Choosing*

as lonely as a pair of gloves left on a bus
ELISABETH YOUNG-BRUEHL *Vigil*

loneliness closed in on me like an iron maiden
NIGEL GRAY *Happy Families*

a knuckle punch of loneliness
ALYSON HAGY *Keeneland*

Under my ribs, loneliness beat inside me like some new and terrible organ
GLEN HIRSHBERG *The Snowman's Children*

look

a look like an unoccupied house with one unconvincing nightlight left on
WALLACE STEGNER *Angle of Repose*

you look as if you spent the night in self-abuse
CHRISTINA STEAD *The Man Who Loved Children*

He looked like a man emerging from a fugue
LIAM HUDSON *The Nympholets*

she looked like a George Grosz idiot, one of those lopsided bitches with a rosary around her neck and yellow jaundice to boot
HENRY MILLER *Tropic of Capricorn*

an old man stood looking criminally like a Michelangelo cartoon
LAWRENCE DURRELL *Monsieur*

She looked like a blob of black-eyed fat crouched at a window
BJ CHUTE *The Story of a Small Life*

he looked like a sacramental taper next to a tallow candle
ROBERT NYE *Captain Rufus Coate*

She looked like a badly carved serving of steamed fowl
PATRICK WHITE *A Woman's Hand*

he looked like an insane genius patiently waiting to take an
examination no one could set him
JG BALLARD *Manhole 69*

He looked like a cross between Franz Kafka and an intelligent
Alsatian
BARBARA BENSON *The Underlings*

he looked like the Artful Dodger with rickets
MARTIN AMIS *Heavy Water*

He looked like a magistrate in hell sentencing people to heaven
HUGO CHARTERIS *A Share of the World*

he looked and behaved like a walking power-surge
MARTIN AMIS *The Information*

He looked like a curator who has heard a midnight noise in the
museum
HUGO CHARTERIS *The Indian Summer of Gabriel Murray*

looked like a sceptic who has persevered at a boring séance and at
last seen a ghost
HUGO CHARTERIS *The Coat*

She looked like a thing on a slide
KEN KESEY *Sailor Song*

he looked like a bird in the second week of hard weather
HUGO CHARTERIS *Marching with April*

she looked awesome and dangerous, like a cracked statue
PETER REDGROVE *The God of Glass*

He looked like one of those dying children who must have
Christmas early
FLANNERY O'CONNOR *The Enduring Chill*

She looked like a hen stupefied by a chalk line
AL BARKER *A Question of Identity*

he looked like a man with twenty seconds to devise an escape from a cul-de-sac
  ROSELLEN BROWN *Civil Wars*

[She looked] like a fundamentalist on the way to heaven
  ROBERT DOWNS *Going Gently*

[She looked] like a house whose lawn was landscaped and whose kitchen was on fire
  NORMAN MAILER *Barbary Shore*

she looked and talked like a pastry-shop cashier
  LOUIS BEGLEY *The Man Who Was Late*

[He looked] like a suit of clothes on a padded hanger or a three-storey house with a fat central chimney
  MICHAEL DORRIS *Cloud Chamber*

he looked like a large rock tilted at an impossible angle
  MATT COHEN *The Bookseller*

you look like the victim of designer drive-by
  CAROL MUSKE-DUKES *Saving St. Germ*

[He looked] like the sort of father a lonely child might invent
  ELIZABETH MCCRACKEN *Some Have Entertained Angels, Unaware*

She ... looked like a child with progeria
  MARK O'DONNELL *Let Nothing You Dismay*

he looked like the last angel Eve ever saw as she left Eden
  REYNOLDS PRICE *Roxanna Slade*

She looks like a Brontë heroine who has lost herself on a bleak upland and emerged in the wrong century
  MARY HOCKING *Indifferent Heroes*

a look as if angels were sliding down her hip
  DJUNA BARNES *Nightwood*

We looked like characters in a Depression wood-cut
  GARY DISHER *Clemency*

He looked like a Bauhaus lamp
  ANNE LEATON *Good Friends, Just*

a look on her face as if she was about to pull the switch at Sing Sing
   T CORAGHESSAN BOYLE *Caviar*

She looked like a giant caryatid just salvaged from the sea
   JACK MATTHEWS *Elma*

He looked like a refugee from one of Rembrandt's group portraits
   T CORAGHESSAN BOYLE *World's End*

She looked like a Renoir trying to be a motorcycle
   ANNE ROIPHE *Loving Kindness*

He looked like a man surrendering to the police
   JAMES HOUSTON *Love Life*

He looked like a stick insect with VD
   NIGEL WILLIAMS *Jack Be Nimble*

He looked like a full hot-water bottle
   SHANE CONNAUGHTON *A Border Station*

she looks ... like ... an electrocuted mop
   MARGARET ATWOOD *The Robber Bride*

he just looks like a mouth-disease illustration
   MARGARET ATWOOD *The Robber Bride*

he looked like he had emigrated from a Dostoevsky novel
   JOHN CROWLEY *The Translator*

[He had] the look of [a] cannibal turning a corner and bumping
into a sumo wrestler
   T CORAGHESSAN BOYLE *A Friend of the Earth*

He looked like a freshly oiled gun
   SUZANNE FINNAMORE *Otherwise Engaged*

he looks like something smooth and salt-dried washed up on a
beach
   JOANNE GREENBERG *Where the Road Goes*

[They] looked like the people of the far long ago, when, we are
told, there was great happiness and heroism in the world
   DOUGLAS DUNN *The Canoes*

He looked meditative, like a vet tending a small mammal
   DOUGLAS DUNN *Mozart's Clarinet Concerto*

He looked like the geek who couldn't say 'when' to a liposuction pump
  IAIN SINCLAIR *Radon Daughters*

he looks like someone who will turn up, later, on a stamp
  MARGARET ATWOOD *Cat's Eye*

He looked haunted, juiceless, withered like last year's apple gone dry in the cellar
  T CORAGHESSAN BOYLE *The Road to Wellville*

I look like a wraith in a windstorm
  KIT REED *@expectations*

[They looked] like warders from a Hogarthian asylum
  IAIN SINCLAIR *Downriver*

that randy, let's-lick-the-sauce-off-the-spoon-together look
  T CORAGHESSAN BOYLE *Drop City*

[He looked like] a halfwit riding shotgun on a doomed stagecoach
  ALYSON HAGY *Keeneland*

He looked like a retail punk, lost in fresh air
  ALYSON HAGY *Keeneland*

A look crossed her face like it was on the way to somewhere else
  J ROBERT LENNON *On the Night Plain*

[He] looks like he ought to rule a country or at least conduct symphonies
  ELIZABETH BERG *Range of Motion*

He looks like a cartoon image of himself after being squashed by a steamroller
  GLEN HIRSHBERG *The Snowman's Children*

He looks abandoned, hanging on to a long-lost purpose, a derelict padlock clinging to a fence
  NICK FOWLER *A Thing (or Two) about Curtis and Camilla*

[He looked] as astonished as an inevitably snipered senator
  STEVE AYLETT *The Siri Gun*

he looked like something water logged that had sunk to the bottom of a crowded aquarium
  MARTHA BERGLAND *A Farm under a Lake*

[He] looked like a tugboat with arms
JACK CADY *The Off Season*

[He] looked like the confused dreams of gently but firmly raped children
JACK CADY *The Off Season*

He [looks like] something on a slab, exsanguinated by shock, one of Weegee's pavement specimens
IAIN SINCLAIR *Radon Daughters*

He looked like something from a nature programme – a snake swallowing an egg
AL KENNEDY *Everything You Need*

he looked like a dark-age warlord in mid-campaign, taking a glazed breather before moving on to the women and the children
MARTIN AMIS *Career Move*

She looked at me as if I had picked up an ax
RICK DEMARINIS *Under the Wheat*

He looked like something you'd see in an anthropology textbook, as if forty thousand years of evolution had skipped over him
RICK DEMARINIS *Horizontal Snow*

He looks like an identikit picture of a waste of time
JANICE GALLOWAY *Foreign Parts*

He looks like a formal portrait, sepia tinted, from some other time
JANETTE TURNER HOSPITAL *Oyster*

[He looked like] something that might hang at a crossroads in winter
JIM SHEPARD *Nosferatu*

The look I got was hydrochloric
TOBY LITT *Beatniks*

he looked at her like a blind organist searching for a chord
JILL NEVILLE *The Love Germ*

She looked like some kind of impatient angel
JOSEPH O'CONNOR *The Salesman*

a closed-down look on her face, like some ancient sage scrutinising
a mystic fire
JOSEPH O'CONNOR *The Salesman*

he looked … like a tyrant with a weakness for chicken jokes
MARY KAY ZURAVLEFF *The Frequency of Souls*

She offers me the insect-in-formaldehyde look
RICHARD YAXLEY *The Rose Leopard*

He looked … like a divinity student out of a Russian novel
JOYCE CAROL OATES *Détente*

Asleep she looks like a collapsed easel, something hard and
angular lying where it shouldn't
JULIE ORRINGER *When She Is Old and I Am Famous*

The … clerk looked up sardonically … like a child who knows
exactly where in the flower bed he has buried his father's wallet
PHILIP HENSHER *The Fit*

she looked like a Modigliani gone to seed
KATE CHRISTENSEN *The Epicure's Lament*

She gave me one of her rare Mother Teresa looks
HUGH LEONARD *A Wild People*

You look like a couch in an old-age home
JANET FITCH *White Oleander*

I look like cobbles with too many centuries
TIBOR FISCHER *The Thought Gang*

[an] I-knew-I-should-have-brought-the-gun-out-tonight look
TIBOR FISCHER *The Thought Gang*

she looked like a photograph someone had taken a pair of scissors
to
TIBOR FISCHER *The Thought Gang*

She looked like a starlet on her day off
SUSIE BOYT *Only Human*

He looks like an erect cotton bud or a stroppy sperm on its tail, but
not in a bad way
TIBOR FISCHER *Voyage to the End of the Room*

he looked like a frozen face ready to melt and pour out words in an unknown tongue, fit to burn down cities
REYNOLDS PRICE *Kate Vaiden*

He looks gray like a prisoner of war, like mangled grade-school clay
LORRIE MOORE *Anagrams*

He looked like a million Mexican dollars
STEVE AYLETT *The Crime Studio*

He [looks like] one of those insects that looks dead on the outside
STEVE AYLETT *Atom*

she looked vacant, like an abandoned house, shutters wind-kicked wide open, a curtain lifting now and then, a reminder that there was once care, attention, a femininity, or even a simple practicality of keeping back some sun
JULIANNA BAGGOTT *The Madam*

[He looked like] a pretty little spotted horse spitting disappointing hay
CYNTHIA OZICK *The Suitcase*

[She looked like] one who has just learned that the Empire has gone, the new Archbishop of Canterbury is black and Winston Churchill was gay
MAVIS CHEEK *Getting Back Brahms*

His quick sideways look was a very creditable combination of damp prawn and gigolo
MAVIS CHEEK *Getting Back Brahms*

She looked like an old photograph, someone's unrestored ancestor
ROSELLEN BROWN *Civil Wars*

[He looked] like an urchin in a daguerreotype
WILL EAVES *The Oversight*

[She] looked like a small, fearless deity
GLEN DUNCAN *Love Remains*

He looked like a plant that had grown up in shadows
LAVINIA GREENLAW *Mary George of Allnorthover*

He looked like a Christmas ornament produced in a shelter workshop
  JEAN THOMPSON *City Boy*

She looks like a sad sandwich between five sets of blankets
  COLUM MCCANN *This Side of Brightness*

he looked like a survivor of Appomattox who with steady rest and diet might soon be attending the officers' ball
  BRUCE WAGNER *I'll Let You Go*

love

Their love is gentle and discreet. If it were a plant it would be a fern, light green and feathery and delicate; if a musical instrument, a flute. If a painting it would be a water lily by Monet, one of the more pastel renditions, with its liquid depths, its reflections, its different falls of light
  MARGARET ATWOOD *The Robber Bride*

their love, which was growing at once more detailed and more unified every day, like an epic poem bristling with events and characters all held together through a mysterious system of balanced echoes
  EDMUND WHITE *Palace Days*

love mounted in cloudlike waves, filling the world with its instantaneous blinding architecture
  ANNA KAVAN *Happy Name*

love ... seems to avoid him, the way a creek flows around a discarded hub-cap
  EMILY CARTER *Zemecki's Cat*

Loving him was a little like spotting an Empire bureau at a garage sale
  RENÉE MANFREDI *Above the Thunder*

your love wears thin like the lead backing of a cheap mirror corroding the glass
  JOYCE CAROL OATES *Demon*

life at home lurched and creaked; love turned into a cross-threaded bolt
  BRET ANTHONY JOHNSTON *Waterwalkers*

Their love is birdlike, full of vibration and scribbled chattering
DEREK BEAVEN *Acts of Mutiny*

the infinitesimal patient breath-held palm and finger touch of his love
ROSELLEN BROWN *Civil Wars*

the long legs of love flash like scissors through the daily silk of life
MARION HALLIGAN *Lovers' Knots*

Love is like rain. Sometimes you can bar your door against it and still find your feet wet the next morning
LAURA KALPAKIAN *Caveat*

the curves and folds, the ivory and gilding, of her love
TOBY LITT *Ghost Story*

luck

bad luck will cling to me like a dry fern for the whole of my formless career
STEVE AYLETT *The Crime Studio*

lust

His lust shows on his face like a knife-gash
STEVEN MILLHAUSER *The King in the Tree*

their little megabombs of lust
MATT COHEN *Nadine*

marriage

couples lugging the weight of their marriages between them like so many stickered steamer trunks
    A MANETTE ANSAY *Midnight Champagne*

the water-holes, the sand-patches, the lost artesian seas where his own marriage pumped a weak current
    THEA ASTLEY *The Slow Natives*

At times her marriage seemed like a saint, guillotined and still walking for miles through the city, carrying its head
    LORRIE MOORE *Like Life*

Her marriage ... is subtle, complicated, like paper that's been balled up again and again
    JULIANNA BAGGOTT *The Madam*

memory

memory has many waiting rooms
    LAWRENCE DURRELL *The Black Book*

memories stirred like the dead turning
    DAVID PIPER *Trial by Battle*

faint memories like so many moths rise up in a powder of velvety dust
    JS MITCHELL *The Pursuant*

memories fell through him like pieces of tarnished cutlery
    SUNETRA GUPTA *A Sin of Colour*

The long thin knife of memory
MATT COHEN *The Bookseller*

[Memories] returned like old mosquito bites
SUNETRA GUPTA *Memories of Rain*

the wordless spaces of mature memory
SUNETRA GUPTA *The Glassblower's Breath*

memories ... flapped like old rags of curtains, the priceless ones
with gold thread, and moths flew out, always grey, or night-
coloured, scattering their suffocating down
PATRICK WHITE *Riders in the Chariot*

memory gathering its material, beady-eyed and voracious, like a
demented photographer
JOHN BANVILLE *The Newton Letter*

in the grip of the straits of memory
WILSON HARRIS *Palace of the Peacock*

memories like small untamed threshing birds
PENELOPE SHUTTLE *Rainsplitter in the Zodiac Garden*

my worn litany of memories
JOAN CHASE *The Evening Wolves*

[memory] like the silver meander of a slug's trail
JENNIFER LASH *Blood Ties*

memory trickled through his mind like an underground stream
against a limestone bed
CHRIS OFFUTT *The Good Brother*

the memory that had been swabbed onto his mind like bacteria
onto a petri dish
NICOLE KRAUSS *Man Walks Into a Room*

the bric-à-brac memories of decades
THEA ASTLEY *Coda*

a whole rosary of strung-together memories
ROLAND MERULLO *In Revere, In Those Days*

the palest brink of memory
CYNTHIA OZICK *The Messiah of Stockholm*

memories like lighthouse beacons flickering in a heavy storm
RICK MOODY *Garden State*

the fetal curl of memory
ALYSON HAGY *Ballad and Sadness*

memory is the lasso with which we capture the past and haul it
from chaos towards us in nicely ordered sequences, like those of
baroque keyboard music
ANGELA CARTER *The Scarlet House*

precious stones set in the gold of his memory, Fabergé'd by his
memory
SEAN THOMAS *Kissing England*

Memory is a hot-lantern thing, spilling burning, sticky stuff on you
HAROLD BRODKEY *The Runaway Soul*

Know-it-all, aide-de-camp Memory
HAROLD BRODKEY *The Runaway Soul*

the memory seeks me out like a bore tapping on my shoulder
MARTIN AMIS *Success*

the *excuse me* of a sick memory
MARTIN AMIS *Success*

the dusty attic of our small-town memories
RICK MOODY *The James Dean Garage Band*

memory is its own animal. It can hibernate, spawn, and rise up
– moths in a well lit room, each thin body lifted by fierce wings
JULIANNA BAGGOTT *The Miss America Family*

I'm coming more and more to see memory as an amalgam, a
millefeuille of fact, interpretation, desire, invention
ITA DALY *Unholy Ghosts*

Individual and perfectly formed memories lifted from and settled
upon her like butterflies
GLEN DUNCAN *Love Remains*

the lantern slides of my memory
DELIA FALCONER *The Service of Clouds*

the memory feathered away
WARD JUST *Ambition and Love*

metaphor

a bad metaphor makes the world seem dim and creaky; a good one
shines a light into the gap for a brief instant
KATE CHRISTENSEN *The Epicure's Lament*

The metaphors are soon backed up nose to tail, honking their
horns, like off-road vehicles in a downtown jam
EDWARD DOCX *The Calligrapher*

mind

... mind was clenched like a fist
WALLACE STEGNER *A Shooting Star*

when the mind dies, it goes belly up, a poisoned fish, the sickly
white of the unconscious nakedly displayed
FRED CHAPPELL *It Is Time, Lord*

the dried-up peanut of a tasteful spinster's mind
PATRICK WHITE *The Vivisector*

her mind was constructed like shelves with numbered volumes
placed along them
YAËL DAYAN *Three Weeks in October*

Her mind was in automatic park
TONI MORRISON *Tar Baby*

minds like kindly air-pockets
PETER VANSITTART *A Little Madness*

His mind set to a letterpress
PK PAGE *The Sun and the Moon*

his mind like damaged fruit
T CORAGHESSAN BOYLE *Two Ships*

a mind like an Emmenthal cheese
ANDREW SINCLAIR *Beau Bumbo*

[a] mind like a butterfly touched by the frost
T CORAGHESSAN BOYLE *World's End*

I made my mind a white sheet ready for his ink
MICHAEL DORRIS *Cloud Chamber*

My mind dragged like a razor back over the days
  SIMON BREEN *Down in One*

My mind flips back and forth, a fish on the deck
  SUZANNE FINNAMORE *Otherwise Engaged*

a mind like a soap opera
  MARGARET ATWOOD *Surfacing*

Her mind is clear, scoured and ready like a bowl in which eggs are
to be beaten, like a board on which green herbs are to be bruised
and chopped
  MICHÈLE ROBERTS *The Visitation*

my shooting star mind
  ALYSON HAGY *Keeneland*

Her mind was emptying out, day by day, like the warehouse of a
business that's starting to fail
  MICHAEL PYE *The Pieces from Berlin*

let your ... mind move like a slow spoon through a second coffee
  WILLIAM H GASS *Emma Enters a Sentence of Elizabeth Bishop's*

Her mother's mind was like an agitated sea that might throw
anything up from its depths
  ROSELLEN BROWN *Half a Heart*

The gray electrical hush of the mind listening
  HAROLD BRODKEY *The Runaway Soul*

His mind soared as if he'd thrown it in the air, high where the
mists of an idea came together into a terrible cloud
  DARIN STRAUSS *The Real McCoy*

his bleary mind on the verge of station sign-off
  STEVEN HEIGHTON *The Shadow Boxer*

[His] mind was like a pond in a blizzard
  STEWART O'NAN *The Night Country*

Her mind was like a hostess-tray with lots of little bits in it and
none of it really satisfying
  JILL NEVILLE *The Love Germ*

His mind was like a Dalí landscape where delirious torsos writhed on burning sands of paranoia
NINA FITZPATRICK *Daimons*

Her mind is a stained porcelain tub on old-fashioned claw feet splashing with frothing water
JOYCE CAROL OATES *Because It Is Bitter, and Because It Is My Heart*

His mind was a maze, an overly ornate metaphor
RICHARD POWERS *Prisoner's Dilemma*

the amoeba-like quality of his mind
THEA ASTLEY *Girl with a Monkey*

Then there was a blank in his mind. It was like the asterisk authors use to separate the chapters of a book
PHILIP HENSHER *Kitchen Venom*

a mind as attentive as a small threatened creature
REYNOLDS PRICE *The Promise of Rest*

My mind is still sometimes more like a damp yard at dusk, fireflies lifting up, lit like a hundred tiny tinderbox fires
JULIANNA BAGGOTT *The Miss America Family*

[Her] mind was like a large, clean, well-lit room in which there was little furniture but that little of the most solid, bulky and hand-crafted kind
ANGELA CARTER *Shadow Dance*

her mind … tends to work like a beautiful, jumbled poem, full of unexpected leaps, without connectors or prepositions
KELLY DWYER *Self-Portrait with Ghosts*

minute

the minutes … tip-toeing past him like a troop of well-marshalled fieldmice in feather slippers
NICOLA BARKER *Behindlings*

The minutes were long highways
LORRIE MOORE *Anagrams*

miracle

a miracle is no cute thing but more like the swing of a sword
LEIF ENGER *Peace Like a River*

misery

a misery that ... is returning to him, like an amnesiac's interlude of clarity
JONATHAN BUCKLEY *Invisible*

mist

mist like skimmed milk in a pig-trough
ANNE RIDER *A Light Affliction*

a mist hanging on the peg of morning
PAUL RADLEY *My Blue-Checker Corker and Me*

mists clung like a momentary hush
DESMOND HOGAN *Afternoon*

bleak mists enveloping ... like a mother embosoming an ugly son
DM FOSTER *The Pure Land*

a dull mist crawling hand in glove over the car roofs
AL KENNEDY *Christine*

the mist above the river is chill and clammy as the interior of another's mouth
JOYCE CAROL OATES *Because It Is Bitter, and Because It Is My Heart*

Mist rose from the creek like dread in our bowels
JOYCE CAROL OATES *Broke Heart Blues*

mood

a new mood invading his face like a troop of horses with bugles, cracking flags
WILLIAM H GASS *The Tunnel*

moon

[the] moon ... frozen and smeared with slate
JACK KEROUAC *Maggie Cassidy*

the moon's strange powdering
ERNEST FROST *It's Late by My Watch*

[the] monastic thought of the moon
JANET FRAME *The Pleasures of Arithmetic*

the bleached C of the moon
    FRED CHAPPELL *The Inkling*

puss-faced moon
    ANGELA CARTER *Several Perceptions*

[the] moon running over the house fronts like a spotlight
    JOYCE CARY *The Horse's Mouth*

[the] moon like an old skull working itself out of a grave
    CYNTHIA OZICK *Trust*

A moon browsed
    DESMOND HOGAN *The Ikon Maker*

The moon's full and needs a shave
    ROBERT NYE *The Voyage of the Destiny*

the tilted broken skylight of the moon
    WILSON HARRIS *Heartland*

a moon with an escort of stars rode the turbulent sea-sky with
thrashing screws
    ANTHONY BURGESS *The Worm and the Ring*

the moon floating like an empty palace
    PETER VANSITTART *Orders of Chivalry*

the moon [with] penciled scabs upon its pale face
    SUNETRA GUPTA *Memories of Rain*

the moon had drifted ... like a boat untied
    ANN HARLEMAN *Nothing*

The full moon grinned down like a lottery winner on a world of
losers
    DAVID IRELAND *The Chosen*

the moon out hanging upside down like some garish, show-offy
bird
    LORRIE MOORE *Who Will Run the Frog Hospital?*

A thin moon haunted the corner of the sky
    RUPERT THOMSON *The Insult*

a half moon hangs like a scrap of lace
    SARAH MYLES *Transplanted*

a crescent moon hanging like an incense boat
  SHANE CONNAUGHTON *A Border Station*

the enormous moon slowly emerged from enveloping clouds,
strongly developing itself like a photograph
  MICHÈLE ROBERTS *Fluency*

a gibbous moon ... with a light as pale and cold as the ambient
light of a dream
  T CORAGHESSAN BOYLE *A Friend of the Earth*

A thin nail-clipping moon
  PETER GOLDSWORTHY *Maestro*

an egg-frail moon
  THEA ASTLEY *Coda*

a moon no larger than a lathe curl
  ALYSON HAGY *Hardware River*

the moon lacing his body with shadows that stroked his flesh like a
signature
  ALYSON HAGY *Ballad and Sadness*

the moon ... was high in the sky, a pure wafer pressed with a holy
image
  ELIZABETH KNOX *The Vintner's Luck*

a milky blind cat's eye of a moon
  WILLIAM GAY *Those Deep Elm Brown's Ferry Blues*

a disorientated moon which was as angry a purple as if the sky had
bruised its eye
  ANGELA CARTER *A Souvenir of Japan*

The moon ... peeked quickly from behind the clouds like a
commuter glancing up briefly from his newspaper
  NICOLA BARKER *Wide Open*

the moon, just a splinter shaved from a cloud
  IRA SHER *Gentlemen of Space*

The moon floated on the still surface of the lake that night, like a
dinner plate floated up from the wreck of a sunken hotel
  IRA SHER *Gentlemen of Space*

the moon came out from behind a cloud like a bright thought
   TIM GAUTREAUX *The Bug Man*

the bright albino watchface moon
   HAROLD BRODKEY *Dumbness Is Everything*

the moon blunders into [the day] from behind like some startled
old woman in a line
   JOE COOMER *A Flatland Fable*

a smoky and defiled moon (a cigarette stub fizzing in a saucer of
yellow milk)
   IAIN SINCLAIR *Radon Daughters*

This new moon, visible at night as a faintly luminous lariat slowly
moving across the paralyzed sprinkle of stars
   JOHN UPDIKE *Toward the End of Time*

a frail horn of moon was rising through the dense fur of the night
mists
   LAWRENCE DURRELL *Sebastian*

a voyeuristically attentive moon
   STEVEN HEIGHTON *The Shadow Boxer*

a cold December moon cradled up out of the apple orchard and
hung like a corpse candle over a haunted wood
   WILLIAM GAY *The Long Home*

the moon was ... like a bounty hunter's far-off torch
   TONI MORRISON *Love*

the moon still bright and mocking as a rounded, wondering eye
   JOYCE CAROL OATES *The Sepulchre*

The scar tissue moon
   STEVE AYLETT *The Crime Studio*

the electric egg of the moon in a slow ovulation across the sky, lone
as a diamond, as one bad eye roaming
   LORRIE MOORE *Anagrams*

Outside, the pussy-cat face of the moon hung in the sky as if
balanced on an invisible jet of water, like the ping-pong balls at
shooting ranges
   ANGELA CARTER *Shadow Dance*

the earth's mad companion, the moon, is shining stainless-steel beams across the bed
    CHARLES BAXTER *Saul and Patsy Are Pregnant*

I could see the moon printed on the sky, exactly like the vaccination mark on your arm
    KATHRYN DAVIS *Labrador*

the moon ... made tracks on the water like mother of pearl, picked out sheds on the reclamation and drew the harbour wall in white crayon and black ink
    MAURICE GEE *The Scornful Moon*

the tropical moon like some ghastly mango sailing in clouds
    LAWRENCE DURRELL *Monsieur*

The moon rummages down in the alleyway like somebody's forgotten aunt
    LORRIE MOORE *Go Like This*

The moon was full like a moon in old mezzotints, Japanese prints
    RUSSELL HOBAN *Kleinzeit*

the moon like a petal of honesty
    GLEN DUNCAN *Weathercock*

The moon in the blue sky is the colour of a crashed wave
    GILLIAN MEARS *Swan Dives*

moonlight

moonlight slipping along the old tramway like vaseline
    TREZZA AZZOPARDI *The Hiding Place*

The moonlight glittered off the lake like electric fish, like a school of ice
    LORRIE MOORE *Terrific Mother*

the white spreadsheet of moonlight on the floor
    NICHOLSON BAKER *A Box of Matches*

the pale moonlight streaked a fault line in the clouds
    DANIEL BUCKMAN *The Names of Rivers*

The moonlight was coagulate in the cloud seams
    DANIEL BUCKMAN *The Names of Rivers*

moonlight that polished [the city] like a great casket
LAWRENCE DURRELL *Justine*

the moonlight ... flared like a war bonnet
JOAN CHASE *The Evening Wolves*

morning

pale upper airs of morning
JOHN BANVILLE *Birchwood*

The morning smelled like school
TONY EARLY *Jim the Boy*

blue-fingered mornings getting up at six
CHRISTINA STEAD *Seven Poor Men of Sydney*

morning standing at his bed like a valet
RANDOLPH STOW *To the Islands*

morning set in a splendour of enamels
PATRICK WHITE *Voss*

a sticky morning, of yellow down, of old yellowed wormy quinces
PATRICK WHITE *The Solid Mandala*

the morning came like a yellow fog along a roll of developing film
LAWRENCE DURRELL *The Black Book*

One day, morning was open like a dish, a glazed Greek wine bowl, and as shallow
DEREK BEAVEN *Acts of Mutiny*

soft slatey grey mornings still as churches
PHILIP CALLOW *The Bliss Body*

mother

[his] mother, a fluster of hardships
JANETTE TURNER HOSPITAL *The Tiger in the Tiger Pit*

mountains

mountains stretching in the distance like a gift of simplicity
COLUM MCCANN *Hunger Strike*

greeting-card mountains, of the sunset-and-sloppy-message variety
MARGARET ATWOOD *Cat's Eye*

mountains ... shadowed the city like a row of brown shrugs
STEVE ALMOND *My Life in Heavy Metal*

the torn tin sheet of the not-very-distant mountains
HAROLD BRODKEY *The Runaway Soul*

the dim humps of the mountains, like some artistically arranged tray in a jeweller's window
ALAN GOULD *Close Ups*

low, mellifluous, rainy mountains
DESMOND HOGAN *Lebanon Lodge*

mountains triggered with autumn hues
STEVEN HEIGHTON *The Shadow Boxer*

Mountains ... the pale blue, the human blue, of Renaissance madonnas
DESMOND HOGAN *A Farewell to Prague*

moustache

[a] moustache like fine rust
PETER VANSITTART *Landlord*

[His] fierce mustache presides over the sensitive lips like a suspicious trustee
LEONARD COHEN *The Favorite Game*

[his] little moustache moving like a cork on the ocean of his lip
BERYL BAINBRIDGE *Harriet Said*

His moustache was short and scratchy, like a midwife's nailbrush
FRANCES JESSUP *The Fifth Child's Conception in the Runaway Wife*

The mustache ... that hairy, ill-tempered circumflex
VERLYN KLINKENBORG *The Last Fine Time*

a moustache ... like the bristle on bacon rind
SHANE CONNAUGHTON *A Border Station*

the small, little loo-mat of a moustache
JENNIFER LASH *Blood Ties*

his grey moustache, so spare as if enamelled into him
EDNA O'BRIEN *House of Splendid Isolation*

mouth

an executive moustache like the shirt ads, the vodka ads
MARGARET ATWOOD *Surfacing*

[his] moustache ... two decorative serifs to garnish his broad smile
ALAN WALL *The School of Night*

his mustache was like a piece of tin
TIM GAUTREAUX *The Clearing*

His moustache rode on his upper lip like something he'd bought in a store
MATT COHEN *Elizabeth and After*

his moustaches – there were clearly two of them – were folded down over his mouth like wind-ruffled ptarmigan wings
DAVID LONG *Eclipse*

He had a ragged mustache that burrowed between his mouth and nose like a pet mouse
WILL CHRISTOPHER BAER *Penny Dreadful*

mouth

... mouth scarlet as the inside of a pomegranate in a tale by Oscar Wilde
MICHAEL ARLEN *The Green Hat*

... mouth shut tight like a sprung trap
JON CLEARY *The Sundowners*

[a] mouth as brutal as Beethoven's
PHILIP ROBINSON *Masque of a Savage Mandarin*

[a] mouth like a circle of weathered rubber
WILLIAM FAULKNER *As I Lay Dying*

... mouth is a mobile liquid crack
JEREMY LELAND *Lirri*

[a] mouth like a slipped thread in a linen sack
CYNTHIA OZICK *The Suitcase*

[His] mouth was loose, as if too many words had worn down the hinge on his lower lip
ELLIOTT BAKER *Pocock and Pitt*

... mouth ... a grim dab of raspberry jam
KEN KESEY *Sometimes a Great Notion*

her mouth, a wet radius
CLARENCE MAJOR *All-Night Visitors*

[a] mouth like the pecking orifice of some unpleasant machine
JG BALLARD *The Atrocity Exhibition*

a mouth like an unawakened angel
RANDOLPH STOW *The Girl Green as Elderflower*

Her red mouth was a sabre-cut of laughter
LAWRENCE DURRELL *Monsieur*

a small fastidious mouth trained for a remark like a tiny sonata
PETER VANSITTART *Pastimes of a Red Summer*

the ribbed red cathedral of his mouth
ANGELA CARTER *The Magic Toyshop*

a hard, square mouth like a money-box
NINA BAWDEN *Familiar Passions*

an ingle-nook of a mouth
PETER VANSITTART *Orders of Chivalry*

a mouth as soft and as gentle as the angels that haunt the heads of babies
PAUL SMITH *Esther's Altar*

Her rewardless mouth
PENELOPE SHUTTLE *Wailing Monkey Embracing a Tree*

Her mouth looked like some Cuban fruit that has no name in English
JAMES PURDY *Garments the Living Wear*

her mouth was like a garment whose elastic has perished
CLARE BOYLAN *Black Baby*

her lipsticked mouth sealed like a knifeslash across her dark face
CONNIE MAY FOWLER *Before Women Had Wings*

her mouth crucified by braces
NIK COHN *Need*

His mouth ... seemed simple, upturned, and amoral as a cat's
ALLAN GURGANUS *Plays Well with Others*

He had the kind of insolent mouth fathers and ticket takers hate
SUSAN SWAN *The Wives of Bath*

His open mouth was an old sea-shell
MICHAEL ONDAATJE *Coming Through Slaughter*

The home of his wife's mouth
MICHAEL ONDAATJE *Coming Through Slaughter*

She had a mouth like a blood-red fruit, Satsuma plum
MAURICE GEE *Prowlers*

His mouth is a sea anemone in the grizzled seaweed thickets of his beard
JENNY HOBBS *The Sweet-Smelling Jasmine*

the slug of a mouth
T CORAGHESSAN BOYLE *The Road to Wellville*

Her mouth was set, clamped shut, a tiny little line of nothing beneath her nose
T CORAGHESSAN BOYLE *After the Plague*

her mouth grubbying the words like dirty hands on bread
KEITH RIDGWAY *The Parts*

Her mouth and nose looked like they had been stolen from a small boy
KEITH RIDGWAY *The Parts*

His mouth open, inside all glossy and viscid, a bit like the innards that sometimes come tightly packed inside a supermarket chicken
JAMES RYAN *Dismantling Mr Doyle*

[a] mouth ... like the slot in a needy box
WILLIAM H GASS *Cartesian Sonata*

her taut mouth like a minus sign
BERNARD COOPER *A Year of Rhymes*

Her mouth slightly open, curled like a chrysalis
IAIN SINCLAIR *Radon Daughters*

[a] mouth like a scarlet insect
  JOHN BANVILLE *Shroud*

his mouth a torn pocket
  RICK DEMARINIS *Billy Ducks among the Pharaohs*

His mouth is a little sauna, hot and wet
  CHRISTINA GARCIA *Dreaming in Cuban*

her mouth bright red like something shiny pressed into soft white
bread dough
  JOYCE CAROL OATES *Man Crazy*

her mouth all tight and straight across like a box lid
  MARGARET ATWOOD *Alias Grace*

Her mouth tightened into a flat line, like an oscilloscope shut
down
  CYNTHIA OZICK *Heir to the Glimmering World*

her mouth like a burst porthole
  DEREK BEAVEN *Acts of Mutiny*

His shiny wet mouth was too loose, slushing away at his words
  PHILIP CALLOW *Some Love*

your mouth was curved in a little smile, like the moon high above
the perfect boat of your collarbones
  KATHRYN DAVIS *Labrador*

He ... had the mouth of a Roman emperor nursing secret vices
  HELENA ECHLIN *Gone*

[Her] mouth drops, like the ramp of a ferry
  WILL EAVES *The Oversight*

move

He moved quickly, jerkily, like a vicious little winter bird
  JOSEPH O'CONNOR *The Salesman*

muscles

His muscles were like crocodile backs in muddy water
  COLIN CHANNER *Waiting in Vain*

his shoulder muscles played under the overhead light with all the

demonic action of a Swiss music box, the big kind with its works
under glass
EDMUND WHITE *Reprise*

my Sistine muscles
DEBORAH BOEHM *The Beast in the Mirror*

music

the music began to move ... like lava with a crust on top
LIONEL SHRIVER *Checker and the Derailleurs*

The music sounded rich ... like brocade or lush curtains,
something plush and prohibited, an odd religion
BRAD KESSLER *Lick Creek*

the [music was] tepid, staggering, reeling without heart, like a tune
wounded but still carrying on down the road in bedroom slippers
BARRY HANNAH *Yonder Stands Your Orphan*

nausea

All day nausea had tried to climb the rope-ladder in her chest
MARTIN AMIS *Other People*

She is swimming in swirls of nausea. Now is the moment for them to be painted by Egon Schiele
TOBY LITT *Alphabed*

neck

her neck was reminiscent of drought-resistant cattle from India
PETER CAREY *The Chance*

a long swooping Modigliani neck
SUMNER LOCKE ELLIOTT *The Man Who Got Away*

a neck thick as an H-bomb
GARY LIVINGSTONE *Exile's End*

a neck like a birthday cake
MARTIN AMIS *Money*

his neck like a flagpole planted deep in the earth
T CORAGHESSAN BOYLE *East Is East*

the riverbend of [her] neck
SUNETRA GUPTA *Memories of Rain*

his neck puffed out of the collar of his shirt like a middle-aged toad
LISA REARDON *Blameless*

The skin of his neck looked as though it had bunched and gathered there through some catastrophe in the face
RICHARD BAUSCH *Violence*

his bedpost of a neck
ROBERT FORD *The Student Conductor*

his skinny neck with bobbling Adam's apple had all the pathos of a featherless young bird
THEA ASTLEY *Girl with a Monkey*

nerves

tarantella nerves
BERYL BAINBRIDGE *Harriet Said*

A current flickered along the tracery of her nerves like St Elmo's fire round the rigging of a ship
A ALVAREZ *Hers*

the blue rim of her nerves
ANAÏS NIN *Houseboat*

the electric alphabet of nerves
WILSON HARRIS *Heartland*

the electric mains of her nerves
JEREMY REED *Blue Rock*

Under my skin the nerves are moving like tiny people trying to get out
BETH NUGENT *Cocktail Hour*

his ... nerves went rackatty-clack like a half-empty train rushing through a countryside at night
HAROLD BRODKEY *The Abundant Dreamer*

night

night lies becalmed in the doomed straits between history and the future
ERNEST FROST *It's Late by My Watch*

a cold night was driven into the city like a lost traveller wanting warmth
ALAN SILLITOE *Key to the Door*

night would come down like a lid of a child's paint-box, hiding till the clean nursery morning the solid squares of vermilion, air-blue, sand-yellow, orange, citron, scorched green, white that was chalk not milk
ANTHONY BURGESS *The Worm and the Ring*

[a] Constable night
JOYCE CARY *The Horse's Mouth*

the sleazy scraps of night
EDWARD CARL STEPHENS *A Turn in the Dark Wood*

the jewelled estuary of night
MARTIN AMIS *Dead Babies*

the house-breaking night
DYLAN THOMAS *Adventures in the Skin Trade*

The night surrounded me, a photograph unglued from its frame
ANAÏS NIN *House of Incest*

a night like the interior of a grape
PETER REDGROVE *In the Country of the Skin*

The childbearing night
PENELOPE SHUTTLE *Rainsplitter in the Zodiac Garden*

the night like a sleeper's breath
T CORAGHESSAN BOYLE *World's End*

the night itself was some kind of aperture, a passage to despair
STEFAN KANFER *The Eighth Sin*

The night was thick with blind men's dreams
RUPERT THOMSON *The Insult*

that cold, unhooked night
NEIL BLACKMORE *Split My Heart*

The night glided toward morning like a dark skater going across a white ribbon of ice toward home
BARBARA CHEPAITIS *Feeding Christine*

a night drilled by mosquitoes
THEA ASTLEY *Vanishing Points*

the caravanserai of night crosses the sky
EMMA TENNANT *Queen of Stones*

The night [was] weighed down like ... police greatcoats
SHANE CONNAUGHTON *A Border Station*

That night was warm and cloudy, as if you were standing at the
bottom of an unchilled glass of beer
JOEL LANE *The Blue Mask*

the night enveloped me with an unaccustomed tightness, like a
favorite shirt shrunk in the wash
MICHAEL LOWENTHAL *Avoidance*

a new, unopened, E Pluribus Unum, United States type of night
AL KENNEDY *Far Gone*

The night was warm and damp like a glass just out of the
dishwasher
ERIC SHADE *Superfly*

Night penetrated the water like an old remorse
ROBERT DREWE *The Drowner*

[night] ... a warning blue-black grimace of octopus ink
NICOLA BARKER *Behindlings*

Night fell like an unbreakable plate
STEVE AYLETT *The Crime Studio*

the nights shrink close like turtleneck collars
ALEXANDER CHEE *Edinburgh*

Outside, the night opens above us like a whale's jaw, a blue,
deepening wedge
ALEXANDER CHEE *Edinburgh*

Night like a dark gas was seeping down on the city
JOHN BANVILLE *Mefisto*

a quicksand of night
ELIZABETH KNOX *Daylight*

[The] night was a black chasuble, sewn with the stars and the
moon, with all the far universes hidden in its folds
ALICE THOMAS ELLIS *The Other Side of the Fire*

nightmare

a nightmare ... will detonate her sleep like a Molotov cocktail
TERRY WOLVERTON *Bailey's Beads*

nightmares rise and fall like gulls on the horizon; something is being unearthed
TREZZA AZZOPARDI *The Hiding Place*

nipple

the great peach thermometers of her nipples
JOE COOMER *Apologizing to Dogs*

Her nipples were tiny and a pale beige colour, like small round servings of coffee ice-cream
NICOLA BARKER *Reversed Forecast*

My nipples were cold and hard like the tips of a Crayola before anyone had ever used it
OLYMPIA VERNON *Eden*

the facelike nipples peering through her nightgown
HAROLD BRODKEY *Waking*

her nipples were spherical, like paler, smokier versions of honeysuckle berries
JOHN UPDIKE *Toward the End of Time*

His nipples were like two wet and fuzzy flowers
LESLEY GLAISTER *Now You See Me*

nose

[a] nose like a Delft pepper-pot, shiny with blackheads
JULIA O'FAOLAIN *Godded and Codded*

[a] cheeseparing nose
ANTHONY BURGESS *Clockwork Testament*

[a] brilliant nose like Petrarch's
GILBERT ROGIN *Judging Keller*

[a] nose like a piece of cuttlefish bone stuck between the wires of a budgerigar's cage
ANTHONY BURGESS *The Worm and the Ring*

a nose like a headlight
  WARD JUST *Stringer*

[a] nose like a proud, wrecked ship on a beach
  NINA BAWDEN *The Birds on the Trees*

a big red nose like a bonfire with pimples
  ALAN BLEASDALE *Scully*

His nose hangs down like Notre Dame in gloom
  LAWRENCE DURRELL *The Black Book*

a nose like a paw
  PENELOPE GILLIATT *Mortal Matters*

[a] nose like a prefabricated garage
  EMMA TENNANT *The Last of the Country House Murders*

[a] nose as narrow and brown as the backbone ridge of a roast turkey
  BRIGID BROPHY *Flesh*

a fail-safe nose
  NEIL BLACKMORE *Split My Heart*

He had an open razor of a nose
  HUGH LEONARD *A Wild People*

the beautiful little bird-bone of her nose
  CYNTHIA OZICK *The Messiah of Stockholm*

[a] nose like a skinned animal pinned to his face
  T CORAGHESSAN BOYLE *Drop City*

[his] nose like something an undertaker had sculpted out of wax then studied with a critical eye
  WILLIAM GAY *Provinces of Night*

a sharp little nose, like a bit of carrot
  HUGH LEONARD *A Wild People*

[a] large nose that sits like an abandoned mining tower over the desolation it inhabits
  RICHARD FLANAGAN *Death of a River Guide*

that long vulpine nose which lay resting against his face like the proud figurehead of an abandoned ship
LAWRENCE DURRELL *Justine*

nostrils

curling nostrils like a Byzantine Saint's
JULIA O'FAOLAIN *Godded and Codded*

nostrils like bolt-holes for imaginary animals
DAVID IRELAND *The Chosen*

long stiff nostrils that stared downward like an extra pair of eyes
CYNTHIA OZICK *An Education*

... nostrils were set in a fixed flare like a woman re-entering a room, noticing a smell that was not there when she went out
ANTHONY BURGESS *The Right to an Answer*

Her elegant nostrils, shaped by the delicate chisel of a carver of Old Testament scenes on the panels of a cathedral door
STEVEN MILLHAUSER *The King and the Tree*

[His] nostrils looked like holes dug under a stump
GRANT BUDAY *A Sack of Teeth*

notes

[Musical] notes looked ugly and hard, like goat droppings
A MANETTE ANSAY *Vinegar Hill*

The precise, separated piano notes were like arrangements of gleaming picked bones, hung up to dissolve in the air
PHILIP CALLOW *Janine*

[musical] notes like unpricked bubbles rising through the netting of the clef
ALAN WALL *China*

notion

The notion ... was as pale now as a match lit on a bright beach
HESTER KAPLAN *Kinship Theory*

nun

the nun moved steadily in her black habit like a piece of night
detached from the rest of the darkness and moving autonomously
toward its own dawn
HELEN HUDSON *Meyer Meyer*

nuns go by quiet as lust
TONI MORRISON *The Bluest Eye*

[Nuns] moved up and down the aisles of the classroom like great
black ships in sea lanes
PAUL CODY *Eyes Like Mine*

ocean

The ocean was a Walt Disney blue
DESMOND HOGAN *The Bomb*

the ocean's slow deep heartbeat
GEORGE JOHNSTON *Clean Straw for Nothing*

the ocean with its lacy edge turned back upon the beach like a
chenille bedspread ready for night
KEN KESEY *Sometimes a Great Notion*

ocean bellows to ocean across the continents like allied
commanders exchanging a salute of guns
ANNA KAVAN *Sleep Has His House*

faint breathing of the ocean ... distant but distinct, like the soft
memory of a colour preserved in dried flowers
DAVID PROFUMO *Sea Music*

The ocean shushed and tittered like an audience when the lights
dim before the main feature
ANGELA CARTER *The Merchant of Shadows*

the whole hump-backed ocean lifted the sky like a blue-green
impossibility
AL KENNEDY *So I Am Glad*

the ocean, so loaded with seafood, is more like a loud and giant
bouillabaisse
LORRIE MOORE *Anagrams*

at the foot of the cliff, [the ocean] shattered its foamy peripheries with the sound of a thousand distant cinema organs
ANGELA CARTER *The Merchant of Shadows*

oppression

I felt oppressed, like a little honeymoon bungalow stranded between a couple of skyscrapers
FRED CHAPPELL *Look Back All the Green Valley*

pain

dull-yellow spotted pain like a poisonous plant
  JANET FRAME *Intensive Care*

long thin aluminium limb pains
  JANET FRAME *Intensive Care*

pain enough to shake a house
  REYNOLDS PRICE *Good and Bad Dreams*

pain spread creeping like conceited monograms
  ROSALIND BELBEN *The Limit*

a slick spurt of pain
  JOHN UPDIKE *The Centaur*

He shakes the pain around like a steel ball in a brandy glass
  HUGH C RAE *The Saturday Epic*

a bracelet of pain
  EDMUND WHITE *Nocturnes for the King of Naples*

The little seeps of their pain fertilise the earth
  PENELOPE SHUTTLE *Rainsplitter in the Zodiac Garden*

a pain like infanticide
  PENELOPE SHUTTLE *The Mirror of the Giant*

A vast pattern of pain, like some formal dance
  JENNIFER JOHNSTON *The Christmas Tree*

round smooth beads of pain
  JANET FRAME *Intensive Care*

The pain was still there, like a jagged door that might open at any time
    PETER REDGROVE *In the Country of the Skin*

pain filled him quickly, like water gushing into a vase
    ELIZABETH JORDAN MOORE *Cold Times*

A little stadium of pain
    MARTIN AMIS *Time's Arrow*

The dull pain was deep in his leg like the ache of a mountain after the coal was removed
    CHRIS OFFUTT *The Good Brother*

a whole string section of pain playing up and down my spine in a mad pizzicato
    T CORAGHESSAN BOYLE *A Friend of the Earth*

their dark choir of pain
    SEBASTIAN BARRY *Annie Dunne*

pain passed through her ... like a cry through a rented room
    WILLIAM H GASS *Emma Enters a Sentence of Elizabeth Bishop's*

The pain ... shredded each nerve individually, picking them apart like faulty embroidery
    JEAN MCNEIL *Private View*

Now and then, pain stops by to ream through the memory root canals with a little taste of gangrene and carbolic soap
    AL KENNEDY *So I Am Glad*

a flower of pain blooming through her body, a jagged steel lotus
    JANET FITCH *White Oleander*

The pain poured up him from ankle to eyes, plain to see as a rat in milk
    REYNOLDS PRICE *The Tongues of Angels*

a *Mahabharata* of pain
    MARTIN AMIS *The Information*

[They hoped] that their pain would soon grow small and manageable, like an origami bird they could carry in their pockets
    CONNIE MAY FOWLER *The Problem with Murmur Lee*

Threads of pain, like the whiplash crackle of an approaching train, fanned out across my forehead
  WILL EAVES *The Oversight*

panic

Panic fluttered in my throat: a dull bird, a sparrow
  HILARY MANTEL *An Experiment in Love*

past

[The] past was being cut out and lugged bleeding away
  PETER VANSITTART *Lancelot*

The gross tonnage of the past
  NIK COHN *Need*

the entire weight of the overloaded past seemed to pour onto her like liquid cement that immediately set solid, incarcerating her in its stiff gloom
  ANITA DESAI *Fire on the Mountain*

Outside, the past is spread, in pools of blue, in black limbs, in felted voices
  PATRICK WHITE *The Twyborn Affair*

[The] past swirls like fingerpaint into [the] present
  ALISON DYE *An Awareness of March*

his past had surfaced, like some barnacled submarine
  RICK MOODY *Garden State*

His past was a cemetery full of dirt
  NICOLA BARKER *Wide Open*

he felt the past shambling over him like a drunken elephant, ponderous, random
  JANETTE TURNER HOSPITAL *The Tiger in the Tiger Pit*

Like cat-hairs, wisps of the past still clung to me
  HUGH LEONARD *A Wild People*

A possible past belled out behind him, a hinterland of shadow
  STEVIE DAVIES *The Element of Water*

She has a past like a paw full of thorns
  LAWRENCE DURRELL *Constance*

[a] grand piano dominating the room like a bier
  EDWARD STEWART *Rock Rude*

the tinny piano gave the hymns the same frothy, tinsel feel of
enamel candies, tasting of salt and molasses
  JOAN CHASE *The Evening Wolves*

a piano cuts the stillness with melodic scimitars
  THEA ASTLEY *Girl with a Monkey*

poem

her poems [are] like the finest diamonds in the finest Fabergés of
the finest Czar, not faltering, defeated by topaz
  LORRIE MOORE *Go Like This*

prayers

prayers like little pieces of white paper
  PATRICK WHITE *Voss*

[Her] prayers are lightweight aluminium; she imagines them
skittering, skimming, flying across the surface of a body of water,
knows they won't be heeded so she fashions them cheap and
disposable
  JOYCE CAROL OATES *Because It Is Bitter, and Because It Is My Heart*

prejudice

deep slits of prejudice
  JANET FRAME *The Edge of the Alphabet*

puberty

the musky outskirts of puberty
  REYNOLDS PRICE *The Tongues of Angels*

pulse

the faintest of pulses – like a distant memory of a canoe turning a
corner
  COLUM McCANN *This Side of Brightness*

pupils

pupils like two tiny black planets floating about in blue outer space
  MARIANNE SINCLAIR *Watcher in the Park*

pupils

Her pupils were two black thorns turned inwards
JOHN UPDIKE *The Witches of Eastwick*

Her pupils like pinholes, stars in negative
TERRY WOLVERTON *Bailey's Beads*

the pupils steely, tiny as the tips of ice picks
STEVEN HEIGHTON *The Shadow Boxer*

questions

    questions swarming through her head like fruit flies
        LISA ALTHER *Kinflicks*

    questions were screws that spiralled down into the brain
        PATRICK WHITE *Riders in the Chariot*

    questions ... hurled like pipe bombs
        TERRY WOLVERTON *Bailey's Beads*

    Questions flared like snake cowls
        TONI MORRISON *Love*

    The question hangs in the air like a little wire poking
        LESLEY GLAISTER *Sheer Blue Bliss*

    The questions trooped nose-to-tail through her mind like a
    wretched convoy of children crawling down an ill-lit corridor
        STEVIE DAVIES *The Element of Water*

queue

    a queue like a film of DNA cloning itself
        JANICE GALLOWAY *Foreign Parts*

quiet

    the quiet was like a kiss
        NICOLA BARKER *Small Holdings*

    the quiet flowed through him like medicine
        TIM GAUTREAUX *People on the Empty Road*

rage

the tight politeness of rage
PAMELA HANSFORD JOHNSON *Catherine Carter*

rage falling over her like handfuls of rice at a wedding
DARYL PONICSAN *The Accomplice*

his rage ... fills up rooms like sourdough and everyone gets a taste
JANICE GALLOWAY *Clara*

a tiny, shrew-footed, virtually inaudible, pitter-patter of rage
NICOLA BARKER *Behindlings*

He could feel the rage of a lifetime rising in him like a thrombosis
swelling and flowering and unfolding its clotted petals
JANETTE TURNER HOSPITAL *The Tiger in the Tiger Pit*

Rage circled and built in him, like a saxophone solo
LORRIE MOORE *Real Estate*

Rage jolted through her like a suddenly inflating parachute
CAI EMMONS *His Mother's Son*

rain

sabres of black rain
JOHN BANVILLE *Birchwood*

icy, thousand-needled rain
ALEXANDER BARON *From the City, From the Plough*

a bewitching of rain
JANET FRAME *The Edge of the Alphabet*

hissing rain like an arched grey cat cornered by the enemy
JANET FRAME *Scented Gardens for the Blind*

a slow rain descended like remorse from the sky
MERVYN PEAKE *Titus Groan*

rain as thin and sour as motorway wheel-squirt
MARTIN AMIS *Money*

rain like dice on the roof
PETER VANSITTART *Landlord*

rain like soft nails being driven into rotten wood
KEN KESEY *Sometimes a Great Notion*

rain set like a seal of misery
ROSALIND BELBEN *The Limit*

rain washed the roof with close slanted sounds
TRUMAN CAPOTE *Other Voices, Other Rooms*

rain like wings in the chimney
TRUMAN CAPOTE *Other Voices, Other Rooms*

the rain began to hiss outside, like the chorus in Bach's St John
Passion demanding crucifixion
ANTHONY BURGESS *Beard's Roman Women*

rain like shot tossed in a tin
EVA HANAGAN *The Upas Tree*

a dove-grey consecrating rain
ROBERT NYE *Merlin*

a soft antique rain
ANNA KAVAN *Sleep Has His House*

rain like a deepening scale of piano notes
TRUMAN CAPOTE *The Grass Harp*

rain like a tap on the shoulder from God
GEOFF PIKE *Golightly Adrift*

rain, the whole sky sobbing potato juice
JAYNE ANNE PHILLIPS *Blind Girls*

vipers of rain
DESMOND HOGAN *A Curious Street*

rain like glass hair
JEAN THOMPSON *Little Face*

royal shuttlecocks of rain
JIM HUNTER *Walking in the Painted Sunshine*

rain ... slanting like steel wire
WILLIAM HOFFMAN *Moorings*

a distant scrim of rain
JIM SHEPARD *Flights*

the angry rain that puts its narrow fingers in through the putty
SEBASTIAN BARRY *The Whereabouts of Eneas McNulty*

the whispered commentary of the rain
ELIZABETH KNOX *After Z-Hour*

the layered insult of dawn rain
MARTIN AMIS *London Fields*

rain in Hell's Kitchen is a curtain of soot draped in lethargic folds
over the crumbling streets and avenues
ALISON DYE *An Awareness of March*

Long stalks of rain
DAVID IRELAND *The Chosen*

The rain like so many little windows going down around us
MICHAEL ONDAATJE *Coming Through Slaughter*

The ... rain has madness in it like an illness, an ague
SEBASTIAN BARRY *Annie Dunne*

rain in the courtyard ... like the sound of newspaper burning
EDMUND WHITE *Palace Days*

rain falls outside, so much rain that it bands together like thick
ribbons unspooling from the sky
SARAH WILLIS *Some Things That Stay*

rain came across the surface of the river like the bristles of a broom
ELIZABETH KNOX *The Vintner's Luck*

The rain was coming down heavily now, like a fall of dirty light
JOHN BANVILLE *Ghosts*

The sound of the rain nuzzled the building, like the fuzz of an old record
  IRA SHER *Gentlemen of Space*

The warm winter rain fell solemn and steady as a litany
  MARGARET SKINNER *Molly Flanagan and the Holy Ghost*

a rain that sinks into you like history and makes the whole world come to pieces in your hands
  CHARLES FERNYHOUGH *The Auctioneer*

the rain comes like a stampede, like horses crossing the roof, Appaloosas, roans, serinas tearing holes in the sky and plunging through them
  ROBERT OLMSTEAD *America by Land*

It was a thin needling rain, white-mouthed and unsmiling in its task
  MARTIN AMIS *Other People*

rain ... drifting aslant in the lamplight like something about to be remembered
  JOHN BANVILLE *Athena*

thin rain like umbrella-spokes
  JOHN BANVILLE *Athena*

a heavy winter rain ... formed unpredictably into eddies and sudden thicknesses, like the folds of a veil, like shot silk
  PHILIP HENSHER *Pleasured*

The rain crept across the polished sea, made it one angry fizzle, and then engulfed us with a deliberate and leisurely bite
  DEREK BEAVEN *Acts of Mutiny*

Rain hit his face – warm, like the saliva of a giant beast
  ROBERT BOSWELL *Imagining Spaniards*

And then, just like a musical note, a little ping, like a clock striking one, like a single word in Chinese: rain had struck the window
  LAURA KALPAKIAN *Caveat*

rat

rats ran like ink in the gutters at night
  DELIA FALCONER *The Service of Clouds*

remark

[His] remarks were like grubby fingerprints
GRANT BUDAY *A Sack of Teeth*

river

river like a slice of alloy moon
KEN KESEY *Sometimes a Great Notion*

the river rides like a clean collar among the parklands
LAWRENCE DURRELL *The Black Book*

a heavy, dark grey river unfolded thickly like the slow thoughts of an old man
JENNIFER DAWSON *The Ha-Ha*

The river looked like cold onion soup, a brown gruel with a soggy cap of bread
PETER GADOL *Light at Dusk*

The river changed like a living thing, sometimes creeping up to our house like a visitor who wouldn't come in
SARAH WILLIS *Some Things That Stay*

the log-lively waters of the river
THEA ASTLEY *It's Raining in Mango*

He listened to the river sucking at the banks like an animal trying to find its way in
WILLIAM GAY *Those Deep Elm Brown's Ferry Blues*

The river runs full and clear as a trout's eye
ROBERT DREWE *The Drowner*

the river, which rippled with moonlight like the slow bulk of a sleeping reptile
JAY McINERNEY *Ransom*

road

[The] road wound like a petrified snake
JG BALLARD *Vermilion Sands*

roads like fresh whip scars
YAËL DAYAN *Death Had Two Sons*

roads stretched like wet rulers
SEAN O'FAOLAIN *In the Bosom of the Country*

the road like a cat flattening its ears
JOHN UPDIKE *The Centaur*

The road ran on like a hypnotism
WILLIAM FAULKNER *Mosquitoes*

The road gleamed like cold fat on a frying pan
ALAN GOULD *Close Ups*

The dirt road rolled down the hill, brown and wet and bumpy, like
some giant cut-out tongue on the ground
GLEN HIRSHBERG *Struwwelpeter*

roofs

roofs that sagged like old marital mattresses
PJ KAVANAGH *A Happy Man*

tiled roofs looming like sinister chessboards
NICK JOAQUIN *May Day Eve*

roofs seem greasily lustrous with sullen inner knowledge
JOHN UPDIKE *The Centaur*

room

[The] rooms became soupy and affectless, like derelict
conservatories in summer thunder
MARTIN AMIS *Denton's Death*

the room as still as a diorama
BERNARD COOPER *A Year of Rhymes*

The room looked like half of something torn in two
MARTIN AMIS *Bujak and the Strong Force*

root

a delicate young oak, with burly roots like the toes of a gryphon
exposed in the wet ground
CYNTHIA OZICK *The Pagan Rabbi*

sadness

sad like chimps destined for the moon
HUGO CHARTERIS *The Indian Summer of Gabriel Murray*

They looked sad, like strangers in a storm
JEROME CHARYN *War Cries over Avenue C*

the proud, sad air of the king of a rainy country
ANGELA CARTER *Reflections*

he felt saddened – as when a hearse passes on a fine summer's day
JANETTE TURNER HOSPITAL *Borderline*

[as sad] as if World War II had never ended
NANCY HUSTON *Dolce Agonia*

sadness, like a spirit hand
DIANE JOHNSON *Lying Low*

sadness oozed around me like primeval silt
DAVID LONG *Eclipse*

snippets, pinches, little sips of sadness
JULIA ALVAREZ *In the Time of the Butterflies*

persistent sadness, like a small rain
ANDREI CODRESCU *Messiah*

a low-grade sadness coursing through me like a virus
GREG BOTTOMS *LSD in Raleigh*

a sadness in those eyes like water seeping into a hole you've dug in the earth
  JOYCE CAROL OATES *Man Crazy*

His sadness began to accumulate, like sand
  TINA DE ROSA *Paper Fish*

sadness like a wall of raw earth
  GLEN DUNCAN *Weathercock*

scar

the scar beneath his eye like the split back of a cicada shell
  SARAH MYLES *Transplanted*

a small white scar like an unwiped white of egg
  WILLIAM H GASS *Omensetter's Luck*

his scar the carved zigzag of a snowmobile across a winter lake
  LORRIE MOORE *The Jewish Hunter*

The scar was someone else's unwanted hand on her, permanently
  GLEN DUNCAN *Love Remains*

sea

a sea calmly pedalling away to a ruled horizon
  LAWRENCE DURRELL *Nunquam*

[the] sea laying its cheek softly on the warm sand, making ministering nurse-movements dressed in its cap of white foam
  JANET FRAME *Scented Gardens for the Blind*

a dejected sea in a thin green dress sitting upon the hearth waiting for the tide to come home
  JANET FRAME *The Edge of the Alphabet*

[the] wheezy loitering sea
  PETER VANSITTART *Sources of Unrest*

[the] vacillating sea
  PETER VANSITTART *Sources of Unrest*

the sea came in arcades
  EMMA TENNANT *Wild Nights*

a Paul Klee sea
  BERNARD KOPS *On Margate Sands*

the thin, pale taunt of the sea
  FRANCIS EBEJER *In the Eye of the Sun*

the steady hushing of the sea
  ANNE MULCOCK *Landscape with Figures*

the steady applause of the sea
  THEA ASTLEY *The Multiple Effects of Rainshadow*

the sea made a far-off sound like dancers
  AL BARKER *Novelette*

the sea that bright metallic four-o'clock blue
  JOHN UPDIKE *S.*

The sea remains, just a wide windswept pavement of water; some wild Doré precinct
  JENNIFER LASH *Blood Ties*

the moon-lusting sea
  ADAM ZAMEENZAD *Love, Bones and Water*

the sea moving like eels
  NEIL GORDON *The Gun Runner's Daughter*

the sea morsing sunlight across the length and depth of the shockingly blue horizon
  AL KENNEDY *Everything You Need*

The sea seems sunken, greasy, like the concave underside of a silver ingot
  JOHN UPDIKE *Toward the End of Time*

the sea was just a noise like nervous cellophane, like cellophane crushing in someone's hands
  JANICE GALLOWAY *Nightdriving*

The varicose blue of the sea
  DESMOND HOGAN *A Farewell to Prague*

the [sea] at the shoreline gray and marbled with white, like a cheap cut of meat
  RENÉE MANFREDI *Above the Thunder*

the lamenting sea, spilling a repetitive grief along the foreshore
  THEA ASTLEY *The Well Dressed Explorer*

The morning sea is an emerald corrugation
ALLISON BURNETT *Christopher*

The sea was brown in daylight, like an endless prairie, the colour of lions
ANGELA CARTER *Heroes and Villains*

The sea, that night, curled and lisped and whispered in a voice which said Dismay, Dismay, Dismay
JIM CRACE *The Gift of Stones*

The sea comes thinly finished at the shingle's edge
GLEN DUNCAN *Love Remains*

The sea sparkled, a colossal sapphire
CONNIE MAY FOWLER *Remembering Blue*

seaweed

seaweed sprawled like names
DESMOND HOGAN *The Ikon Maker*

sentence

a full-dress sentence
MARTIN AMIS *The Rachel Papers*

sentences clipped like hedges and lawns into strange shapes that surprise you in the dark
JANET FRAME *Scented Gardens for the Blind*

sentences poured effortlessly out like ectoplasm
JOHN GARDAM *Black Faces White Faces*

Every sentence sticks out its li'l mouse neck
ALLAN GURGANUS *Plays Well with Others*

Her sentences never waved white flags before coming over the crest of the hill
ELIZABETH KNOX *Treasure*

Every sentence was a board laid in place and her pauses the nails that clenched them in
FRED CHAPPELL *Look Back All the Green Valley*

this glowing sentence ... opening like a casement
JOHN CROWLEY *The Translator*

her sentences stood in parcels above her head
MAURICE GEE *Prowlers*

The sentences floated through the air like scraps of old thread
ROLAND MERULLO *In Revere, In Those Days*

sentences circle me like a toy train
WILLIAM H GASS *The Tunnel*

The sentence knocked around in my mouth like a hard candy
AIMEE BENDER *An Invisible Sign of My Own*

that sour half-sentence still hanging in the cold midday air, still
ringing in his head like a small pebble in a milk bottle, rolling and
bouncing down a steep, cobbled hill
NICOLA BARKER *Behindlings*

sex

Sex stirred like a ship on the Thames
DESMOND HOGAN *The Airedale*

Sex undoubtedly played its moonshine tune across the gap
between them
STEVIE DAVIES *The Element of Water*

shadow

an afternoon shadow, like mauve lichen invading by creeping
inches
PATRICK WHITE *The Twyborn Affair*

shadows sharp and small as deadly penknives
JANET FRAME *Intensive Care*

shadows like tear channels
AL BARKER *John Brown's Body*

shadows, huge, moving, like a procession of sins
ANTHONY BURGESS *Devil of a State*

Deep shadows lay like spilled sleep
JACK MATTHEWS *Elma*

Shadows walked like eighteenth-century figures proclaiming The
Rights of Man, proclaiming Revolution
JACK CADY *The Off Season*

whirling shadows are sometimes like the splashed gray letters of a restless alphabet slipping over rocks and dead branches
HAROLD BRODKEY *What I Do for Money*

the shadows were like loose sacks tied to branches or eaves or tractors, or were like sheets of dark paper on weeds
HAROLD BRODKEY *The Runaway Soul*

The black shadow of the house lay across the lawn like a fallen stage-flat
JOHN BANVILLE *The Book of Evidence*

Long warm shadows moved along the spines of my books like fingers choosing the story best for that night
THYLIAS MOSS *Tale of a Sky-Blue Dress*

sunlight in the street and a diagonal shadow by de Chirico sharp as the blade of a guillotine
JOHN BANVILLE *Athena*

Blue shadows climbed the tawny round slopes of the mountain, like hands modelling the shape of a lover's thigh
JANET FITCH *White Oleander*

The shadows of the clouds draw giant petals and paw prints on the surface of the pale-green sea
JANE MENDELSOHN *I Was Amelia Earhart*

shame

scarlet shame, scarlet like chilies drying in the sun
ROBERT OLMSTEAD *America by Land*

Shame suffused his being like a blood mist
JOYCE CAROL OATES *The Ice Pick*

shame shook her like an ague
PETER CONRAD *Underworld*

she

she was becoming a desert, thirsty and tearless, a layer of sand that could be carried off by any brief wind
AD NAUMAN *Scorch*

she was a kind of rockface, a staring, greedy, monitoring promontory, full of unspoken demands
  JENNIFER LASH *Blood Ties*

She is a sort of laughing knife of a woman
  HAROLD BRODKEY *The Runaway Soul*

She had an airbrushed quality, a touch of a smile, as if she'd spent her life looking out through a train window
  DAVID LONG *Attraction*

[She was] dreadfully stooped, the letter S in a Victorian alphabet
  KATE JENNINGS *The Magazine for Pool Families*

she was thin, dreamy, as full of odd angles as a Picasso mademoiselle
  JANET FITCH *White Oleander*

She was like a person whose light has been extinguished. Like a stripped Christmas tree thrown beside a snowy sidewalk for collection
  JANETTE TURNER HOSPITAL *The Ivory Swing*

[She] was a road. She heaved me down it with a few naughty wriggles and I was out at the other end going somewhere
  PHILIP CALLOW *The Bliss Body*

sheep

sheep bleating plaintive arpeggii
  JANET FRAME *Faces in the Water*

sheep grazed like fallen clouds in an inverted sky
  SUSAN KERSLAKE *Middlewatch*

shoes

shoes lining the wardrobe like motionless lizards
  CATHERINE CHIDGEY *Golden Deeds*

shoulders

His shoulders lay across his body like a bench
  CHRIS OFFUTT *The Good Brother*

her shoulder blades flashing through her skin like hatchets
  COLIN CHANNER *Satisfy My Soul*

His shoulders were Detroit fenders
  IAIN SINCLAIR *Downriver*

shrub

He thought the shrubs looked like circles of children gossiping at recess
  TIM GAUTREAUX *The Bug Man*

sigh

a sigh like a pious wee bagpipes
  ROBERT NYE *Faust*

... sighed like the shift of sand dunes
  TONI MORRISON *Song of Solomon*

sighing like a mermaid stranded in a supermarket
  ELIZABETH TROOP *Woolworth Madonna*

when he sighed you could hear the distant seagulls falling through his lungs
  MARTIN AMIS *The Information*

She sighed heavily, glancing heavenwards as if in memory of all sorts of dear departed royalty mown down before her eyes
  ISABEL COLEGATE *The Summer of the Royal Visit*

[a] sigh shaped exactly like a dove
  JOHN UPDIKE *Four Sides of One Story*

A drifting sigh comes up and out of her lungs, through her open mouth, like a butterfly on a warm day
  SARAH WILLIS *Some Things That Stay*

a single effort-filled balloon-blow of a sigh
  JAMES RYAN *Dismantling Mr Doyle*

My carbonated lovesick sighs
  DEBORAH BOEHM *The Samurai Goodbye*

she lets out a basketball of a sigh
  ALBERT GOLDBARTH *Pieces of Payne*

She'll sigh at the end of prayers like her heart has just been aired
  JULIANNA BAGGOTT *The Madam*

she sighed and it seemed as if the sigh were taken up by the room
and settled in sad corners
ITA DALY *Dangerous Fictions*

silence

silence like an unbroken hieroglyph
W WATSON *Better Than One*

silence like breath held at the ribs
MERVYN PEAKE *Titus Alone*

silence like the clash of toothless gums
PETER VANSITTART *Sources of Unrest*

the silence of a stilled typewriter
MICHAEL BALDWIN *The Cellar*

Streams of enormous silence slid in ghostly loneliness through
the bones of the house and crept in like a sly dream to finger the
stillness that had descended on the room
PAUL SMITH *Come Trailing Blood*

silence is a fuel: it whistles through the rigging of the nerves like a
Force 8 gale
LAWRENCE DURRELL *Monsieur*

silence like a piano under a cloth
EMMA TENNANT *Wild Nights*

X-ray silence
ALFRED HAYES *The End of Me*

a windy threadbare silence
MARTIN AMIS *Dead Babies*

The cotton of silence
ANAÏS NIN *Children of the Albatross*

silence like a river about to overflow its banks
DERMOT HEALY *Love*

a nasty silence ... like a morgue just before it's filled
ANDREW SINCLAIR *The Hallelujah Bum*

a silence like a future
ELIZABETH KNOX *Black Oxen*

The silence was a callus. It formed a blister, like a heavy-hanging sky, a blister with blood in it
ELIZABETH KNOX *Black Oxen*

the passionless, critical silence of a sickroom
SHIRLEY HAZZARD *A Place in the Country*

She wears silence around her neck like garlic against vampires
MARGARET ATWOOD *Life Before Man*

And silence drops down from out of the night, into this city, the briefest of silences, like a falter between heartbeats, like a darkness between blinks
JON MCGREGOR *If Nobody Speaks of Remarkable Things*

There was a long, windy silence, desolate as a stretch of midnight interstate
NICK FOWLER *A Thing (or Two) about Curtis and Camilla*

a dry small-town silence
HAROLD BRODKEY *The Shooting Range*

What I like are moneyed chasubles of silence
MARTIN AMIS *Success*

Given an opportunity, silence would enter the house and sit down like a bold intruder
RICK DEMARINIS *Romance: A Prose Villanelle*

The silence became one of those cartoon balloons designated to be filled in with suitable captions
THEA ASTLEY *Coda*

An embarrassed silence slapped like a wet net over the table
ALLISON BURNETT *Christopher*

silent as a cat in velvet
REYNOLDS PRICE *Kate Vaiden*

His silence was a moat
CYNTHIA OZICK *Heir to the Glimmering World*

The silence in the room is like copper in my mouth
WILL CHRISTOPHER BAER *Hell's Half Acre*

sin

sins stacked up like vertebrae
STEVE AYLETT *The Crime Studio*

Sin can multiply like mosquitoes' skeins of eggs, a gritty scrim on stagnant water, a new breed always rising
JULIANNA BAGGOTT *The Madam*

skin

skin like blue stained glass to the sky
JANET FRAME *The Adaptable Man*

skin very quiet over sharp bone
PETER VANSITTART *Sources of Unrest*

photogravure grain of her skin
ANGELA CARTER *Several Perceptions*

your skin might have been for sale in a Buchenwald dress shop
FRANCES JESSUP *The Fifth Child's Conception in the Runaway Wife*

skin patinated and toned as if painted by Modigliani
JEREMY LELAND *A River Decrees*

skin slick as a piston after a valve job
JAMES BARKER *Fuel Injected Dreams*

his white skin pale and damp like a dandelion under a stone
SEBASTIAN BARRY *The Whereabouts of Eneas McNulty*

her skin wallpapered with grief
COLUM McCANN *Step We Gaily, On We Go*

His skin had the pallor of a sixties educational TV host
RICHARD POWERS *Galatea 2.2*

His skin looks like old cat food
MERLE DROWN *The Suburbs of Heaven*

skin like the paper you put at the bottom of a cake tin
JOHN BERGER *King*

His skin smells clean, like paper. The thick brown kind, from grade school. His skin smells like a good memory
SUZANNE FINNAMORE *Otherwise Engaged*

my skin was sickly white, like one of those old dinner plates you see glimmering out at you in a dark corner of an antique shop
  STEVEN MILLHAUSER *The King in the Tree*

Your skin was an ocean of sky sliding toward me
  WILLIAM H GASS *The Tunnel*

Her skin was wrinkled in pinpricks like the surface of Parmesan cheese
  ANGELA CARTER *The Merchant of Shadows*

her unnaturally taut skin like a Noh drum
  DEBORAH BOEHM *The Samurai Goodbye*

fair, hairless skin haunted by the ghosts of freckles
  LOUIS BAYARD *Fool's Errand*

skin like hail damage
  ROBERT DREWE *The Drowner*

tracing-paper skin
  CHARLES FERNYHOUGH *The Auctioneer*

[her] skin like vacuum-cleaner bags hanging from between her elbows and armpits
  CLYDE EDGERTON *In Memory of Junior*

The skin on her face like heaps and heaps of dead porridge
  DESMOND HOGAN *Lebanon Lodge*

[his] skin ... weathered like a network of dried riverbeds
  JANETTE TURNER HOSPITAL *The Tiger in the Tiger Pit*

her skin looked a bit like the celluloid negative of a photograph of a lamington made in a factory where they are slightly miserly when they sprinkle on the desiccated coconut
  RICHARD KING *Kindling Does for Firewood*

her skin, white as an unscuffed softball, felt like one as well
  MARY KAY ZURAVLEFF *The Frequency of Souls*

her skin rippled with pimples like risotto
  PHILIP HENSHER *The Fit*

the skin on his face seemed lifeless and crushed, a second-hand substance from the bottom shelf in the scullery
  PETER CAREY *Oscar and Lucinda*

His skin was barnacled with cold
JIM CRACE *The Gift of Stones*

your skin was the thinnest wash of moonlight on snow, the snow
across which the rabbit leaps at the sound of approaching footsteps
KATHRYN DAVIS *Labrador*

her skin felt like the underside of old, soft fabric left to age in attic
trunks and brought out once a year to be dusted
THOMAS GLYNN *Watching the Body Burn*

tanned skin as smooth as honey spilled on a table
KEVIN MCCOLLEY *Praying to a Laughing God*

A network of fine lines etched her near-translucent skin. She could
have been crystal dropped just hard enough on the floor
KEVIN MCCOLLEY *Praying to a Laughing God*

Her skin … was flat, chill white, like a milk carton
JEAN THOMPSON *City Boy*

His skin felt like wet rubber, like a hand hidden in a surgeon's
glove
JESSE LEE KERCHEVAL *The Museum of Happiness*

sky

the sky swipes with the back of its hand
JANET FRAME *The Edge of the Alphabet*

pomegranate sky
CHRISTINA STEAD *Seven Poor Men of Sydney*

the sky had been stabbed and has been left to die above the world,
filthy, vast and bloody
MERVYN PEAKE *Gormenghast*

[the] sky, hurtfully blue
WALLACE STEGNER *Angle of Repose*

the entire sky was a warm blanket of eyes and mouths
ANAÏS NIN *A Spy in the House of Love*

a needlepoint sky
KEN KESEY *Sometimes a Great Notion*

the sky opened like the clockwork Easter eggs the Tsars gave one another
    Angela Carter *Elegy for a Freelance*

the terrific eyeballs of the night sky
    Lawrence Durrell *The Black Book*

The sky looked like a vast and friendly ocean, in which drowning was forbidden
    James Baldwin *Another Country*

skies like lead from the deck of a ship
    Donald Hutley *The Swan*

The sky looks like its throat is cut
    Geoff Pike *Golightly Adrift*

powdery blue sky the color of a hymnal
    John Updike *Couples*

the sort of sky that forms the backdrop for so much bad literature
    Nora Keeling *The Driver*

A sky by John Constable, R.A.
    John Updike *A Madman*

A magnificent bold-blue quattrocento sky
    Anthony Burgess *Honey for the Bears*

The satsuma sky
    Penelope Shuttle *Rainsplitter in the Zodiac Garden*

a thick keel of sky
    Hugo Barnacle *Promise*

the sky a vast empty ache
    T Coraghessan Boyle *Riven Rock*

the sky was indigo, almost black, like the mind at the point of unconsciousness
    Gretel Ehrlich *Heart Mountain*

a sky that wouldn't sit still
    Michael Doane *Legends of Jesse Dark*

sky with mother-of-pearl veins
    Joyce Cary *The Horse's Mouth*

sky the colour of a dead furnace
TERENCE WHEELER *The Conjunction*

a cumulus sky with heavy patches like iodine on a bruised leg
JOHN GOODING *People of Providence Street*

the long granite lid of the sky pulled over everything
SEBASTIAN BARRY *The Whereabouts of Eneas McNulty*

the lonesome batter of the sky
SEBASTIAN BARRY *The Whereabouts of Eneas McNulty*

the sky overhead is an old boarding-house sheet flapping eastward
VERLYN KLINKENBORG *The Last Fine Time*

the sky turned to gore
LISA ALTHER *Five Minutes in Heaven*

the darkish purple sky, like the extra eyelid over a seal's eye
KEN KESEY *Sailor Song*

many fathoms of impossible, enclosed, frozen, baked-Alaska sky
ELIZABETH KNOX *Treasure*

clear, choral, late-winter sky
ELIZABETH KNOX *Treasure*

The sky was empty, blown clean, an unblinking Africa of blue
MARTIN AMIS *London Fields*

The sky ... turned blue, as if it had never tried the color before and
wasn't sure anyone would like it
TONY EARLY *Jim the Boy*

the sky a distant drum
JENNIFER DAWSON *Judasland*

the sky had taken on the color of dead grass, darkening in yeasty
gusts
SUNETRA GUPTA *Memories of Rain*

a sky that looked so tight and shiny it might squeak
LESLEY GLAISTER *Partial Eclipse*

Way above, the sky was blue like potato spray
SHANE CONNAUGHTON *The Run of the Country*

the night sky was suspiciously perfect, a planetarium sky
DAVID IRELAND *The Chosen*

Dark blue sky arced, a shell starred with barnacles
DAVID PROFUMO *Sea Music*

a damaged El Greco sky
DESMOND HOGAN *A New Shirt*

the big sky and its zoo of cumulus – its snow leopards and polar bears
MARTIN AMIS *Time's Arrow*

the rain-filled sky dipping to ... seal the whole world in slate
LOUIS OWENS *Nightland*

The sky is bright, bright blue like a fist pushed into an eye, that puddle of hot colour
MARGARET ATWOOD *The Robber Bride*

The sky changed channels from purple to gray
MICHAEL HORNBURG *Bongwater*

the sky had the unreal brightness of a bulb that's about to blow
IAIN SINCLAIR *Landor's Tower*

the sky is the colour of a dressing over a wound which bleeds
JOHN BERGER *To the Wedding*

The sky reared above me, oceanic, untroubled; blue waves tipped in a glass bowl
IAIN SINCLAIR *Landor's Tower*

The black sky sagged like a doom over our heads
ANNA KAVAN *Ice Storm*

The sky was too deep to be called purple, belonging more to the hateful family of black
MELINDA HAYNES *Mother of Pearl*

The rain had just stopped and the sky was settling like a wash of winter rags, eggshell and pewter
MOLLY GILES *Iron Shoes*

The sky was assembled from contradictory recipes for smoke
IAIN SINCLAIR *Radon Daughters*

The sky closer to liquid or paint than sky
  CHARLOTTE BACON *Lost Geography*

Cross-section skies
  IAIN SINCLAIR *Radon Daughters*

the sky was the color of the primer you saw on pickups and wagons awaiting the benediction of paint
  T CORAGHESSAN BOYLE *Drop City*

The sky was bruised and purple, racing, livid with threat and prophecy
  IAIN SINCLAIR *Downriver*

the sky was a low washboard of white sliding above a light, tasteless wind
  ALYSON HAGY *Keeneland*

The sky began to come back: like a pale cloth
  MICHAEL PYE *The Pieces from Berlin*

the sky receding like an illustration in a physics book
  WILLIAM H GASS *The Tunnel*

a sky cornered by clouds
  WILLIAM H GASS *The Tunnel*

The sky, a star-eaten blanket
  JEFFERY RENARD ALLEN *Rails under My Back*

an immense sky of the most innocent blue, blue of a bowl from which a child might have drunk its morning milk and left behind a few whitish traces of cloud around the rim
  ANGELA CARTER *The Scarlet House*

The sky soared like a violet-blue paperweight
  EMILY CARTER *Zemecki's Cat*

the sky is a freshly scrubbed blue, as permanent-looking as the first day of the holidays
  JON MCGREGOR *If Nobody Speaks of Remarkable Things*

a fried-rasher sky
  JOHN BANVILLE *The Untouchable*

the giant sky above her. No sun left, no moon up, no stars yet. Just shadow. A great, wide, hugely improbable inky blink
NICOLA BARKER *Wide Open*

the sky is jittery with pale stars
DEBORAH BERGMAN *River of Glass*

The sky gleamed the kind of bionic, stainless blue that makes people believe there's a heaven
MICHAEL LOWENTHAL *Avoidance*

The sky was the blue that makes you smell lakes
MARTHA BERGLAND *A Farm under a Lake*

a cloud-written sky
SIMON BREEN *Down in One*

[a] well-audited sky
HAROLD BRODKEY *Bookkeeping*

an operatically cumulonimbus sky
ALBERT GOLDBARTH *Pieces of Payne*

In winter, the sky is a cloud-jammed attic, noisy and hollow
HAROLD BRODKEY *Ceil*

the billion-acre sky
JAMES BUCHAN *The Golden Plough*

the sky a big goose highway south
MATT COHEN *Elizabeth and After*

It was a sky so perfect it should have been sold to a museum
MATT COHEN *Nadine*

an evening sky lay swathed in its girlish pinks and boyish blues
MARTIN AMIS *Straight Fiction*

The fast-clouding sky became a grotesque menagerie of strange animal shapes and cages of burnt-edged coral
DARIN STRAUSS *The Real McCoy*

The sky was grey and gristly, with interesting bruises
MARTIN AMIS *Bujak and the Strong Force*

the boiling acne of the dying sky
MARTIN AMIS *The Time Disease*

The sky lay heavy in the west, a curved platinum sheet
  CHRISTOPHER COOK *Robbers*

a sky as pale as birdlime
  ROBERT DREWE *The Drowner*

a harsh cobalt sky, an electric sky in a failed painting
  WILLIAM GAY *Provinces of Night*

the sky opened like a tear in a shop awning
  JANICE GALLOWAY *Clara*

the sky, a great gray veto
  TIBOR FISCHER *Fifty Uselessnesses*

the star-inscribed sky
  CHRISTINA GARCIA *Dreaming in Cuban*

Thick royal sky
  JANICE GALLOWAY *Need for Restraint*

the sky was already nagging its way peevishly towards a tight and grey and implacable evening
  NICOLA BARKER *Behindlings*

The sky was high and grey and couldn't care less
  LESLEY GLAISTER *Now You See Me*

the sky so far away, a black wound
  IAIN SINCLAIR *White Chappell, Scarlet Tracings*

The sky so blue that it penetrated my alcoholic daze like the wet tongue of the most brutal lover
  GABY NAHER *The Underwharf*

Through the windshield the sky looks like a blue idea the earth is having
  RALPH LOMBREGLIA *Good Year*

perpetually bloated, premenstrual skies
  NINA FITZPATRICK *Daimons*

The evening sky is a darkening dove-grey still luminous with a Caspar David Friedrich long, long blue that is like a memory, like prayer, like regret
  RUSSELL HOBAN *Her Name Was Lola*

the industrial-waste sky
JOYCE CAROL OATES *Faithless*

a pebbled-white soiled sky that was like a thin chamois cloth about to be lifted away
JOYCE CAROL OATES *The Sky Blue Ball*

the sky like an enamel table that's been scratched and the dark underside's showing through
JOYCE CAROL OATES *Man Crazy*

the sky ... mottled and luminous like old wavy glass
JOYCE CAROL OATES *You Must Remember This*

the sky is a blinding bowl of leaves and birds
KATE CHRISTENSEN *The Epicure's Lament*

days lengthened under the sky's stained egg
RICHARD POWERS *Plowing the Dark*

the sky has become sulky with a huge boil-up of cloud from the sea
THEA ASTLEY *A Kindness Cup*

A sky like a window in a portrait of a Renaissance cardinal
JANET FITCH *White Oleander*

this blue was tender, warm, merciful, without white, pure chroma, a Raphael sky
JANET FITCH *White Oleander*

the sky was a polished silver, a big, upended tureen of a sky
T CORAGHESSAN BOYLE *The Inner Circle*

The sky is a speckless white cheek
CYNTHIA OZICK *Bloodshed*

a wide pitched sky as royal-blue as the eyes of a watchful year-old boy or the banner at a high chivalric tilt in dark-age France
REYNOLDS PRICE *The Promise of Rest*

the skies just beginning to ink
JULIANNA BAGGOTT *The Madam*

The sky has clouded over, dun colored, like the breast of a bird
JULIANNA BAGGOTT *The Madam*

The sky is charcoaled cantaloupe, some oranges and pinks caught in the night clouds like gases
  LORRIE MOORE *Anagrams*

Above, the creases of the sky glimmered like cellulite
  MARTIN AMIS *The Information*

after the strain of being without a cloud all day [the sky] had softened to Wedgwood
  HUGH LEONARD *Fillums*

The sky covers you over with a metallic blue, watercolor wash over tinfoil
  CHARLES BAXTER *Westland*

the sky seemed to billow and unfurl over us like the banner of Christ
  PHILIP CALLOW *Going to the Moon*

The sky was rich with day
  DEREK BEAVEN *Newton's Niece*

The sky, grinning blandly, insisted that it had seen nothing
  PETER CONRAD *Underworld*

The sky was celebration blue
  MAVIS CHEEK *Mrs Fytton's Country Life*

the sky going about its enormous, stealthy business
  JOHN BANVILLE *Mefisto*

the hurt blue of a bare September sky
  JOHN BANVILLE *Mefisto*

the sky above stretching into a streaky winter sunset like a cheap balloon
  AMANDA CRAIG *In a Dark Wood*

the sky folded and pinned like fabric between the buildings
  TINA DE ROSA *Paper Fish*

The sky overhead is a molten blue, like a perfect silk scarf that has been soaked in cerulean ink and then left to dry on a line
  PAUL BRANDON *The Wild Reel*

the sky like an endless open lid
  MYLÈNE DRESSLER *The Deadwood Beetle*

the sky is still clouded the thin white of skimmed milk
HELENA ECHLIN *Gone*

The sky today was like a tramp's overcoat
ALICE THOMAS ELLIS *The Other Side of the Fire*

the gray-blue sky over the bay is marbled with luminous purple clouds, elegant as the frontispiece of an antique book
CAI EMMONS *His Mother's Son*

the sky telling of winter, evening-colored at four in the afternoon
LEIF ENGER *Peace Like a River*

the sky flat and silent as a stone
WILL CHRISTOPHER BAER *Penny Dreadful*

The sky had gone red and pink, like an exposed membrane
WILL CHRISTOPHER BAER *Penny Dreadful*

The sky in London is like the water-bowed ceiling of an old house
ANONYMOUS *The Bride Stripped Bare*

[the] sky like a spittoon
ALAN WALL *China*

the sky was familiar Chicago no-color
JEAN THOMPSON *City Boy*

An intolerably calm placid smiling cheap vulgar insensitive neo-classical blue sky
RUSSELL HOBAN *Kleinzeit*

the steel-gray sky, a sky no poet in history ever attempted to approach with verse, nor any filmmaker with camera, a sky that defies definition, mocks metaphor, confounds hope, a nasty November sky so blank it turns the trees and fence and shed to dun
NANCY HUSTON *Dolce Agonia*

the raked evensong of sunset skies
BRUCE WAGNER *I'll Let You Go*

It was after five, though the sky would claim that it was later
SUE HALPERN *The Book of Hard Things*

The sky went black as a limousine
JANE MENDELSOHN *Innocence*

skyscraper

skyscrapers shone ... like extra-large bottles of caffeinated soda
MARK O'DONNELL *Let Nothing You Dismay*

skyscrapers blazing like exorbitant lamps
STEVE ALMOND *The Pass*

sleep

light sheet of sleep
ANITA DESAI *Voices in the City*

black gorge of sleep
GLADYS SCHMITT *Electra*

sleep crouched malignantly over the houses
CHRISTINA STEAD *Seven Poor Men of Sydney*

sleep ... seized her like an undertow
PETER CRAIG *Hot Plastic*

sleep, like a seamless cylinder
EL WALLANT *The Human Season*

the vanishing hem of sleep
ANNA KAVAN *Machines in the Head*

sleep finally folded me in like a coal-black blanket, old heavy rough wool
REYNOLDS PRICE *Roxanna Slade*

A sleep more tranquil than the curve of eggs
TONI MORRISON *Sula*

cold thimblefuls of sleep
SUNETRA GUPTA *Memories of Rain*

the liqueur of sleep
SUNETRA GUPTA *The Glassblower's Breath*

sleep came on him like a layer of loam
CHRIS OFFUTT *The Good Brother*

sleep came and went like a slug crawling over my belly
NICOLA BARKER *Small Holdings*

She was impossible in the morning, crawling out of the blood-red cave of her insomniac's sleep like a lioness poked with a stick
  T Coraghessan Boyle *Acts of God*

the helpless molasses-slow muscle of sleep
  Janette Turner Hospital *The Ivory Swing*

He slept the sleep of lead: dark, heavy, immobile, malleable and, ultimately, molten
  Richard Flanagan *Death of a River Guide*

smile

[a] smile like the curve of a knife
  Peter Vansittart *Lancelot*

smiles as mean as watered gin
  Ernest Frost *It's Late by My Watch*

smiling like the profile of a saucer
  Andrew Sinclair *The Project*

aching fugue of smiles
  John Banville *Birchwood*

smiling like Rothschild
  Robert Aickman *The Inner Room*

smiles were offered like canapés
  Peter Vansittart *Quintet*

a teaspoon of smile
  Peter Vansittart *Pastimes of a Red Summer*

[a] smile wide as octaves
  Cynthia Ozick *Trust*

smiled like a cancer patient at the doctor's joke
  Hugo Charteris *A Share of the World*

His smile dug one's grave
  Lawrence Durrell *Balthazar*

a half-smile – Huckleberry Finn trapped in the body of a Hapsburg
  Anne Roiphe *Torch Song*

a smile like a torch with a weak battery
  Hugo Charteris *The Indian Summer of Gabriel Murray*

fully-rigged smiles
AL BARKER *Next Door*

her smile is a dolphin's wake
ANDREW SINCLAIR *The Hallelujah Bum*

[a] lazy-looking trompe l'oeil smile
EL WALLANT *Tenants of Moonbloom*

[a] housebroken smile
PENELOPE SHUTTLE *Rainsplitter in the Zodiac Garden*

a smile flung backward like a handful of flowers
WALLACE STEGNER *Crossing to Safety*

a frail ET-like smile
JAMES BAKER *Fuel Injected Dreams*

a little what-hath-God-wrought smile
EUGENE WALTER *The Untidy Pilgrim*

smiles lit distances
SHANE CONNAUGHTON *The Run of the Country*

... smile was like tea made of finger-nails
PETER VANSITTART *Pastimes of a Red Summer*

a smile like a ticket dispenser
NIK COHN *Need*

a flashing smile that uncovered far too much pink enthusiasm
SHEILA KOHLER *The Perfect Place*

[her] polite going-visiting smile
CONNIE MAY FOWLER *Before Women Had Wings*

a peculiar, distant smile that stank of sacrifice
DAVID HART *Come to the Edge*

smiling forth such hard-wired wattage
ALLAN GURGANUS *Plays Well with Others*

a demi-smile, in dimple eighth notes
ALLAN GURGANUS *Plays Well with Others*

the smile of a disturbed entertainer
SUNETRA GUPTA *The Glassblower's Breath*

[She] pays out a thin smile
ANN HARLEMAN *The Cost of Anything*

Her parting smile ... put me in mind of a word. Millivolts, that was
it
DAVID IRELAND *The Chosen*

a slow smile won its way on his mouth
REYNOLDS PRICE *Roxanna Slade*

smiled like a roomful of mirrors
JON CLEARY *Man's Estate*

her smile was so wide she might have been related to the sun
MICHAEL FELD *The Short Cut Life of Bacchus Pocock*

that nervous, thin smile that's like a child's scribble on a magic
erasing slate
EMMA TENNANT *The Ballad of Sylvia and Ted*

[a] smile that made him look like a toad with an oversized insect
clamped in its jaw
T CORAGHESSAN BOYLE *Captured by the Indians*

a full-on, interplanetary dreamer's smile
T CORAGHESSAN BOYLE *The Black and White Sisters*

the tight composed smile of a man running for office
T CORAGHESSAN BOYLE *Sorry Fugu*

a smile like a fluorescent light
MICHAEL ARDITTI *Easter*

narrow over-zealous first-world smiles
THEA ASTLEY *Vanishing Points*

she smiled one of her thousand-watters
JOYCE WEATHERFORD *Heart of the Beast*

her shiny prefab smile
FRED CHAPPELL *Look Back All the Green Valley*

It's a smile that wavers like a gasoline slick on water, shining,
changing tone
MARGARET ATWOOD *Wilderness Tips*

He gave his version of a smile – a thin crack in his face, like mud drying
  MARGARET ATWOOD *The Blind Assassin*

The sort of smile memories are not so much made of as repaired by
  A MANETTE ANSAY *Midnight Champagne*

His smile ... seemed to have become less a smile and more an instrument, a tool of inquiry, like a lockpick
  JOHN CROWLEY *The Translator*

he sits, with no more smile to him than there is on a hammer
  MERLE DROWN *The Suburbs of Heaven*

an excellent smile like a person might draw
  SEBASTIAN BARRY *Annie Dunne*

your klieg-light smile
  EDMUND WHITE *Watermarked*

He smiled, but it was wrong. Like seeing bits of your safari guide's clothes wedged between the lion's teeth
  SUZANNE FINNAMORE *Otherwise Engaged*

a smile like the smile on the Patron Saint of Maple Syrup
  JOANNE GREENBERG *Where the Road Goes*

her sky-tinting rainbow smile
  JOANNE GREENBERG *Where the Road Goes*

her ancient Attic smile
  THEA ASTLEY *Coda*

he smiled, a warm, welcoming smile in F major. Or no, with a touch of insolence, so F-sharp major
  CHRISTOPHER BRAM *The Notorious Dr August*

... smiled like a clown penny bank, white teeth slightly open and acquisitive
  MARGARET ATWOOD *Life Before Man*

that tripwire smile of his
  ALYSON HAGY *Hardware River*

a smile becalmed on his face
  MOLLY GILES *Iron Shoes*

He scrawled his famous smile across his face, hastily, like an autograph
WILLIAM H GASS *The Tunnel*

smiling like a half-opened tin
WILLIAM H GASS *The Tunnel*

his smile widening like a syrup spill
WILLIAM H GASS *The Tunnel*

his smile fighting out of his mouth like an animal in his skin
KEITH RIDGWAY *The Long Falling*

she displays the thin blade of her smile
JAY McINERNEY *Model Behaviour*

your smile as fiercely hopeful as a dog biting the fleas on its back
KEVIN McILVOY *Hyssop*

She was smiling faintly, like someone at the rail of a boat drifting toward the open ocean
GLEN HIRSHBERG *The Snowman's Children*

It's not that he doesn't smile; it's that if his smile were something you drew, you'd erase it, thinking, Wrong
ELIZABETH BERG *Range of Motion*

an almost contrite, impossibly white, there-were-just-no-cabs-to-be-*had*-darling smile
NICK FOWLER *A Thing (or Two) about Curtis and Camilla*

the wasteland shore of her smile
SEAN THOMAS *Kissing England*

smiles like wounds
LOUIS BAYARD *Endangered Species*

Her formidable microtoothed smile
LOUIS BAYARD *Endangered Species*

smiling like Hansel and Gretel setting out
MARTHA BERGLAND *A Farm under a Lake*

a cheese-sauce smile
SIMON BREEN *Down in One*

her dazzling book-jacket smile
DEBORAH BOEHM *An Itching in the Heart*

a cute little gumbo-ladling smile
TIM GAUTREAUX *The Courtship of Merlin LeBlanc*

He smiles like a juvenile paratrooper
HAROLD BRODKEY *The Boys on Their Bikes*

a hideous feral-cat-little-pointed-teeth-and-licking-its-whiskers
smile, shamed as if after eating carrion
HAROLD BRODKEY *Profane Friendship*

the launched-arrows-the-battle-is-joined-smiles of hers
HAROLD BRODKEY *The Runaway Soul*

smiling awkwardly, like a single mussel placed on a large platter
and destined for the invited guest
MATT COHEN *Elizabeth and After*

His smile curled all the way round a room
TALITHA STEVENSON *An Empty Room*

[She] smiled the way sunlight came from behind the clouds
PAUL CODY *Eyes Like Mine*

a smile like a slice of watermelon
MARGARET SKINNER *Molly Flanagan and the Holy Ghost*

a need-a-drink smile
CHARLES FERNYHOUGH *The Auctioneer*

a smile on her like a downward crack on a yellow teapot
DESMOND HOGAN *Miles*

a cinematic, mid-twentieth-century smile
ANNE SCOTT *Calpurnia*

He flashed a smile like a torn photograph
JONATHAN LETHEM *The Fortress of Solitude*

[She] smiled into the room, radiating a look that would have gone
well as dessert after a magnificent meal
DAVID IRELAND *A Woman of the Future*

a phantom smile camped about the lips
DAVID LONG *The Daughters of Simon Lamoreaux*

[his] smile [like] some private store of sunlight he bestowed on you and only you
  RENÉE MANFREDI *Above the Thunder*

I have a smile like the core of an apple
  ANDREW SEAN GREER *The Confessions of Max Tivoli*

don't-bother-your-little-head smiles
  KATE JENNINGS *Moral Hazard*

she cracks a smile and it has an imperfection to it, frail Dresden china with a crack
  NANI POWER *Crawling at Night*

A smile tiptoed across the licked lips
  THEA ASTLEY *The Well Dressed Explorer*

a smile that crept out like a mouse
  THEA ASTLEY *The Slow Natives*

[His] smile is macho, backlit with an innuendo of violence
  JANETTE TURNER HOSPITAL *Due Preparations for the Plague*

[She] smiled mildly like some nineteenth-century portrait of a handsome young mother
  HAROLD BRODKEY *Innocence*

A smile, a weird one, nestled in his mouth like an egg
  LORRIE MOORE *You're Ugly, Too*

He finally smiled – something he did seldom enough to make it like the blast when you throw phosphorus off a bridge
  REYNOLDS PRICE *Kate Vaiden*

the sparse twist of his smile was a dry inchworm
  CYNTHIA OZICK *Heir to the Glimmering World*

a bright woman-of-the-house smile
  HUGH LEONARD *Fillums*

I thought of her smile, so like the light from a distant star
  TOM ENGELHARDT *The Last Days of Publishing*

her spun-steel-and-stardust smile
  CHARLES BAXTER *The Feast of Love*

an open-sewer smile
  CHARLES BAXTER *The Feast of Love*

her heated smile was chipped, hazy
  CYNTHIA OZICK *The Doctor's Wife*

She wore an odd smile, a neatly tied bow which only just kept the
trembling parcel of her face together
  PETER CAREY *Oscar and Lucinda*

a smile like open day in a porcelain factory
  ANGELA CARTER *The Merchant of Shadows*

a freshened-up smile that had sympathy for sons of ill mothers
in it
  PHILIP CALLOW *The Subway to New York*

her smile a piece of the moon
  ROBERT BOSWELL *Brilliant Mistake*

her marble memorial smile
  JOE COOMER *Beachcombing for a Shipwrecked God*

disconsolately smiling, like a dark Madonna in the brownish sea-
light of some old painting
  JOHN BANVILLE *Mefisto*

At street corners armies of youths lounged … their smiles splitting
into decay
  ITA DALY *A Singular Attraction*

He smiled a carrion smile
  STEVIE DAVIES *The Element of Water*

There was his smile, the smile that made her soul go wrong, that
blurred her mind like music
  TINA DE ROSA *Paper Fish*

[I] smiled my warmest smile – a Tuscan sun shimmering across
a valley of ripening vines that whisper to one another of
forthcoming Montepulciano
  EDWARD DOCX *The Calligrapher*

her smile with the one indented tooth, like a sticking piano key
  PETER CRAIG *Hot Plastic*

His smile, like an umbrella whooshed inside out
ANONYMOUS *The Bride Stripped Bare*

smiling in that just-baptized manner of hers
ANTHONY GIARDINA *Recent History*

She smiled with a certain unsurprising hardness, allowing nothing,
a Margaret Thatcher sort of smile
ANTHONY GIARDINA *Recent History*

the smile of a woman who has just dined off her husband
LAWRENCE DURRELL *Justine*

[Her smile] was without guile, like scallops cut in an apple turnover
THOMAS GLYNN *Watching the Body Burn*

the contours of his smile celebrating the whole of creation
ALAN WALL *China*

the smile was like the crêpe on a coffin
LAWRENCE DURRELL *Livia*

a smile you could warm your hands on
ANGELA CARTER *Wise Children*

[his] bogus, in-patient smile
BRUCE WAGNER *I'm Losing You*

her bravest smile-face (smile back along the hospital ward, smile in
the rain outside the crematorium)
TOBY LITT *Ghost Story*

smiling like a kid in a swimming pool
ROLAND MERULLO *A Little Love Story*

smog

smog lay thick over the valley, like a vast headache over a defeated
terrain
JANET FITCH *White Oleander*

smoke

city smoke like a stole
JANET FRAME *The Edge of the Alphabet*

smoke went up like a prayer
CHRISTINA STEAD *Seven Poor Men of Sydney*

smoke like the disturbed dressing of a Christmas tree
ALEX HAMILTON *Not Enough Poison*

[A] column of smoke curled like a black long stocking into the sky,
its head quickly dispersing at the shock of finding nothing to keep
it in shape
ALAN SILLITOE *Key to the Door*

a thin, frost-blue plume of smoke, sinuous, hurrying, like a chain
of shivery question marks
JOHN BANVILLE *The Untouchable*

the softness of the smoke that gathers like tulle over the town
RICHARD YAXLEY *The Rose Leopard*

smooth

smooth as the toes of kissed stone R.C. saints
LEONARD COHEN *Beautiful Losers*

smooth as paper in a dictionary
STANLEY ELKIN *The Condominium*

snow

snow, white hyphens dropping evenly
JANET FRAME *A Sense of Proportion*

snow fell like a great armistice
ELIZABETH HARDWICK *Sleepless Nights*

the snow like a rumpled dining table in the woods
LAWRENCE DURRELL *Monsieur*

the snow sifts down like crushed bone
T CORAGHESSAN BOYLE *Water Music*

A parachute of fresh snow
HUGH C RAE *The Saturday Epic*

The edges of the snow were molars in the mouth of night
TODD MCEWEN *Fisher's Hornpipe*

snow spun down the street ... like a flock of fiercely white and tiny
birds
CHARLOTTE BACON *Lost Geography*

All that snow, hip deep, as though the clouds had snagged themselves on the earth and unraveled
   GLEN HIRSHBERG *The Snowman's Children*

[Snow] would come down like a soundless rain of white hankies from shy and lonely ladies
   THYLIAS MOSS *Tale of a Sky-Blue Dress*

the continual blur of more snow, falling like soft boulders
   JANICE GALLOWAY *The Trick Is to Keep Breathing*

it is snow without any laughter in it, a pale gray pudding thinly spread on stiff toast
   WILLIAM H GASS *In the Heart of the Heart of the Country*

the snow was beautiful that night, lilting down from above like the notes of a symphony
   ROBERT BOSWELL *Century's Son*

a snow like nothing you have ever seen – white as a whip, blank, edible, maddening
   ALISON FELL *Mer de Glace*

sorrow

sorrow rose in her like a pair of wings
   KAREN E BENDER *Like Normal People*

sudden moments of sorrow that hurt like saw teeth across a careless thumb
   FRED CHAPPELL *Look Back All the Green Valley*

A sepia tone of sorrow glows within me
   DJ LEVIEN *Swagbelly*

soul

Their souls are miniscule, like commas in the compact *OED*
   ANDREI CODRESCU *Messiah*

She searched through her soul like a capuchin seeking fleas
   WILLIAM H GASS *The Tunnel*

I have a soul of hard-packed dung
   KEVIN MCILVOY *Hyssop*

her soul quivering like a huge mouth in a fairy tale
HAROLD BRODKEY *The Runaway Soul*

a soul as tender as an opal when it is freshly dug up from the earth
and fingernails can break it
DELIA FALCONER *The Service of Clouds*

speak

[He] spoke like a man obeying someone at a funeral
ANDRE DUBUS *Deaths at Sea*

she spoke with a flourish, as if her words were meant to be drawn
in calligraphy
COLIN CHANNER *Waiting in Vain*

He spoke ... as if he held cinnamon in his mouth
TRACY CHEVALIER *Girl with a Pearl Earring*

They spoke as if each word were being served with scones and
china cups
COLUM MCCANN *Hunger Strike*

he speaks like a man rewriting the Bible
SALLY RENA *The Sea Road West*

[He] spoke slowly and assuredly, like a lecturer, shaping his
sentences and stacking them on end with the palms of his hands
LLOYD JONES *Biografi*

She ... spoke in the way of a biblical moll
STEVE ALMOND *The Pass*

She spoke like popular fiction
HAROLD BRODKEY *Largely an Oral History of My Mother*

he spoke at moron rpm
JONATHAN LETHEM *The Fortress of Solitude*

[He] spoke ... like something whispered in the bowl of a radar dish
STEVE AYLETT *Atom*

staircase

[a] staircase that went up in florid curves, like Mae West
ANGELA CARTER *Wise Children*

star

stars like luminous breadcrumbs on some mighty tablecloth
  ALAN SILLITOE *Key to the Door*

oxy-acetylene stars
  ALAN SILLITOE *A Tree on Fire*

taut stars
  LAWRENCE DURRELL *The Black Book*

the stars hugely unconcerned
  JOHN RECHY *City of Night*

Singly, like delayed guests arriving at a dance, appearing stars
pierced the sky
  TRUMAN CAPOTE *The Grass Harp*

stars were scarcely visible, spies from the banked-down furnace of
the universe
  PETER VANSITTART *A Little Madness*

the stars were white and blue and yellow in the sky like a bowl of
delirium
  FRED CHAPPELL *Brighten the Corner Where You Are*

stars were slipping overhead like a thick fabric
  BRAD KESSLER *Lick Creek*

a spongy field of algal stars
  IAIN SINCLAIR *Radon Daughters*

stars like a run of the right hand in a piece by Liszt
  WILLIAM H GASS *The Tunnel*

stars as lonely as a single spat tooth rattling around in a cuspidor
  ALBERT GOLDBARTH *Pieces of Payne*

A star ... shimmers like a tear anxious to drop
  DARIN STRAUSS *The Real McCoy*

The sky was black, its stars digitally bright
  DAVID BOWKER *The Death You Deserve*

stars rioting away
  COLUM McCANN *Songdogs*

Sometimes the stars are thrillingly sharp ... private needle-holes of exactitude in the stygian diorama

NICHOLSON BAKER *A Box of Matches*

the last star still hanging in the [dawn] sky like a hanky someone forgot on the clothesline

LAURA KALPAKIAN *And Departing Leave Behind Us*

stare

you stare like a wife murdered a century ago

PENELOPE SHUTTLE *The Mirror of the Giant*

[He] stared like a man in a Fuseli painting

VICTOR SAVAGE *Little Goethe*

staring like a man casing the ocean

DAVID WAGONER *The Escape Artist*

Her stare could have drilled a hole through a diamond

BERNARD COOPER *A Year of Rhymes*

He stares at me like I'm a piece of slime with three heads of former US Presidents

TIBOR FISCHER *The Collector Collector*

I saw [him] staring behind me like a stretch of bad road

TIBOR FISCHER *The Thought Gang*

[He] had the proud, moistened, middle-distance stare of a man who believes himself to have been gravely and perhaps insupportably traduced

MARTIN AMIS *The Information*

He could feel the stares harden from a ticklish cloud into something wiry like cat whiskers

CHRISTOPHER BRAM *Lives of the Circus Animals*

They continued to stare, mouths open, exactly like figures in a very depressed Aunt Sally

MAVIS CHEEK *Mrs Fytton's Country Life*

a waxy faraway stare like someone gazing through the smoked-glass windows of purgatory

DENIS HAMILL *Sins of Two Fathers*

She stared at him, as if he were a portrait in a gallery, searching for flaws or signature brush strokes
DENIS HAMILL *Long Time Gone*

still

as still as a railway sleeper
DONALD HUTLEY *The Swan*

still as plate glass
LAWRENCE DURRELL *Monsieur*

as still as the oceans of the moon
ANDREW HOLLERAN *Dancer from the Dance*

story

the indiscriminate birdshot of her life story
DAVID LONG *Life As We Know It*

stream

a slow, tiny stream, which trickled and glided gingerly over rocks, like something afraid of hurting itself
LORRIE MOORE *What Is Seized*

street

[The] street lay drugged in sleep
CHRISTINA STEAD *Seven Poor Men of Sydney*

[The] street was always in a state of sleazy undress
EL WALLANT *Children at the Gate*

Lamplit streets passed by like trills of piano-played light
JEREMY LELAND *While the Country Sleeps*

the sun-burnt, brain-burnt streets
KATHY ACKER *Empire of the Senseless*

through rain, the streets ... looked like the insides of an old plug
MARTIN AMIS *The Information*

one of the small, depopulated streets that laced downtown like blocked veins
STEPHEN AMIDON *The Primitive*

The street looked like a woman who'd seen enough of life and wanted to sleep it off, push the guy away from her, go home, except she couldn't. She was home
LYNNE TILLMAN *No Lease on Life*

streets like throats
ROSALIND BELBEN *The Limit*

the afternoon-soaked streets
RICHARD POWERS *Plowing the Dark*

The streets seeming longer and longer. Stretching out like a ribbon unrolled in a fit of rage and then not put back up again. Left out and unfurled. Somebody's hard work
MELINDA HAYNES *Mother of Pearl*

streets that ran away like bad children
JAMES BUCHAN *The Golden Plough*

the street silver, like the trail of a slug
MARTHA BERGLAND *Idle Curiosity*

the granite-crushing street
JANICE GALLOWAY *Clara*

Four stories below, the street was its usual furnace-clot of cars
ALLISON BURNETT *Christopher*

The street looks like an old movie shot through a vaselined lens
JANICE GALLOWAY *The Trick Is to Keep Breathing*

summer

summer went on emptily, like TV with the sound turned off
PETER VANSITTART *Quintet*

summer was moving forward, a perfectly launched ship
PETER VANSITTART *Pastimes of a Red Summer*

summer has shut down on us like handcuffs
LAWRENCE DURRELL *The Black Book*

summer had come to the city like a youth gang appearing suddenly on the corner: sullen, physical, odorous and exciting, charged up with ungrounded electricity
JAY MCINERNEY *Brightness Falls*

sun

[The] sun twitched like an extra nerve in the mind
    JANET FRAME *The Mythmaker's Office*

[the] sun erupting its contagious boils of light
    JANET FRAME *The Mythmaker's Office*

the sun a hammer at midday
    NICOLAS FREELING *This Is the Castle*

[the] powerful sun policing the earth
    JANET FRAME *Faces in the Water*

[The] sun sat in the empty sky like a judge
    PETER VANSITTART *Sources of Unrest*

[the] pale sun like a ball of pollen
    MERVYN PEAKE *Gormenghast*

[The] sun fell warm as gloves
    ANGELA CARTER *Several Perceptions*

a raw sun was sawing at them
    PATRICK WHITE *The Solid Mandala*

each evening, the shipwrecked sun unloaded its cargoes of
marigolds
    DANNIE ABSE *Ash on a Young Man's Sleeve*

the sun like a forgotten spotlight
    JG BALLARD *The Unlimited Dream Company*

the sun appeared like the pale flag of a foreign country
    SUSAN KERSLAKE *Middlewatch*

a miserable sun all salted by a little bladed wind
    SEBASTIAN BARRY *The Whereabouts of Eneas McNulty*

The sun was pinned to the creaseless sky – a medal on a soldier's
chest
    COLIN CHANNER *Waiting in Vain*

The sun pressed against the earth like a paw on a bird
    ELIZABETH JORDAN MOORE *Cold Times*

the sun is coming up like a small red tranquilliser
    COLUM MCCANN *Stolen Child*

the obscured sun straining through like a cyclamen bruise
DAVID PROFUMO *Sea Music*

the sun in its autumn yawn
PETER GADOL *Light at Dusk*

It was gloomy now, the sun sickening behind them
KEITH RIDGWAY *Never Love a Gambler*

The late sun was a warm hand on my throat
ALYSON HAGY *Ballad and Sadness*

a brochure sun
EMMA TENNANT *Queen of Stones*

There was a bit of watery sun about, like a light bulb behind a
shower curtain
BRUCE ROBINSON *The Peculiar Memories of Thomas Penman*

the sun's bare ribs poking through the clouds
JEFFERY RENARD ALLEN *Rails under My Back*

the sun felt soft as a cat
SONYA HARTNETT *Of a Boy*

the sun like a fevered hand resting on the back of our necks
MARK SLOUKA *God's Fool*

[the] sun, looking down at us like an eye at a telescope
AL KENNEDY *So I Am Glad*

The sun was a twitchy lip-color ribbon across the Hudson
DARIN STRAUSS *The Real McCoy*

The sun rode up high and white like a pearl wrapped in alabaster
CHRISTOPHER COOK *Robbers*

The sun – a great burnished ingot emerging from the ocean like
salvaged treasure
JANETTE TURNER HOSPITAL *The Tiger in the Tiger Pit*

the sky was streaky, with this little punk-point of a sun
DAVID LONG *The Daughters of Simon Lamoreaux*

the sun shining through the layers of [mist] all blurred and rosy
like a peach gently on fire
MARGARET ATWOOD *Alias Grace*

the sun suddenly bursts through again, lighting up the trees like an idea
  LORRIE MOORE *Anagrams*

There was a pale winter sun lemoning the sky
  MAVIS CHEEK *Pause Between Acts*

the sun inching its complex geometry across the dusty floors
  JOHN BANVILLE *Mefisto*

The sun was dropping towards the rooftops, slowly, slowly, and it looked for all the world like a large spoonful of golden sweetness slipping from the sky
  MAVIS CHEEK *Sleeping Beauties*

The sun's like a coin that's been buried for years
  SONYA HARTNETT *Surrender*

The sun burned like a silver sore place low in the gray November sky
  JOHN UPDIKE *Killing*

The late sun was hazing the valley, like a huge gauzy bee dusting the plushy fields with pollen
  MARION HALLIGAN *Spider Cup*

Sunday

Sunday is always a bad day. A sort of gray purgatory that resembles a bus station with broken vending machines
  LORRIE MOORE *Anagrams*

Sunday like a whole day of evenings sewn together, vacant
  PHILIP CALLOW *Clipped Wings*

sunlight

the sunlight climbed the hillside, rolling its ladder up after it as it went
  ELIZABETH KNOX *Treasure*

sunlight is glittering on the godly Hudson River like some sudden fad
  ALLAN GURGANUS *Plays Well with Others*

The sunlight peers in ... like the hand of a stranger in the
possessions of an old woman
SEBASTIAN BARRY *Annie Dunne*

The dying sunlight bled on us, warm and cidery on the back of my
neck
PHILIP CALLOW *The Bliss Body*

In the hall a rhomb of sunlight basked on the floor, like a reclining
acrobat
JOHN BANVILLE *Mefisto*

we ... watched the sunlight as it faded like applause
DELIA FALCONER *The Service of Clouds*

sunrise

sunrise was opening the kitchen
BRET ANTHONY JOHNSTON *The Widow*

sunset

a deep stippled cracked egg of a sunset
T CORAGHESSAN BOYLE *A Friend of the Earth*

a beautiful sunset is the day taking a bow
SARAH WILLIS *Some Things That Stay*

a joke pink sunset
CANDIDA CREWE *The Last to Know*

the sunset gets redder and looks like a treasure chest being creaked
open
ELIZA MINOT *The Tiny One*

Sunsets fell through the western sky, the colour of blood through a
fistful of water
COLUM MCCANN *Songdogs*

an unframed Turner sunset burned itself slowly
LAWRENCE DURRELL *Livia*

the sun went down ... in a gradual catastrophe of reds and golds
JOHN BANVILLE *Ghosts*

The sun going down in old gold scraggles like in a Flemish painting
DESMOND HOGAN *A Farewell to Prague*

the sun declining in ghastly blood-streaked splendour like a public execution across, it would seem, half a continent
ANGELA CARTER *Nights at the Circus*

Outside, it was one of those sunsets that nobody looks at, a red and orange and purple massacre, spilling its guts out above the city
JANE MENDELSOHN *Innocence*

our magnificent smoggy New York sunsets, creamy purple, amber and pink suspended over the river like a slice of melting spumoni
LYNNE SHARON SCHWARTZ *The Fatigue Artist*

sunshine

The sunshine seems hollow and buoyant as the bones of birds
RALPH LOMBREGLIA *Monarchs*

suspicion

The edge of suspicion in the room seemed to sharpen the tines of forks
DELIA FALCONER *The Service of Clouds*

sweat

sweat on his forehead like a field of blisters
GREG BOTTOMS *A Seat for the Coming Savior*

he feels her sweat like a sweet acid from dead leaves
HAROLD BRODKEY *Lila and S.L.*

his forehead suddenly sweating like a picnic cheese
CINTRA WILSON *Colors Insulting to Nature*

syllables

The syllables seemed stitched with their own spangles of last century history, thrown together by no accident to spell out a past in this area
THEA ASTLEY *Vanishing Points*

Syllables ... alight ... like geese in a dimly lit yard
HAROLD BRODKEY *Religion*

syntax

every syllable washing him into fears he didn't want to have
AL KENNEDY *Everything You Need*

the raw tick of syllables
AL KENNEDY *Everything You Need*

The long syllables slid down his tongue like gravy
RICK DEMARINIS *Experience*

He was helpless before the segue of her syllables
JANETTE TURNER HOSPITAL *Borderline*

[my] syllables deliberate, tidy as needlepoint
LORRIE MOORE *Anagrams*

syntax

the syntax spat like rivets
IAIN SINCLAIR *White Chappell, Scarlet Tracings*

taillights

[The] taillights of the car receded, red eyes of a night animal racing backward
SARAH STONICH *These Granite Islands*

talk

talk that traveled like roads into the night
LORRIE MOORE *Who Will Run the Frog Hospital?*

You talk like some book you've reviewed
WILLIAM H GASS *The Tunnel*

bright gouges of talk
JOYCE CAROL OATES *Because It Is Bitter, and Because It Is My Heart*

tear

[His] tears make tiny trails … like lonely little rivers that have really nothing to water
ALISTAIR MACLEOD *In the Fall*

the tears left his eyes like small creeks running, like rain on long bony land
GILLIAN MEARS *In the Heart of the Sky*

teeth

long clean teeth jumped out like bayonets from ambush
CLIVE BARRY *Crumb Borne*

ivory gears of teeth
JEREMY LELAND *The Jonah*

teeth like headstones under a winter moon
  PAUL SMITH *Come Trailing Blood*

yellowed teeth like discoloured choirboys
  ANGELA CARTER *The Magic Toyshop*

teeth which lean this way and that like terraced houses propping
each other after a bomb explosion
  DIANA FARR *Choosing*

[His] teeth were like a rank of men in macs on a stadium terrace,
tugged into this or that position by the groans of the crowd
  MARTIN AMIS *The Information*

harp-strung teeth
  SUNETRA GUPTA *The Glassblower's Breath*

her straight white teeth glamorizing the air surrounding her
  JOYCE WEATHERFORD *Heart of the Beast*

an ivory gate of young teeth
  CHRISTOPHER BRAM *The Notorious Dr August*

Her teeth were crowded to the front of her mouth as if they were
ready for an argument
  ALICE MUNRO *Hateship, Friendship, Courtship, Loveship, Marriage*

His teeth dazzled like Mexican bone dice
  IAIN SINCLAIR *Downriver*

her teeth ... were large and folded slightly in on one another as if
they refused to let her face forget its childhood
  STEPHEN MARION *Hollow Ground*

the teeth of a sunbelt golf pro
  MARTIN AMIS *Yellow Dog*

Teeth like a row of alabaster Britannicas
  JOE COOMER *Kentucky Love*

his teeth ... those rotting, crooked, dun-colored enamel placards of
his
  DJ LEVIEN *Swagbelly*

his little corn-niblet teeth
  KRISTIN WATERFIELD DUISBERG *The Good Patient*

the way her teeth snap, like a toy lock
WILLIAM H GASS *Omensetter's Luck*

her teeth shone generous and wet, the creamy incisors curved as cashews
LORRIE MOORE *Terrific Mother*

a skeleton staff of teeth
MARTIN AMIS *The Information*

his teeth, like unregistered weapons
CAI EMMONS *His Mother's Son*

her big smile ... that offered a view of her hundred-octane teeth
ANGELA CARTER *Wise Children*

thighs

... thighs bulge out like cream from an éclair
JEREMY LELAND *Lirri*

the upturned hulls of her thighs
JEREMY LELAND *A River Decrees*

her Bambi thighs
MARTIN AMIS *Success*

Her thighs were the covers of an open book – a journal lined with fantasies and fears
COLIN CHANNER *Waiting in Vain*

her thighs like a triumphal arch but unable to speak the Latin tongue
ROBERT NYE *A Portuguese Person*

'Cello thighs
BERYL BAINBRIDGE *Harriet Said*

Her thighs and hips had an unyielding engineered quality: I imagined them moving things: steel beams, drawbridges
LOUIS BAYARD *Endangered Species*

thighs like big logs gone to termites
DANIEL BUCKMAN *The Names of Rivers*

thought

a vast newsprint of thought
WILLIAM SANSOM *The Body*

... thought tadpoled through her mind
JULIA O'FAOLAIN *Godded and Codded*

thoughts spilled out like a crowd angry at being deluded
JEREMY LELAND *The Tower*

a thought suddenly set fire to the virgin steppes of her brain
ANDREW SINCLAIR *The Project*

[a] thought at the back of his mind, like the tiny persistent
scratching of a broken-backed mouse
WILLIAM VINCENT BURGESS *Second-Hand Persons*

The thought depressed him, like a glimpse of some great undone
task
STEPHEN AMIDON *The Primitive*

the thought of being apart ... had gathered like a monsoon gloom
within his veins
SUNETRA GUPTA *Memories of Rain*

the slightest thought working its way across her face, like a bit of
weather
LORRIE MOORE *Who Will Run the Frog Hospital?*

thoughts crept like cold oil around her brain
JEFFREY CAINE *The Cold Room*

like an invisible rusty crane, thought was beginning to heave and
grind and crank
RT PLUMB *A Pebble from Rome*

his thoughts ... felt like a large handful of slippery and
uncooperative credit cards
DAVID IRELAND *The Chosen*

squadrons of passionless mouse-grey thoughts trooping without
hitch round his skull
LINDA ANDERSON *Cuckoo*

thoughts rising like baroque remains in a tropical jungle
PATRICK WHITE *The Twyborn Affair*

My thoughts move like a man who has to pass from his salon to his library and is disturbed by what he encounters on the way
    PETER VANSITTART *Pastimes of a Red Summer*

thoughts gripped like a row of oily hands from a torpedoed crew
    HUGO CHARTERIS *The Coat*

her thoughts coursed thinly through her consciousness like the veiny desiccation of ivy on old church walls
    SUNETRA GUPTA *Memories of Rain*

My thoughts were bumping together like moored boats
    NICOLA GRIFFITH *Stay*

her thoughts ... gradually gain on each other like the slow-moving curves on the back of a centipede
    JACQUELINE ROSE *Albertine*

my thoughts ... came like doors opening and faces looking in
    BARBARA ESSTMAN *Night Ride Home*

there was a terrible thought trapped by the weight of his panic, like a spider under an upturned glass
    KEITH RIDGWAY *The Parts*

A thought passes through my mind like a cat walking on my shoulders behind my neck
    HAROLD BRODKEY *A Guest in the Universe*

[Her] thoughts come sniffing like underfed dogs
    CHRISTINA GARCIA *Dreaming in Cuban*

Her thoughts swirl like smashed embers
    JANETTE TURNER HOSPITAL *Oyster*

a thought bombing like an electron across the dark screen of his brain
    STEWART O'NAN *The Night Country*

she held the thought in her mouth, like a cupped bird
    ANDREW SEAN GREER *The Confessions of Max Tivoli*

thoughts whirling like flimsy [fish] scales flashing in a sink's wetness
    NANI POWER *Crawling at Night*

The thought … felt as distant and cool as a handsome old house
seen from a fast car, trailing off in the dusk of a rearview mirror
  REYNOLDS PRICE *The Promise of Rest*

The thought burrowed in me like a fever tick
  LORRIE MOORE *Anagrams*

Thoughts came relentlessly and in a pattern but not a logical one,
more like the pattern on a carpet
  ROBERT BOSWELL *Century's Son*

thoughts moving in her, hard as little glaciers
  PAULETTE JILES *Sitting in the Club Car*

the thought flashed up like a nasty fin out of the water
  ROSELLEN BROWN *Before and After*

the *camera obscura* of the thoughts which filled his mind
  LAWRENCE DURRELL *Justine*

a cumulus of thought
  LAWRENCE DURRELL *Livia*

thought stirring his face like a spoon
  SUSAN WHEELER *Record Palace*

the thought grew like a confident sapling
  RICHARD FLANAGAN *The Sound of One Hand Clapping*

throat

the tulip-stem stance of your throat
  JOHN UPDIKE *The Centaur*

a throat like a brick-kiln
  CHRISTOPHER LEACH *The Send-Off*

a throat clearing like a rusty bolt
  PHILIP CALLOW *The Bliss Body*

thunder

the Michelangelo thunder of an Indian summer storm
  JOYCE WEATHERFORD *Heart of the Beast*

the coughing of faraway thunder
  NICK FOWLER *A Thing (or Two) about Curtis and Camilla*

The blackberry sickness of incipient thunder
IAIN SINCLAIR *Radon Daughters*

time

time works like a damp brush on water-colour
JOHN STEINBECK *East of Eden*

time seemed to be turning from a liquid into a powder
STEFAN KANFER *The Eighth Sin*

time passed like ivory beads on a black thread
JOHN HAWKES *Travesty*

time like cement blocks tied to a stool pigeon's leg
ANNE ROIPHE *Long Division*

time was a slow, sweet secretion
ELIZABETH KNOX *Treasure*

time compressed itself into a crystalline trinket, lodging on the
highest shelf of [her] memory
SARAH STONICH *These Granite Islands*

[She] felt time drag like a rusted tailpipe, abrasive and combustible
TERRY WOLVERTON *Bailey's Beads*

bits of time disappeared like old pennies
GREG BOTTOMS *A Seat for the Coming Savior*

Time bent away from me like a tail-dancing rainbow
RICK DEMARINIS *Weeds*

[He] spent time like linty change fished up from the pockets of his
jeans
WILLIAM GAY *The Long Home*

time wore on her nerves like a road drill
JILL NEVILLE *The Love Germ*

Time wound its Möbius strip
MICHAEL LOWENTHAL *The Same Embrace*

Time cleared its throat and tapped its brand-new watch
EDWARD DOCX *The Calligrapher*

Time crawled past on leaden hands and knees
SONYA HARTNETT *Surrender*

This is how time runs: like some stoked-up, stage-sick kid in his first talent show
RICHARD POWERS *The Time of Our Singing*

tiredness

tiredness as soft as padded satin, the tiredness of a seaside day
GRACE INGOLDBY *Bring Out Your Dead*

toes

toes ... like five little red tugboats all ready to dock
LEON ROOKE *A Good Baby*

tongue

[his] tongue hanging out of his mouth like a fish dried in sulphur
ROBERT SHAW *The Man in the Glass Booth*

... tongue lay in its mouth as harmless as a sandwich
TONI MORRISON *Song of Solomon*

tongues curled back to the roots of forgotten words
JOHN HAWKES *The Cannibal*

Her tongue a biblical lash
SHANE CONNAUGHTON *The Run of the Country*

the rag folds of his damp tongue
SUNETRA GUPTA *The Glassblower's Breath*

her tongue flashed briefly between her teeth like the bright, licentious opening of a flower
ANDREW CRUMEY *Mr Mee*

Hostilities make her tongue an iron spike
MAURICE GEE *Sole Survivor*

His tongue felt like a foreigner. A king-sized Polish sausage gone bad
MELINDA HAYNES *Mother of Pearl*

Big pink tongue sitting in his mouth like a meal
MAURICE GEE *Prowlers*

her sweet-sherry tongue
MARTIN AMIS *Success*

his tongue rolled in his mouth like a frightened frankfurter
ANGELA CARTER *Shadow Dance*

toupee

his coal black toupee fit his head like a single sock drying on a tin mailbox
JOE COOMER *One Vacant Chair*

town

[the] town looking like a jumble of wool bales dropped from some passing wagon
JON CLEARY *The Sundowners*

wet towns in the distance were like wooden uneven nailheads hammered into the earth
ALAN SILLITOE *The Death of William Posters*

stuffy, chapel-ridden little towns
HE BATES *The Fabulous Mrs V*

The town looked over-laundered
SERENA HILSINGER *Still Life*

The town was a blur of grey, like a model waiting to be painted
LAVINIA GREENLAW *Mary George of Allnorthover*

traffic

the cyclotron of one-way West End traffic
MARTIN AMIS *London Fields*

traffic hurrying to make way for the silence of the small hours
RUSSELL HOBAN *Angelica's Grotto*

The traffic sounds below ride the night air in waves of trigonometry, the cosine of a siren, the tangent of a sigh, a system, an axis, a logic to this chaos, yes
LORRIE MOORE *Go Like This*

an outrage of traffic like the silent forced evacuation of Hell
REYNOLDS PRICE *The Promise of Rest*

The traffic slurred in the street far below
CHRISTOPHER BRAM *Lives of the Circus Animals*

the iron centipede of traffic
DENIS HAMILL *Sins of Two Fathers*

train

Deep in the woods, a train blew a mournful chord, like a great harmonica
STEWART O'NAN *A World Away*

The train is going through evening like a detective through somebody's drawers
PAULETTE JILES *Sitting in the Club Car*

The train charges down the tracks into the blackening happy night, down the typeface of the double rails and ties, as if it were a typewriter carriage engaged upon an endless sentence
PAULETTE JILES *Sitting in the Club Car*

tree

trees like men stooping
JEREMY LELAND *The Tower*

trees wringing their hands behind your back
MARTIN AMIS *Success*

formal trees stood like guests
PETER VANSITTART *Landlord*

old trees ranged like solemn guests
ALICE THOMAS ELLIS *The Birds of the Air*

trees like fixed explosions on the afternoon
WILLIAM FAULKNER *Mosquitoes*

trees laden to the plimsoll-line with a dreaming cargo of birds
ANGELA CARTER *The Magic Toyshop*

trees tilted like named corpses
JOHN EHLE *The Winter People*

trees as fragile as the legs of listening deer
LEONARD COHEN *The Favourite Game*

trees were thin and bare like hurried cobwebs
JENNIFER FITZWILLIAM *Anyway, This Particular Sunday*

begging trees on the mountain crisp as a child's brain
DERMOT HEALY *First Snow of the Year*

the trees stood in their fall leaves like nerves in a burned hand
CLAIRE CRESWELL *Ten Seconds*

trees ... looked like shadowy dignified bankers
RT PLUMB *A Pebble from Rome*

Outside ... trees plotted and spied upon our half-shuttered evening windows, sending leafy warnings to the lonely men sprawled with their sticky dreams upon their bachelor beds
THEA ASTLEY *The Multiple Effects of Rainshadow*

the particularly massive carcass of a tree lay like an ancient beast, gray in weird decay
TIM FARRINGTON *Blues for Hannah*

great trees rocking like a Pentecostal choir, thrashing in a wind invisible but moving like the Holy Ghost
COLIN CHANNER *Satisfy My Soul*

trees like bombers coming in low
T CORAGHESSAN BOYLE *Drop City*

trees ... dark-foliaged as etchings
MARGARET ATWOOD *The Grave of the Famous Poet*

the Rorschach trees
WILLIAM GAY *I Hate to See That Evening Sun Go Down*

trees like runs of ink on a white page
WILLIAM GAY *The Man Who Knew Dylan*

trees ... like masked attendants at a ceremony
JOHN BANVILLE *Ghosts*

The trees around me were in new leaf, shyly pointillist
HAROLD BRODKEY *Hofstedt and Jean – and Others*

The stubby trees hunched up like pinched and twisted spinsters
NICOLA BARKER *Behindlings*

the trees were big graffiti scribbles happening on the sky
LESLEY GLAISTER *Now You See Me*

The tree lay back against the sky like a licked postage stamp
CYNTHIA OZICK *The Pagan Rabbi*

The trees groped each other in bony clusters, sharp-edged against
a quilted sky
WILL EAVES *The Oversight*

One bare black tree was pressed against the sky, like the cross
section of a lung
GLEN DUNCAN *Love Remains*

trees at the edge of the lawn nodded like bishops in convocation
MAURICE GEE *The Scornful Moon*

the autumn trees which fretted the sky with shattered Gothic
tracery
ALAN WALL *China*

Nearby, a bulbous conifer tilted like a giant microphone awaiting a
quote from the sky
GLEN DUNCAN *Death of an Ordinary Man*

above them, a dinosaur fig tree ... bowed over them like a hand in
its hundredth year of slowly closing
KEVIN MCILVOY *Hyssop*

palm trees rising up out of the smog like the tapering, reticulated
necks of Mesozoic beasts
T CORAGHESSAN BOYLE *A Friend of the Earth*

the mountain poplars are spending their yellow coins like
gamblers
PAULETTE JILES *Sitting in the Club Car*

The willows at the foot of the lawn looked exhausted this morning,
like the unwashed hair of overworked waitresses
KATE CHRISTENSEN *The Epicure's Lament*

an old man willow, its branches and leaves trailing in the still water
like hands hanging lazily from an Oxford punt
PAUL BRANDON *The Wild Reel*

willow trees bent over the wide river like things about to drink
GREG BOTTOMS *Levi's Tongue*

truth

His truth was thin as prison soup
IAIN SINCLAIR *Dining on Stones*

twilight

When twilight shadows the sky it is as if a soft bell were tolling dismissal
TRUMAN CAPOTE *Other Voices, Other Rooms*

twilight ran in like a quiet violet dog
WILLIAM FAULKNER *Mosquitoes*

the twilight wandered down ... stooping like a willow bough
JOHN WRAY *The Right Hand of Sleep*

vague

[She] is as vague as a bowl of rice
JAY MCINERNEY *Model Behaviour*

vein

long veins like wind-swept branches
BETH ARCHER BROMBERT *A Concert of Hells*

veins rose like moleruns
FD REEVE *White Colours*

the veins ... ripped through her legs like blue barbed wire
SHANE CONNAUGHTON *A Border Station*

veins that tree and knot under the skin of her hands
RON HANSEN *Mariette in Ecstasy*

two veins that intersect like rural routes on a map
STEVE ALMOND *Geek Player, Love Slayer*

red veins squiggling in every direction like secondary roads on an old map
GREG BOTTOMS *The Metaphor*

The blue of her veins was even clearer on her breasts, under the clear white skin, like some gorgeous secret
JOE COOMER *Kentucky Love*

A vein pulsed bright as embered stick along his hairline
LEON ROOKE *A Good Baby*

Her veins bleating in her neck
JANETTE TURNER HOSPITAL *The Tiger in the Tiger Pit*

A vein flutters and twitches like a blemish in finest porcelain
JANETTE TURNER HOSPITAL *The Tiger in the Tiger Pit*

the vein across his calf is almost repulsive, like a lizard on a rock
JONATHAN BUCKLEY *Invisible*

Veins rose, eskers on the back of his hand
COLUM McCANN *Songdogs*

The spidery veins at his temples seemed like things under water, tentacular and drowned
LORRIE MOORE *The Jewish Hunter*

the veins in his forehead standing out like ill-advised volunteers
STEVE AYLETT *The Crime Studio*

a little insect of a vein battled against his skin
ROSELLEN BROWN *Before and After*

My veins were like rivers bringing warm bliss on the king tide through the glacial landscapes of my taut muscles
LUKE DAVIES *Candy*

veins that run like underground utilities
THOMAS GLYNN *Watching the Body Burn*

The veins in his temples swelled like candelabra
BRUCE WAGNER *I'm Losing You*

village

villages looked like faint negatives
JOAN ALEXANDER *Thy People, My People*

the whole wintry village looks like a Nazi medical experiment
LEONARD COHEN *Beautiful Losers*

Here and there, isolated half-timbered villages poked out between new industrial terrains, like traces of fresco from under annihilating renovations
RICHARD POWERS *Galatea 2.2*

[The village] lay before him like an unpainted model of a town made by a boy with a dull pocketknife
TIM GAUTREAUX *The Clearing*

There were villages pressed into [the valley's] curves, like cups lined with scales of slate
AL KENNEDY *Bracing Up*

the sucked-in bones of a village after an aerial bombardment
COLUM McCANN *Songdogs*

voice

an undressed voice
JANET FRAME *The Edge of the Alphabet*

[a] voice as small as a moth
RICHARD CHOPPING *The Fly*

[a] voice like a plantation overseer's
AC CLARKE *Amongst Thistles and Thorns*

[a] voice almost tweedy, almost clubman
PETER VANSITTART *Landlord*

[a] voice like hundreds and thousands
JANET FRAME *Owls Do Cry*

[a] voice intense and brilliant as a streak of blood
SALLIE BINGHAM *A New Life*

his voice floated out of his soft head like a paper streamer
MERVYN PEAKE *Gormenghast*

[a] voice like the warm, sick notes of some prodigious mouldering bell of felt
MERVYN PEAKE *Titus Groan*

voices like tiny knives scratched on very small plates
ANGELA CARTER *Several Perceptions*

a small cornucopia of a voice
JEREMY LELAND *The Jonah*

the voice crumbled, becoming a rusty outraged squeak like a well sucking dust
KEN KESEY *Sometimes a Great Notion*

[a] leatherbound meeting-house voice
  KEN KESEY *Sometimes a Great Notion*

[a] voice like soft soot pouring through the twilight
  LYNNE REID BANKS *Two Is Lonely*

a more than averagely plastic-and-offal lilt in his mealy new voice
  MARTIN AMIS *Success*

a voice which sounded as though he was perpetually swallowing a
mouthful of expensive whisky together with a few fox hairs
  ALICE THOMAS ELLIS *The Birds of the Air*

a stop-watch voice
  PATRICK WHITE *The Vivisector*

a voice that could bring bodies up from deep waters
  PAUL SMITH *Come Trailing Blood*

the voice of magnolia blossoms and Corinthian columns
  ANNE ROIPHE *Torch Song*

a voice like a pat of butter
  LAWRENCE DURRELL *The Black Book*

The sound of a father's voice is various: like film burning, like
marble being pulled screaming from the face of a quarry, like
the clash of paper clips by night, lime seething in a lime pit, or
batsong
  DONALD BARTHELME *The Dead Father*

[the] voice of a crow reared on honey
  ANGELA CARTER *Black Venus*

her voice was flat, like a wide river without any undertow
  TONI MORRISON *Tar Baby*

[a] voice like an earache in the brain
  TONI MORRISON *The Bluest Eye*

her voice like a hand over his hair
  PHILIP CALLOW *Flesh of Morning*

his voice was tipped with tungsten
  FORBES BRAMBLE *Fools*

a breaking E-string voice
ANTHONY BURGESS *The Right to an Answer*

a voice like a note of a distant hymn heard in moonlight
HUGO CHARTERIS *Marching with April*

a voice suitable for laying a foundation stone
SUMNER LOCKE ELLIOTT *Careful, He Might Hear You*

a voice like a sixteen foot organ-stop
ANTHONY BURGESS *Tremor of Intent*

[a] voice like an army with banners
ANGELA CARTER *The Passion of New Eve*

his voice was formal, like an arrest
PETER VANSITTART *Landlord*

a voice sludged with the bottom of wine bottles
KATHARINE MOORE *Fitter's Night*

Her voice was on English tip-toe
SHIRLEY HAZZARD *The Transit of Venus*

their voices sounded like a wireless left on in a burning room
HUGO CHARTERIS *A Share of the World*

a wire-clipping voice
CHRISTY BROWN *Wild Grow the Lilies*

... diner-club-car voice
ALEX HAMILTON *Flies on the Wall*

Her voice goes on the prowl
PENELOPE SHUTTLE *Wailing Monkey Embracing a Tree*

a voice like bone marrow
WILL CHRISTOPHER BAER *Kiss Me, Judas*

Gentle voices in incessant talk surrounded him ... like an aviary with no roof where the birds had been taught to speak Russian
LOUIS BEGLEY *The Man Who Was Late*

The tenor voice that pulled the heart tight as the cross-stitch of a doubled thread
MICHAEL DORRIS *Cloud Chamber*

her voice slapping just like salt water
  KEN KESEY *Sailor Song*

a voice like a sulky hornet
  KEN KESEY *Sailor Song*

[her] voice ... like a cloudy palace of uncountable ramparts
  DAVID HART *Come to the Edge*

her voice was weighted down as if her words were little balls of
buckshot that fitfully rolled up through her windpipe without any
firm sense of direction
  CONNIE MAY FOWLER *Before Women Had Wings*

a salesman's voice, full of unearned bonhomie
  ANN HARLEMAN *Happiness*

his voice a grappling-iron
  DAVID IRELAND *The Chosen*

her voice had a laugh in it, like a display of fresh vegetables
  DAVID IRELAND *The Chosen*

[her] voice like the cry of a bird lost in a storm
  GREG HRBEK *The Hindenburg Crashes Nightly*

her voice as ominously level as thin ice
  MARK O'DONNELL *Getting Over Homer*

His voice is nothing fancier than a sweet knotty rope that he lets
out of his throat
  BART SCHNEIDER *Blue Bossa*

[His] voice strongly resembled a Phantom jet in the hands of a
developing nation
  RICHARD POWERS *Three Farmers on Their Way to a Dance*

His voice was embalmed
  JAMES BAKER *Fuel Injected Dreams*

His voice [was] thin and quaint, like the high notes on a mouth
organ
  RUPERT THOMSON *The Insult*

a voice like a nail coming out of the wood slowly
  DIANNE BENEDICT *Crows*

a voice like a boulder tearing apart
FRED CHAPPELL *I Am One of You Forever*

There were abandoned wells in that voice and haunted caves and
rotten graves opening from inside
FRED CHAPPELL *I Am One of You Forever*

a voice that could scour streets
T CORAGHESSAN BOYLE *Water Music*

her big white blotting-paper voice that craved for moisture
PATRICK WHITE *The Aunt's Story*

His voice carefully decontaminated words
PATRICK WHITE *The Aunt's Story*

a Statue-of-Liberty voice
CHARLES BAXTER *First Light*

his voice was B-flat with innuendo
ANDREW SINCLAIR *Beau Bumbo*

[His] voice was a low rumble, like the revving of his Pontiac
AMY TAN *The Bonesetter's Daughter*

[a voice] like an English lesbian preventing some rude tribesman
from maltreating a donkey
WILLIAM S BURROUGHS *Exterminator*

her creaking, octave-challenged voice
T CORAGHESSAN BOYLE *My Widow*

the man's voice, deep and alien, like an engine in another room
BRAD KESSLER *Lick Creek*

Her voice trails out over the small dunes hunting the sea and
becomes part of the endless pulse of water chatter, hoists sail and
drifts away
THEA ASTLEY *Vanishing Points*

his voice rumbling like a cordon of cement trucks
T CORAGHESSAN BOYLE *The Champ*

pale unhappy voices like those at the edge of sleep
MARGARET ATWOOD *The Robber Bride*

a man with a voice like logs hauled over rocks
  RUPERT THOMSON *Air & Fire*

The voice was deep, dark-tawny, clubbable: lungs, lights and vintage port
  IAIN SINCLAIR *Landor's Tower*

a voice as cold as a frozen gate on bare fingers
  MERLE DROWN *The Suburbs of Heaven*

Our voices were volatile – like swallows in flight seen through a window
  JOHN BERGER *Photocopies*

His voice is surprising because it is both light and delicate. It poses on a sentence like a butterfly on a flower, wings upright and fluttering
  JOHN BERGER *King*

His voice sounds deep and low, like a tree bending against the wind
  SUZANNE FINNAMORE *Otherwise Engaged*

A voice that reminded him of grilling sausages: a faint, constant spitting of sibilants in the background
  PETER GOLDSWORTHY *Maestro*

A voice, I thought, like a beaten-copper shield, phoney but antique-looking, and when he wanted to he turned it edge on and chopped with it
  MAURICE GEE *Sole Survivor*

His voice is still sleep-furred
  JENNY HOBBS *The Sweet-Smelling Jasmine*

the smallest rupture of a voice
  T CORAGHESSAN BOYLE *The Road to Wellville*

His voice was a whisper in a closet on the far side of the street
  T CORAGHESSAN BOYLE *The Road to Wellville*

a voice that grated on him like a harrow dragged the length of his body
  T CORAGHESSAN BOYLE *The Road to Wellville*

a deep-diving puff of a little floating wisp of a voice
   T CORAGHESSAN BOYLE *After the Plague*

[a] voice like a faulty cement-mixer
   IAIN SINCLAIR *Radon Daughters*

pushing his voice out of himself like it was something he did not want
   KEITH RIDGWAY *The Parts*

His voice was death beds and boiling, rusted locks and cheap paint, chains and plasterboard partitions and second hand cutlery
   KEITH RIDGWAY *The Parts*

his voice was like the sound of a zipper going down
   KEITH RIDGWAY *The Parts*

a voice like the starter of a car that won't catch
   JOHN BERGER *Lilac and Flag*

[her] big-enough-to-eat-you voice
   JAMES RYAN *Dismantling Mr Doyle*

the smooth-sided cedar-box voice
   BRIAN HALL *The Saskiad*

Her voice had a quality of suspended motion, like a spun dime
   J ROBERT LENNON *On the Night Plain*

[Their] voices were impeccably coiffed
   WILLIAM H GASS *The Tunnel*

The woman's voice, high and clear as the sound of a glass rapped with a spoon to summon a waiter
   ANGELA CARTER *A Very, Very Great Lady and Her Son at Home*

It was a soft, rustling, unemphatic, almost uninflected, faded, faintly perfumed voice, like very old lace handkerchiefs put away long ago in a drawer with potpourri and forgotten
   ANGELA CARTER *Reflections*

Their voices glittered like tossed beer cans on traffic islands
   EMILY CARTER *East on Houston*

She's got this high-pitched voice that sounds like talking shellac
   EMILY CARTER *WLUV*

her voice was dry and brittle, like an old letter recovered and preserved after a season of rain and snow
   JAY MCINERNEY *Brightness Falls*

his voice rumbling, gravelly, like a tire spinning on rocks
   GLEN HIRSHBERG *The Snowman's Children*

The mother's voice is like a bird's wing brushing glass
   SONYA HARTNETT *Of a Boy*

a shiny toy gun of a voice
   NICK FOWLER *A Thing (or Two) about Curtis and Camilla*

His voice was like a dry cork twisting in the neck of a bottle. A tight voice
   NICOLA BARKER *Small Holdings*

a voice like treacle and lye
   DEBORAH BOEHM *The Samurai Goodbye*

her voice ... like a flock of crows that blackly sail out and attack, peck at, eat everything
   HAROLD BRODKEY *Innocence*

The voice laid hands on him
   TIM GAUTREAUX *People on the Empty Road*

his loud cigarette voice squalling like a needle dragged across a record
   MICHAEL CAHILL *A Nixon Man*

The voice was nakedly peeled
   HAROLD BRODKEY *The Bullies*

her voice is like a bunch of robins pulling worms from him
   HAROLD BRODKEY *Waking*

a voice as dry and light as the pages of a Bible
   JOE COOMER *One Vacant Chair*

a voice like thin corrugated tin
   JOE COOMER *One Vacant Chair*

her voice like syrup with words of fruit
   JOE COOMER *One Vacant Chair*

Her voice was weak and ragged, like the slow dry turning of a wire and screen flour sifter
JOE COOMER *One Vacant Chair*

His voice is like pushing a big oak table across a concrete floor, or ripping the bass string out of a piano and shooting arrows with it
JOE COOMER *A Flatland Fable*

[His voice] comes quietly but in a high pitch like a mouse burning
JOE COOMER *A Flatland Fable*

Her voice was deep like a furnace
PAUL CODY *Eyes Like Mine*

His voice seemed lost in the physics of the room, baffled by bad acoustics
AL KENNEDY *So I Am Glad*

Her voice emptied to grey
AL KENNEDY *Everything You Need*

[her voice like] a cartoon mouse in a bell jar
JOHN UPDIKE *Toward the End of Time*

a voice swerving like some brilliant bird from register to register
LAWRENCE DURRELL *Sebastian*

the tone of her voice like an admiring curtsy
DARIN STRAUSS *The Real McCoy*

her voice small, like a remnant of childhood
RICK DEMARINIS *Desert Places*

her Portia voice
ROBERT DREWE *The Drowner*

his voice like a kite's tail, looping at the back end of something lifted up
ERIC SHADE *Blood*

his thin but rather distinctive pebble dash voice
NICOLA BARKER *Behindlings*

his voice worryingly moss-lined and springy
NICOLA BARKER *Behindlings*

The kind of voice that paused to draw on an imaginary cigarette
JANICE GALLOWAY *Foreign Parts*

the women's voices rise and fall like traffic on a quiet street
ANNE SCOTT *Calpurnia*

Her voice was thin, like a little squeak against the thumb
TIM GAUTREAUX *Resistance*

his voice like a cloud of hammers
JONATHAN LETHEM *The Fortress of Solitude*

The voice is breathless and rapid-fire yet somehow composed, in control, like a virtuoso on antic ragtime piano
STEVEN HEIGHTON *The Shadow Boxer*

Her voice was harsh … like a prime minister's voice when he has a record majority
DAVID IRELAND *A Woman of the Future*

Her voice … like a rattle of hailstones in a well
JANETTE TURNER HOSPITAL *Oyster*

a thin vermouth'd voice
IAIN SINCLAIR *White Chappell, Scarlet Tracings*

The stiff, high, crackly voice of church hymnals
TRUDY LEWIS *Private Correspondences*

Her voice cuts through the night like a line of fire burning all that is in its path
BETH NUGENT *Locusts*

his voice issuing forth like gravel
ROBERT FORD *The Student Conductor*

voices like slipper satin across your bare chest
JANET FITCH *White Oleander*

his voice like a hand between my legs
JANET FITCH *White Oleander*

His voice was metallic, laminated with a thin layer of outrage
T CORAGHESSAN BOYLE *The Inner Circle*

[a] voice like lighted sparklers
JANICE GALLOWAY *The Trick Is to Keep Breathing*

The voice is oily, whiskey-colored
    DAVID LONG *Saving Graces*

His voice stilled, like the clotting of a wound
    DAVID LONG *Morning Practice*

his voice like fresh gauze
    DAVID LONG *Home Fires*

her voice trailed off … like a violin plummeting down through the melody of some baroque canon
    RICK MOODY *The Preliminary Notes*

his voice full of warm minerals
    CAROL SHIELDS *Unless*

His voice was slow with prairie, thick with Great Lakes
    LORRIE MOORE *The Jewish Hunter*

a voice that implied she was doing a temporary fill-in for Sisyphus
    MAVIS CHEEK *Getting Back Brahms*

her voice was like wind in graveyards
    ANGELA CARTER *Nights at the Circus*

My voice thudded into the fog, like bullets into a mattress
    JOE COOMER *Beachcombing for a Shipwrecked God*

He had the kind of peachy voice that could soften stone
    JIM CRACE *Arcadia*

Her voice very dry, like salt
    WILL CHRISTOPHER BAER *Hell's Half Acre*

Her voice has disappeared down a shaft of memory
    ITA DALY *Unholy Ghosts*

a voice as cold as a night crawler
    LISA REARDON *The Mercy Killers*

The voice was clear and rigid, as if it had never been softened through use, like a shirt pinned to a piece of cardboard
    KATHRYN DAVIS *Labrador*

a voice like the sea raking back the tiny pebbles of a beach
    PAUL BRANDON *The Wild Reel*

[his] voice ... cold and powerful as a splitting glacier
PAUL BRANDON *The Wild Reel*

[her] voice raised in song, like music wrung from a wet sock
KATHRYN DAVIS *Labrador*

her voice sounded tremulous as windblown tinsel
CAI EMMONS *His Mother's Son*

the glint of a razor shimmering in her voice
CONNIE MAY FOWLER *Remembering Blue*

big brash voices, just dripping with testosterone and ready-made ideas
NANCY HUSTON *Dolce Agonia*

vowel

his fruitily slanted vowels
THEA ASTLEY *It's Raining in Mango*

vowels crawling out from all corners of my mouth like crabs
NICOLA BARKER *Small Holdings*

a cantata of vowels
DEBORAH BOEHM *The Samurai Goodbye*

her long vowels moaning like the wind in pines
ANGELA CARTER *Shadow Dance*

waiter

The waiter came towards us like a tanker spill reaching the beach
EDWARD DOCX *The Calligrapher*

walk

She walked like a sawblade into the night, her elbows, knees and chin carbide tipped
JOE COOMER *A Flatland Fable*

waves

waves like choppy grey ruffs on the neck of a worn-out lion
JANET FRAME *The Edge of the Alphabet*

tight-lipped waves
ALAN SILLITOE *A Tree on Fire*

little waves like the flat side of a cheese grater
JOYCE CARY *The Horse's Mouth*

the waves coming towards the boat like rank after rank of emulsified infantry
JEREMY LELAND *A River Decrees*

waves drumming in triplets of dotted eighths
EDMUND WHITE *Nocturnes for the King of Naples*

waves like circumflexes
JOYCE CARY *A House of Children*

The waves are like a constant heartbeat that tells you the world is still alive
  JENNY HOBBS *The Sweet-Smelling Jasmine*

the great carry of the waves
  MARTIN AMIS *Yellow Dog*

weather

the weather here comes in pockets, like oil
  MARGARET ATWOOD *Surfacing*

the weather ... coming like a giant roll of silver dough on the horizon
  RICK DeMARINIS *Under the Wheat*

weekend

The weekend loomed like a Sahara
  ERICA ABEEL *Women Like Us*

wind

Outside, axes of wind ... chopped at [the] landscape
  THEA ASTLEY *The Multiple Effects of Rainshadow*

[The] wind was alligatoring the blue-green bay
  CHRISTOPHER BRAM *Gossip*

wind like a rope burn
  T CORAGHESSAN BOYLE *The Tortilla Curtain*

the wind ran through the trees like a black hound
  ELIZABETH JORDAN MOORE *Cold Times*

winds fingered the tree like apple-pickers testing the fruit
  JEREMY LELAND *The Tower*

[The] wind passed like an X-ray through people
  JANET FRAME *The Edge of the Alphabet*

wind brisk as a bargain hunter
  ANNE MULCOCK *Landscape with Figures*

wind softly moaning under the big front doors of the cathedral like sinners trying to get in
  JON CLEARY *Mask of the Andes*

the sketchings of the night wind
DOMINIC COOPER *Sunrise*

a bluff commercial wind
JULIAN MITCHELL *A Circle of Friends*

a catspaw of wind
LAWRENCE DURRELL *Monsieur*

song-snatching winds
GEOFF PIKE *Golightly Adrift*

a creative elbow of wind
PAUL RADLEY *My Blue-Checker Corker and Me*

pine-snoring wind
WILLIAM FAULKNER *The Hamlet*

[The] wind whistling like shrieks from a shut-up thing
LEON ROOKE *The Birth Control King of the Upper Volta*

[The] wind had already begun to sling carving knives at the city
DAN JENKINS *Baja Oklahoma*

a very blue wind, like the surface of an estuary in late light,
stripped off by a clever knife in the thinnest layer, and hung up by
its fists in the sky
SEBASTIAN BARRY *The Engine of Owl-Light*

the wind tugging ... like a roomful of kittens
PJ KAVANAGH *Only by Mistake*

The wind moved like a huge hand through the valley
KATE CHRISTENSEN *In the Drink*

The wind held only a whisper of coldness, like one stream of
basement air leaking into a warm room
KATE CHRISTENSEN *In the Drink*

The wind gave the slaps and kisses of children in a game
JOANNE GREENBERG *Where the Road Goes*

the wind's smothered complaints
ELIZABETH KNOX *The Vintner's Luck*

the wind, swishing the last leaves on the tree outside [is] like the hiss of bubbling varnish
  TREZZA AZZOPARDI *The Hiding Place*

The clamberings of the wind under the moon brushed and tickled me like cherubs
  HAROLD BRODKEY *Profane Friendship*

The wind was committing murders in the night, sudden abductions, terrible smotherings
  MARTIN AMIS *Yellow Dog*

A dervish of wind raked the valleys and combed each purlieu and harbor
  LEON ROOKE *A Good Baby*

The wind … a harmony of old moans
  STEWART O'NAN *The Night Country*

the wind went hungry about the bare-limbed trees
  WILLIAM H GASS *Omensetter's Luck*

The wind rushed in the young corn leaves like the coming of surf
  DANIEL BUCKMAN *The Names of Rivers*

the wind passes through [the trees] like a running line to some giant, lost sail
  ALEXANDER CHEE *Edinburgh*

The wind, finger by finger, was playing my face like a wooden flute
  ROSELLEN BROWN *Tender Mercies*

the sort of wind that … sent [his] hair on streaming errands from his head
  JIM CRACE *The Gift of Stones*

The sky would empty, and the wind give up its dead
  CLINT McCOWN *The Weatherman*

the wind hauled its silvery vestments overhead, snagging occasionally on the moon's thin hooks
  KATHRYN DAVIS *Labrador*

A wind had risen outside and was mourning in the eaves
  LEIF ENGER *Peace Like a River*

windows

stained-glass windows glowing like mammoth playing cards
CHRISTOPHER BRAM *The Notorious Dr August*

winter

That year the winter ran at us like a sword
T CORAGHESSAN BOYLE *We Are Norsemen*

Winter with its deserted trees came in like a harsh white shadow
and seared the ground with insult
ELIZABETH COX *The Ragged Way People Fall Out of Love*

women

women like mortar between the rough slabwork of men
DOMINIC COOPER *Sunrise*

swarms of women jostling along like bugs in a crack
JOYCE CARY *The Horse's Mouth*

word

the word slips a wreath around his neck
VINCENT O'SULLIVAN *The Club*

words ... flapping like old underwear on a windy washing line
NICOLA BARKER *Five Miles from Outer Hope*

A word heaped with famine
SHANE CONNAUGHTON *The Run of the Country*

the dangerous mishandling of a single word so that a story
softened, collapsed like a fragile set of lungs
JACK DRISCOLL *Wanting Only to be Heard*

warm round words swollen like kisses
JOHN BANVILLE *Birchwood*

words lopping out like white-of-egg
JANET FRAME *Faces in the Water*

the words hung poised upon the edges of a lake of disbelief
SUNETRA GUPTA *Memories of Rain*

words like plants, either grow poisonous tall and hollow around
the rusted knives and empty drums of meaning or like people

exposed to a deathly weather, shed their fleshy confusion and show luminous, knitted with force and permanence
  JANET FRAME *The Edge of the Alphabet*

an endlessness of words spread like butterflies, like folded inkblots
  SUNETRA GUPTA *The Glassblower's Breath*

his words drifting like clots of milk
  SUNETRA GUPTA *A Sin of Colour*

she put down the word like a bad cigarette
  PETER VANSITTART *Landlord*

words staggered on in his head like big numbers on a board
  IAN MCEWAN *First Love, Last Rites*

soft mendicant words falling like dead birds in the dark street
  WILLIAM S BURROUGHS *The Naked Lunch*

I saw words with wild lives of their own until trapped on paper and fixed down by men of conscience
  PETER VANSITTART *Pastimes of a Red Summer*

her words falling like pollen through a fog
  HENRY MILLER *Tropic of Capricorn*

I turned the words over suspiciously, like round, sea-polished pebbles that might suddenly put out a claw and change into something else
  SYLVIA PLATH *The Bell Jar*

his words as heavy as marble and nearly as mute
  ALAN PASSES *Big Step*

short words that sounded like ball bearings being dropped into wet gravel
  KURT VONNEGUT JR *Mother Night*

a eunuch of a word
  STEFAN KANFER *The Eighth Sin*

The escalator of words
  ANAÏS NIN *Under a Glass Bell*

The bleat of a white word
  PATRICK WHITE *The Living and the Dead*

The words curled back on themselves like offended feelers
JOHN UPDIKE *The Centaur*

the word opens the windows of a room like the first four notes of a hymn
TONI MORRISON *The Bluest Eye*

dark brown words with soft centres
PETER CAREY *Bliss*

The words on the page were evil and unruly children, bent on undermining him
LESLIE HALL PINDER *Under the House*

She turned this word in the palm of her dreaming hands, like some tiny hieroglyph with meaning on four sides
ANAÏS NIN *Winter of Artifice*

words lightly coloured like Litmus paper
SHIRLEY HAZZARD *The Bay of Noon*

words like Chinese writing in flames
PETER REDGROVE *In the Country of the Skin*

His words were like an affectionate pet cat's paws running across my taut back
ANITA DESAI *Cry, the Peacock*

a merciless moon tide-pull of words
CHRISTY BROWN *A Shadow on Summer*

harpoonless words
PENELOPE SHUTTLE *Wailing Monkey Embracing a Tree*

words dropping off his tongue like bits of solder
T CORAGHESSAN BOYLE *Water Music*

a beautiful word that went like a watch
HUGO BARNACLE *Promise*

words ... were at most frail slat bridges over chasms
PATRICK WHITE *The Aunt's Story*

The word ... stuck like an isotype just inside [her] ear
JUNE ARNOLD *Sister Gin*

words bunched up in her brain like cars at the toll booth
    AD NAUMAN *Scorch*

The words ... were ... like ... flat closed doors on an empty landing
    JENNIFER LASH *Blood Ties*

weighing his ... words as if they were coins he was placing one by
one on a scale
    KATE CHRISTENSEN *In the Drink*

These words had meaning; they bore weighty planets of meaning
    FRED CHAPPELL *Look Back All the Green Valley*

words are so often like window curtains, a decorative screen put up
to keep the neighbours at a distance
    MARGARET ATWOOD *The Robber Bride*

Silent words waft out of her like stale talcum powder
    MARGARET ATWOOD *The Age of Lead*

words so solid they were practically tools
    CHARLOTTE BACON *Lost Geography*

his words a used thread of his own weaving
    ALYSON HAGY *The Grief Is Always Fresh*

speech to him was a task, a battle, words mustered behind his
beard and issued one at a time, heavy and square like tanks
    MARGARET ATWOOD *Surfacing*

words that stuck under your fingernails like tiny jewels and were
scented and sharp
    MICHÈLE ROBERTS *Impossible Saints*

I listened to each word come around the bend like a tightly
coupled freight car
    ALYSON HAGY *Keeneland*

His words sounded paved in ice
    ALYSON HAGY *Keeneland*

The ring of words in his mouth like the ring of rain in a steel
bucket on a concrete yard in a cold place in the shadow of a hill
    KEITH RIDGWAY *The Long Falling*

She savours the word like a strawberry
    JON MCGREGOR *If Nobody Speaks of Remarkable Things*

The words skein out of my mouth, like a Latin declension
   Louis Bayard *Endangered Species*

uttered words passed through me like a psalm
   Robert Bingham *Bad Stars*

the words came one by one, like birds landing on a wire at sunset
   Tim Gautreaux *The Clearing*

words [like] polite touches remembered on the back of the neck
   Tim Gautreaux *People on the Empty Road*

his words hitting her face like grit
   Martha Bergland *Idle Curiosity*

words hit your brain like garbage churning in a breakwater
   Craig Clevenger *The Contortionist's Handbook*

His words sounded like individual bean bags thrown into a pillow
   Joe Coomer *One Vacant Chair*

a bustling grey sawmill of a word
   Steven Heighton *The Shadow Boxer*

The word ... hangs there between them like the echo of a pistol shot
   Anne Scott *Calpurnia*

Words we spoke there were like stones skipped on water falling with mild echoes to the bottom and becoming treasure
   Thylias Moss *Tale of a Sky-Blue Dress*

Agent Orange words
   Kate Jennings *Moral Hazard*

Her own muddled words trailed a V of dubiousness
   Thea Astley *The Slow Natives*

I shall say eucalyptus: beautiful word, with that goitrous upbeat in the middle of it like a gulp of grief
   John Banville *Athena*

Words trailing their streamers of judgement
   Janet Fitch *White Oleander*

his words limp out from his face and creep like tattered tramps
   Reynolds Price *The Promise of Rest*

I don't actually say these last words; I just bump along on their short, stubbed feet, their little dead declarative syllables
CAROL SHIELDS *Unless*

words pouring out of her, tumbling one after the other, like a paper-doll chain from her mouth
JULIANNA BAGGOTT *The Miss America Family*

The sibilant [word] rustled, like a small, silk undergarment, the petticoat of some dwarf
ANGELA CARTER *Shadow Dance*

the words I want to say fly in my throat like swallows lost in a church
ALEXANDER CHEE *Edinburgh*

her breath so close he felt the words like cobwebs across his face
WILLIAM LYCHACK *The Wasp Eater*

His words are projectiles, high and hostile as fighter jets
CAI EMMONS *His Mother's Son*

their words sank to the floor and remained there, draped across the parlour like so many uninflated balloons
RICHARD FLANAGAN *Death of a River Guide*

The final word came out of [his] throat with a peculiar harshness, as if the word itself carried chains and could be summoned up only with some effort from his guts, as if it had flagellated his throat and tongue on its journey to his lips
RICHARD FLANAGAN *Death of a River Guide*

words that become active boils in the heart
TONI MORRISON *Jazz*

The words flew out of her mouth as if they had been hammered in machine shops, as if banners had been designed for their inauguration, as if through long trumpets they had been blown
THOMAS GLYNN *Watching the Body Burn*

the words came in clusters like curious fruits that asked to be bitten and chewed and rolled around the tongue, and if they were poisonous well that was their nature
MARION HALLIGAN *Wishbone*

worry

Tentacles of worry leaked out of him
JENNIFER STEVENSON *Trash Sex Magic*

wrinkles

wrinkles ... running through his cheeks as through a dry
topography
JOHN CROWLEY *Dæmonomania*

The wrinkles on her forehead plunged into her hairline like waves
into salt grass
JOE COOMER *Beachcombing for a Shipwrecked God*

A new pair of quotation marks had wrinkled around her eyes
MICHAEL LOWENTHAL *The Same Embrace*

wrinkles ... running like precious fault lines across his face
LAURIE LYNN DRUMMOND *Taste, Touch, Sight, Sound, Smell*

wrists

wrists thin as pine kindling
RON HANSEN *Mariette in Ecstasy*

year

the verdigris of the years
MARK SLOUKA *God's Fool*

the whole span of his skin-and-grief years
PHILIP CALLOW *Going to the Moon*

Index of Authors

A

Abeel, Erica 265
Abrahams, Peter 58
Abrams, Linsey 117
Abse, Dannie 231
Acker, Kathy 229
Aickman, Robert 215
Aldiss, Brian W 127
Aldridge, James 58
Alexander, Joan 95, 251
Allen, Jeffery Renard 77, 131, 208, 232
Almond, Steve 30, 78, 163, 214, 226,
   250
Alther, Lisa 185, 206
Alvarez, A 170
Alvarez, Julia 192
Amidon, Stephen 16, 124, 229, 240
Amis, Martin 9, 10, 11, 12, 19, 24, 30,
   34, 37, 42, 47, 50, 51, 59, 60, 68, 74,
   78, 79, 85, 92, 101, 102, 103, 124,
   125, 137, 139, 142, 146, 153, 169,
   171, 180, 187, 188, 189, 191, 195,
   199, 200, 201, 206, 207, 209, 212,
   228, 229, 238, 239, 244, 245, 246,
   253, 265, 267
Anderson, Linda 240
Anonymous 213, 223
Ansay, A Manette 36, 119, 129, 151,
   175, 218
Arditti, Michael 29, 76, 86, 98, 119,
   129, 217
Arlen, Michael 27, 164
Arnold, June 29, 270
Astley, Thea 24, 38, 39, 41, 63, 67, 76,
   80, 90, 99, 114, 122, 151, 152, 156,
   159, 170, 171, 183, 190, 194, 201,
   211, 217, 218, 221, 235, 247, 256,
   263, 265, 272
Atlas, James 74
Atwood, Margaret 14, 19, 22, 25, 29,
   37, 48, 51, 53, 62, 63, 75, 76, 77, 86,
   90, 92, 98, 102, 107, 108, 127, 130,
   131, 144, 145, 149, 155, 162, 164,
   167, 201, 207, 217, 218, 232, 247,
   256, 265, 271

Aylett, Steve 21, 26, 68, 81, 103, 120,
   121, 123, 133, 134, 145, 148, 150,
   160, 172, 202, 226, 251
Azzopardi, Trezza 161, 173, 267

B

Bacon, Charlotte 26, 53, 112, 125, 130,
   208, 224, 271
Baer, Will Christopher 13, 53, 98, 136,
   164, 201, 213, 254, 262
Baggott, Julianna 39, 148, 151, 153,
   156, 199, 202, 211, 273
Bainbridge, Beryl 90, 133, 163, 170,
   239
Baker, Elliott 53, 164
Baker, James 129, 216, 255
Baker, Nicholson 45, 88, 161, 228
Baldwin, James 58, 100, 137, 138, 182,
   205
Baldwin, Michael 19, 200
Ballantyne, Sheila 85
Ballard, JG 36, 85, 142, 165, 190, 231
Banks, Lynne Reid 253
Banning, MC 182
Banville, John 10, 12, 32, 33, 38, 39,
   44, 45, 46, 67, 86, 87, 90, 95, 104,
   105, 107, 110, 116, 123, 128, 135,
   137, 140, 152, 162, 167, 172, 186,
   188, 189, 197, 208, 212, 215, 222,
   224, 233, 234, 247, 268, 272
Barker, AL 21, 29, 44, 58, 59, 97, 142,
   194, 196, 216
Barker, Dudley 32
Barker, James 22
Barker, Nicola 11, 19, 24, 31, 32, 40,
   50, 64, 66, 78, 84, 89, 91, 108, 136,
   139, 156, 159, 172, 173, 181, 185,
   186, 196, 209, 210, 214, 247, 259,
   260, 263, 268
Barnacle, Hugo 205, 270
Barnes, Djuna 49, 143
Baron, Alexander 186
Barrett, Susan 182
Barry, Clive 44, 237
Barry, Sebastian 13, 180, 188, 202, 206,
   218, 231, 234, 266

G

Gadol, Peter 190, 232

Galloway, Janice 9, 49, 65, 80, 87, 94, 102, 108, 132, 146, 185, 186, 194, 210, 225, 230, 261

Garcia, Christina 65, 167, 210, 241

Gardam, John 195

Gass, William H 18, 19, 31, 38, 47, 64, 80, 84, 91, 98, 108, 109, 115, 131, 134, 135, 139, 155, 157, 166, 180, 193, 196, 203, 208, 219, 225, 227, 237, 239, 258, 267

Gautreaux, Tim 11, 38, 55, 56, 64, 84, 87, 102, 108, 119, 160, 164, 185, 199, 220, 252, 259, 261, 272

Gay, William 17, 42, 65, 79, 109, 159, 160, 174, 190, 210, 243, 247

Gee, Maurice 89, 106, 114, 128, 161, 166, 196, 244, 248, 257

Giardina, Anthony 125, 223

Gibson, Miles 138

Gilchrist, Ellen 117, 138

Giles, Molly 13, 63, 108, 124, 207, 218

Gilliatt, Penelope 28, 53, 72, 85, 110, 113, 174

Glaister, Lesley 96, 103, 173, 185, 206, 210, 247

Glynn, Thomas 34, 70, 107, 204, 223, 251, 273

Goldbarth, Albert 106, 199, 209, 227

Goldsworthy, Peter 37, 159, 257

Gooding, John 72, 206

Gordon, Giles 138

Gordon, Neil 46, 53, 62, 194

Gostin, Jennifer 109, 118

Gould, Alan 19, 43, 107, 163, 191

Gray, Nigel 141

Green, Angela 65, 135

Green, Annie 93

Green, Henry 44, 104

Greenberg, Joanne 144, 218, 266

Greene, Harlan 25, 115

Greenlaw, Lavinia 148, 245

Greer, Andrew Sean 54, 66, 82, 137, 221, 241

Griffith, Michael 40, 86

Griffith, Nicola 15, 34, 54, 62, 136, 241

Gupta, Sunetra 33, 36, 47, 83, 88, 138, 151, 152, 158, 169, 206, 214, 216, 238, 240, 241, 244, 268, 269

Gurganus, Allan 36, 97, 166, 195, 216, 233

H

Hagy, Alyson 13, 50, 63, 77, 111, 141, 145, 153, 155, 159, 208, 218, 232, 271

Haldeman, Charles 41, 55, 72, 97

Hall, Brian 258

Hall, Rodney 116

Halligan, Marion 17, 70, 82, 96, 122, 123, 150, 233, 273

Halpern, Sue 213

Hamill, Denis 34, 43, 228, 229, 246

Hamilton, Alex 224, 254

Hanagan, Eva 58, 187

Hannah, Barry 62, 168

Hansen, Ron 38, 250, 274

Harding, Michael 115

Hardwick, Elizabeth 224

Harleman, Ann 50, 61, 158, 217, 255

Harris, Wilson 36, 90, 117, 129, 152, 158, 170

Hart, David 216, 255

Hartnett, Sonya 26, 64, 113, 232, 233, 243, 259

Hawkes, John 111, 243, 244

Hayes, Alfred 200

Haynes, Melinda 14, 62, 207, 230, 244

Hazzard, Shirley 73, 136, 201, 254, 270

Healy, Dermot 200, 247

Heighton, Steven 18, 39, 84, 87, 109, 155, 160, 163, 184, 261, 272

Hensher, Philip 42, 67, 80, 83, 87, 96, 113, 147, 156, 189, 203

Herrick, William 115

Hignett, Sean 97

Hilsinger, Serena 134, 245

Hirshberg, Glen 30, 47, 86, 102, 135, 141, 145, 191, 219, 225, 259

Hoban, Russell 28, 48, 77, 88, 107, 118, 161, 210, 213, 245